THE JEWISH WORLD OF
ALEXANDER HAMILTON

The Jewish World of Alexander Hamilton

ANDREW PORWANCHER

PRINCETON UNIVERSITY PRESS

PRINCETON & OXFORD

Published by Princeton University Press
41 William Street, Princeton, New Jersey 08540
6 Oxford Street, Woodstock, Oxfordshire OX20 1TR

press.princeton.edu

Library of Congress Cataloging-in-Publication Data

Names: Porwancher, Andrew, author.
Title: The Jewish world of Alexander Hamilton / Andrew Porwancher.
Description: Princeton : Princeton University Press, [2021] |
    Includes bibliographical references and index.
Identifiers: LCCN 2021009022 (print) | LCCN 2021009023 (ebook) |
    ISBN 9780691211152 (hardback) | ISBN 9780691212708 (ebook)
Subjects: LCSH: Hamilton, Alexander, 1757–1804—Religion. |
    Protestantism—Social aspects—United States—History—17th century. |
    Judaism—Social aspects—United States—History—17th century. |
    Judaism—Social aspects—Nevis—History—17th century. | Statesmen—
    Religious life—United States—History—18th century. | United States—
    Politics and government—1775–1783. | United States—Politics and
    government—1783–1809. | New York (N.Y.)—Biography. | Nevis—
    Biography. | BISAC: HISTORY / United States / Revolutionary Period
    (1775–1800) | POLITICAL SCIENCE / History & Theory
Classification: LCC E302.6.H2 P67 2021 (print) | LCC E302.6.H2 (ebook) |
    DDC 973.4092 [B]—dc23
LC record available at https://lccn.loc.gov/2021009022
LC ebook record available at https://lccn.loc.gov/2021009023

British Library Cataloging-in-Publication Data is available

Editorial: Fred Appel, James Collier
Jacket Design: Henry Sene Yee
Production: Erin Suydam
Publicity: Kate Hensley, Kathryn Stevens
Copyeditor: Don Burgard

Jacket art: Photograph of miniature watercolor and ink portrait of Alexander Hamilton at age fifteen, drawn from life, January 11, 1773 / Library of Congress.

Background texture: Shutterstock

This book has been composed in Arno Pro

10 9 8 7 6 5 4 3 2 1

In memory of Arthur Mogilesky

In Jewish history, there are no coincidences.

—ELIE WIESEL

CONTENTS

FIGURES

ACKNOWLEDGMENTS

I OWE MY FIRST debt of gratitude to the great Rabbi Dr. Meir "Solly" Soloveichik. When we initially met over breakfast on the Upper West Side in the early days of my research for this book, Solly told me that he would help me in any way. Indeed, no other scholar has done more to make this book a reality. As the rabbi of Congregation Shearith Israel, he is the leader of America's oldest Jewish congregation, whose membership in the early years of the republic had numerous ties to Alexander Hamilton. I'm appreciative for his inexhaustible enthusiasm and deep knowledge of Jewish history. I had the pleasure of spending a semester on sabbatical as a senior research fellow under Solly's auspices at the Zahava and Moshael Straus Center for Torah and Western Thought at Yeshiva University, and I am grateful to the Straus family. Happily, my time at the Straus Center coincided with its Program on Early America and the Jews. Robert and Ellen Kapito merit special attention for their generosity and support of this project. Thank you also to Rabbi Dr. Stu Halpern and Rabbi Aryeh Czarka, who both helped facilitate my involvement with the Straus Center.

Princeton University Press has been a wonderful publisher to work with, owing in large part to the efforts of my editor there, Fred Appel. He is just the kind of attentive and thoughtful editor for whom an author hopes. Many thanks to the rest of the team at Princeton University Press for their efforts in bringing this book to fruition. The anonymous reviewers provided helpful feedback on the manuscript. Thomas LeBien immeasurably improved the project with his insights.

I was fortunate to spend a semester down the street from the press while on sabbatical at the James Madison Program, housed within Princeton University's Department of Politics, where I served as the

Garwood Visiting Fellow. I'm grateful to the program leadership—Professor Robert George and Dr. Bradford Wilson—for the opportunity. The fellowship provided me with critical time to write and the company of a wonderful cohort of fellows. I grew up in the town of Princeton and perhaps have the unique distinction among visiting scholars in the university's long history of having an office on the same street as my childhood home. At the age of twelve, I snuck into the university's football stadium with some friends. When a security guard apprehended us, he informed us that we had a lifetime ban from the campus. If he caught wind of my return to the university during my fellowship, I wish now to express my thanks to him for extending me clemency with his silence.

I am deeply appreciative for the support of a number of scholars at the University of Oklahoma. Foremost among them is Alan Levenson, director of the Schusterman Center for Judaic and Israel Studies. Alan was the first historian anywhere whom I consulted about this undertaking, and he can testify that I actually did begin my research before the *Hamilton* musical debuted. Wilfred McClay advocated for me time and again over the course of the project; he is as generous as they come. Oklahoma is home to a rich cohort of scholars across multiple disciplines with a strong interest in religious history, and I've been fortunate to call many of them friends, especially David Anderson, Scott Fitzgerald Johnson, Louis Cortest, Kyle Harper, and Jill Hicks-Keeton. I had the pleasure of taking up a fellowship at the OU Humanities Forum under the leadership of Janet Ward and thank her for her tireless efforts. This project also received support at OU from the Institute for the American Constitutional Heritage, the Department of Classics and Letters, the Digital Scholarship Lab at Bizzell Memorial Library, and the College of Arts and Sciences. Thanks as well to my diligent research assistants: Elizabeth Bagwell, Austin Coffey, and Rachel Averitt.

The preparation and publication of this volume was made possible by a grant from the Memorial Foundation for Jewish Culture. The Gilder Lehrman Institute of American History awarded me a research fellowship to subsidize my archival work. The American Jewish Historical Society named me the Sid and Ruth Lapidus Fellow, which allowed me to undertake research in its collections; I am particularly indebted to the staff at the Center for Jewish History for its assistance. The George Washington Institute for Religious Freedom and Dr. Michael Feldberg provided resources when I first began this endeavor.

Much gratitude to the countless librarians and archivists across the United States, the Caribbean, and Europe who assisted me, particularly at the Library of Congress, the Danish National Archives, the British Library, the Columbia Rare Book and Manuscript Library, the New York Historical Society, the New York Public Library, the New York State Archives, the American Jewish Archives, the Nevis Historical and Conservation Society, and the Research Library and Archives at Estate Whim. Andrew Fagal deserves many thanks for his close reading of several chapters. Dan Gerstle generously gave me his considered comments on the entire manuscript. Professor Stephen Knott extended this book the benefit of his vast expertise on Hamilton. Thanks as well to Professor Robert Paquette for hosting me at the Alexander Hamilton Institute. David Lynch shared his thorough knowledge of the records on St. Croix. Nathan Carr lent me his insights into religious rites. Any merit there may be in this book is due in large part to all those aforementioned; any errors are mine alone.

Beyond the scholars who and institutions that made this research possible, I have been fortunate to have a loyal circle of friends and family. This project occasioned opportunities to share my findings with audiences in Boca Raton and Chicago, where each set of grandparents hosted me. Thank you to my sister, Kara, who is a font of good advice and good cheer in equal measure. I am grateful, too, for the kindness of her husband, Jonathan, and their children—Abigail, Noah, and Talia. Special thanks is owed to Kristen, who shares much in common with Hamilton: a move to New York to pursue education, a reliance on the courts to defend democratic principles, and a keen appreciation for Jewish history.

Above all, I want to recognize my parents, Donna and Rick Porwancher, who lent their moral support through the painstaking process of my working on this book over the course of many years. They still reside in my childhood home, and during my sabbatical at Princeton, the meals there were free, the linens fresh, and the conversations unfailing. Studying the tragic events that left Hamilton bereft of both his parents has made me appreciate my own all the more.

Finally, I wish to acknowledge my grandfather, Arthur Mogilesky. His family, like so many other Jewish families, had journeyed westward across the Atlantic in the hopes that future generations might find opportunities that would have been foreclosed to them in the old country. Arthur's time was cut tragically short, and so he never fully realized those hopes—but his children and grandchildren certainly have. It is in his memory that I dedicate this book.

Norman, Oklahoma

AUTHOR'S NOTE

SPELLING, capitalization, italicization, abbreviation, and punctuation in quotations from primary sources have been modernized for readability.

Introduction

ON A TINY ISLAND at the edge of the West Indies, Alexander Hamilton began an unlikely journey. He overcame the perils of orphanhood and decamped from the tropics as a teenager to become a vital figure in the birth of the United States. From the battlefield and the bank to the courtroom and the cabinet, Hamilton shaped the republic to a degree that few others could boast. The remarkable events of his American years have long intrigued scholars and, more recently, theater audiences. While Hamilton biographers are exhaustive in their study of his adulthood, research into his obscure upbringing remains scarce. Yet his Caribbean past is not merely an exotic footnote to the high drama of his American life. Hamilton, like all people, was a product of his roots, and so his West Indian youth matters—not least because he was probably born and raised a Jew.

For more than two centuries, the scant treatment of Hamilton's boyhood has proceeded from a default assumption that he and his relatives were cradle-to-grave Christians. That assumption warps how historians approach his Caribbean background and leads to a double error. For one, they make a series of claims about Hamilton's origins that comport with the premise of his Christian identity but have little grounding in evidence. Moreover, archival sources that should prompt scholars to question this premise are mistakenly interpreted so as to preserve the presumption that he was Christian. By subjecting untested claims to scrutiny and reckoning anew with the historical record, this book concludes that Hamilton, in all likelihood, grew up as a member of the Jewish people.

To be sure, Hamilton did not maintain any identity as a Jew in America. Still, his early engagement with Judaism is hardly just a trivial curiosity. It provides critical context for understanding why the adult Hamilton, more than any other founding father, was connected to Jews and fond of their faith.[1] Many founders commended Jewry and Judaism in one breath only to condemn them in the next. In contrast, Hamilton's favorable relationships with Jews and reverential sentiments about the Jewish religion stand unblemished by bias.

The Hamiltonian-Jewish alliance, in turn, opens a unique window onto the early American republic writ large. A paradox vexed the nation from its inception. The United States was conceived in the name of equality yet defined by hereditary hierarchy—free over slave, white over Native, propertied over landless, man over woman, Christian over Jew. American Jewry challenged the country to confront this paradox directly. Having spilled blood and spent treasure in service of the Revolution, Jews began advocating for a status that Europe denied them for centuries and the Declaration of Independence championed: equality.

The rightful role of Jewry became a subject of fierce debate among Americans of the era. Many Gentiles had long resented Jewish participation in commerce and now balked at the prospect of full-fledged Jewish involvement in civic life. They responded with consternation as Jews grasped for access to the courthouse, ballot box, and elected office. That the Jewish population was miniscule—about one-tenth of a percent—yet prompted such outsized angst speaks to the depth of contemporary antisemitism. Against these reactionary forces, Alexander Hamilton sought an economic and legal order where his Jewish compatriots would stand equal to their Christian neighbors.

The successes Hamilton achieved to that end illustrate the democratic possibilities of the new nation. Just the same, the obstacles he encountered mark the limitations of an America still rife with inherited inequality. The following chapters are as much about the Jewish world of the early republic as they are about Hamilton—and it is the relationship between the two that shows us afresh how the aftermath of the Revolution was neither an undeviating march toward modern equality nor a pure perpetuation of traditional hierarchy. We instead find a young country uneasily navigating the contested terrain between New World promises and Old World prejudices.

———

Any claim concerning Hamilton's Jewishness must begin with his mother, Rachel, given the matrilineal nature of Jewish identity. She was unquestionably from a Christian family in the British Caribbean. Rachel wedded a colonist in the Danish West Indies named Johan Levine. Although numerous scholars assume he was not Jewish, considerable evidence suggests otherwise, including the unambiguous declaration from Hamilton's own grandson that Johan was a "rich Danish Jew."[2]

There are compelling reasons to think Rachel converted to Judaism for marriage. When the couple had a son, Peter, they abstained from the standard Christian practice of infant baptism. Peter Levine would later be baptized as an adult under circumstances that indicate he was converting to Christianity and thus not a Christian in childhood. Hamilton scholars do not entertain the possibility that Peter had been Jewish and so remain baffled by his adult baptism.

Rachel fled her marriage and bore Alexander out of wedlock to a Christian, yet she chose to enroll Alexander in a Jewish school. His Jewish education is a well-established fact. Some biographers presume that Alexander attended a Jewish school because his illegitimacy must have precluded him from church schooling. Yet the church records do not support the supposition that out-of-wedlock birth posed an obstacle to church membership. And a host of communal, theological, and political factors give us ample cause to believe that the Jewish school would have accepted Alexander only if the local Jewish community considered him one of its own.

His matriculation at the Jewish school also stands as the best evidence that Rachel had earlier converted to Judaism. Because Jewish identity passes through the mother, any recognition by the Jewish school of Alexander as a coreligionist means that it necessarily would have regarded Rachel in the same light. If we assume that she had no prior identity as a Jew, it is hard to make sense of why Rachel would, or how she even could, choose to arrange a Jewish education for her son. Allow for the possibility of her Jewish identity, however, and such difficulties disappear. Two other long-known details about Rachel, which Hamilton biographers mention but treat with no particular significance, harmonize with the notion that she was Jewish. Rachel kept the surname "Levine" long after she severed ties to Johan—until her death, in fact. And upon her passing she was not buried in a church cemetery.

Hamilton was only thirteen when his mother succumbed to a fatal illness, and he stayed in the Caribbean until the age of eighteen. A recently unearthed legal case from those intervening years makes plain that he presented himself as Christian at seventeen—but it also suggests that his affiliation with Christianity had not been lifelong. When assessed for his competency to swear on the Bible as a witness, Hamilton described himself as Anglican. Yet the court prevented him from giving sworn testimony after Hamilton conceded that he had never before received communion. His failure to have participated in the sacrament of communion would be an oddity if he were raised Anglican but is far more explicable if he were a latecomer to the Christian faith.

Tellingly, Hamilton in his American years was both willing and able to conceal parts of his West Indian background. Newly uncovered records reveal that he fabricated his year of birth after leaving the islands. Hamilton maintained this myth for the duration of his adulthood without any Caribbean contemporary ever exposing him, rendering it all the more plausible that he could obscure a Jewish heritage with similar success.

The theory that Alexander Hamilton probably had a Jewish past may seem, on its face, provocative. But were the foregoing facts presented about the early life and family history of any ordinary Caribbean colonist rather than an American founder, it would be uncontentious to claim that the balance of evidence points to his status as a Jew. And if indeed the evidence of Hamilton's Jewish identity is not controversial, but the idea of it remains so, then perhaps the question of Jewish belonging in the United States is as fraught in our time as it was in his own.

———

This inquiry requires important caveats. Jewish identity has many dimensions—religious, cultural, legal, communal, and ethnic, among others. Often these dimensions overlap for a given individual; sometimes they conflict. The eighteenth-century Atlantic world featured a diverse array of people who were Jewish in some senses and not others, from crypto-Jews to Afro-Caribbean Jews to Gentiles who converted for marriage. An investigation into whether Hamilton was Jewish cannot, therefore, force him into either of two categories: Jew or non-Jew. It must instead center on the likelihood that he had a Jewish identity in any number of the term's multiple meanings for any period of his life.

Furthermore, the process of recreating the personal history of an inconspicuous adult from the West Indies of that time period is an admittedly thorny enterprise, much more so a child. Hurricanes and fires have degraded the historical record. Many of the documents that do survive have been partially eaten by termites. We are left with remnants of individual lives, scraps of evidence that must be read within the context of what is known about the region and era. A great deal of what might be said about most aspects of Hamilton's upbringing and kin are matters of probabilities rather than certainties. The case for his Jewish identity is no different.

———

If Hamilton were likely Jewish, then the question arises of how such a significant feature about a historical icon escaped notice for so long. It is, in fact, unsurprising that a principal part of his boyhood could have evaded his numerous biographers. After all, the adult Hamilton refrained from discussion of his youth with few exceptions. He was notoriously outspoken—often to a fault—about every vital matter in his American life, making his self-censorship around his Caribbean origins especially striking. Undoubtedly, Hamilton's illegitimate birth was a topic he preferred to avoid.[3] And the United States suffered from antisemitic biases; for a statesman whose acceptance into the highest echelons of national politics required at least a nominal pretense to a Christian identity, keeping quiet about any Jewish roots would have been highly prudent.

Hamilton scholars have largely followed the lead of their subject in glossing over his beginnings. Their interests lie in the spectacle of his American years. Excavating the details of Hamilton's West Indian past is not only a peripheral but relatively recent undertaking. Even a fact as basic as his mother's name remained unknown to historians until the twentieth century.[4] It should come as little wonder, then, that his religious upbringing is an underdeveloped field of study.

What's more, materials pertaining to Hamilton's origins are much less accessible, both linguistically and geographically, than those concerning his adulthood. The latter sources are overwhelmingly in English and either available in published form or conveniently located in archives in the United States. By contrast, documents germane to his Caribbean background appear in a variety of languages—Danish, Portuguese, French, Dutch, and German—and are scattered across West Indian islands as well as the European countries that colonized them. The arduous task of reconstructing Hamilton's elusive childhood is hardly worth the effort for his typical biographer whose native tongue is English and whose attention focuses on topics like the Federalist Papers or the Treasury Department.

When historians do write about Hamilton's youth and family of origin, they usually proceed in cursory fashion and recycle untested claims from other scholars. Many of these claims, which take as an article of faith the Christian identities of Hamilton and his relatives, do not withstand scrutiny. And so it is a litany of factors—Hamilton's secrecy, biographers' interests, lingual barriers, remote sources, and faulty assumptions—that have all coalesced to inadvertently obscure important facets of his past.

———

The adult Hamilton never presented himself as Jewish. Nor is there evidence that he covertly practiced Judaism in his maturity. We have, moreover, no indication that upon reaching America he divulged to anyone a prior identity as a Jew. Yet his links to Jewry did not end with his Caribbean boyhood.

Hamilton is best remembered for his financial wizardry, and Jews were pivotal players in his bid to turn the United States into a banking and commercial power. He also served as a distinguished lawyer in New York City, where he represented Jewish citizens in the courts. And at his alma mater, Columbia, Hamilton helped spearhead reforms that were friendly to Jews. He proved instrumental in placing the first Jew on the college board, abolishing mandatory forms of Christian worship for undergraduates, and repealing a religious test that had disqualified Jews and other non-Anglicans from the Columbia presidency.

Keenly aware of the recurrent persecution that Jews suffered, Hamilton viewed their survival since antiquity as beyond remarkable—God's hand was surely at work. He marveled that the "progress of the Jews . . . from their earliest history to the present time has been and is entirely out of the ordinary course of human affairs. Is it not then a fair conclusion that the cause also is an *extraordinary one*—in other words, that it is the effect of some great providential plan?"[5] Perhaps he saw some divine intervention at play in his own improbable rise from Caribbean obscurity to American founder.

Hamilton well understood that the historical train of abuses against Jews continued in the United States. After all, many of his adversaries weaponized antisemitism against his various endeavors throughout his career. During the ratification debates over the U.S. Constitution, Hamilton ranked among its premier defenders while a number of his antagonists denounced the Constitution because it would open federal office to Jewish candidates. The sweeping economic programs that he then advanced as treasury secretary were repeatedly maligned as nefarious plots to benefit Jews. And in a high-profile trial, Hamilton's Jewish witnesses in court were accused of dishonesty owing to an invidious myth that their religion encouraged them to lie under oath. That the forces of anti-Jewish bigotry assailed Hamilton's agenda so frequently is itself noteworthy testament to his alliance with Jewry. Arguably no other self-professed Christian in the early republic confronted more antisemitism.

Despite this fraught environment, Hamilton never wavered in his affection for the people and faith of Judaism. Indeed, the most impassioned denunciation of antisemitism in the annals of any founder came from Hamilton amid the closing arguments of the aforementioned trial. After opposing counsel impugned his Jewish witnesses, Hamilton responded by exalting Jews as the Chosen People: "Has he forgotten, what this race once were, when, under the immediate government of God himself, they were selected as the witnesses of his miracles, and charged with the spirit of prophecy?" Hamilton then alluded to the Roman conquest of the Holy Land and resulting diaspora for Jews throughout the Roman Empire. He recounted how the Jewish people fractured into "remnants of scattered tribes . . . the degraded, persecuted, reviled subjects of Rome, in all her resistless power, and pride, and pagan pomp." The Jews were rendered "an isolated, tributary, friendless people." Hamilton would not abide his own legal system perpetuating this age-old animosity. By his lights, the Judaism of his witnesses was not a stigma to be borne but a religion to be honored. "Were not the witnesses of that pure and holy, happy and Heaven-approved faith?" he asked rhetorically. Invoking the allegorical figure Lady Justice, Hamilton declared that she protected Jews the same as she did all others: "Be the injured party . . . Jew, or Gentile, or Christian, or Pagan, Foreign or Native, she clothes him with her mantle, in whose presence all differences of faiths or births, of passions or of prejudices—all are called to acknowledge and revere her supremacy."[6] Here was a giant of the early republic demanding that Jews, the downtrodden of Europe for centuries, stand equal to Gentiles in an American courtroom. Hamilton's contemporaries remarked that no other trial in his illustrious legal career elicited from him a more emotional performance. Plainly, the case touched something deeply personal within him.

Hamilton's affinity for Jewry undermines the conventional depiction of him, advanced first by rivals and then by scholars, as an aspiring aristocrat with a measure of disdain for those on the periphery.[7] True, he was no populist firebrand. But neither does Hamilton deserve condemnation as an elitist. To reflexively dismiss him as a lackey of the moneyed classes is to overlook how the urban marketplace was more meritocratic than other realms of American life. An enterprising Jew—all too often closed off from the world of law, politics, and colleges—could far more readily access the commercial and financial spheres that Hamilton invigorated. And while many Jewish merchants and brokers in Hamilton's orbit did enjoy a degree of economic security, they were hardly invulnerable to antisemitism. His ties to a Jewish community that was subjected to cultural and legal discrimination call into question the antidemocratic caricature that his foes imagined him to be. It is not without irony that other founding fathers, despite sometimes peddling prejudice against Jews, were far less likely than Hamilton to have charges of elitism leveled against them in their day and afterward.

By fighting for an America where Jew and Gentile would partake alike in civic and economic affairs, Hamilton began to make real the principle of equality in whose name the Revolution had been waged. But the antisemitic resistance that he faced underscores the limits of a hierarchical society still marred by religious intolerance. The experience of American Jewry is certainly not the only one by which to measure the feats and failures of the founding era. Nevertheless, the Hamiltonian-Jewish connections offer us an enriched perspective on the early republic, one that suggests the egalitarian rhetoric of the Declaration of Independence was not an empty promise, even if progress was halting.

Hamilton's appreciation for both Judaism and Jews also has implications for understanding church-state relations. Scholars often presume that historical figures who promoted the separation of church and state were the most compassionate toward minority religions and, correspondingly, that those who saw a role for faith in civic life must have had the least sympathy for religious dissenters. Hamilton's approach complicates these assumptions. In word and deed, he exhibited great esteem for the Jewish faith and its followers. Hamilton *also* argued for a harmony between devotional and civic ends, contending that religion could help nurture the new American republic. Consider, conversely, Thomas Jefferson. He stood as the foremost proponent of the separation of church and state; Jefferson himself coined the phrase. Yet he was blunt in his contempt for Judaism. Jefferson maligned the Hebrew Bible as "defective," the ethics of biblical Judaism as "repulsive," and the Jewish conception of God as "degrading."[8] Hamilton and Jefferson, in opposite ways, illustrate the same point: there was no necessary relationship between respect for Judaism and the principle of separation in their age.

————

This book does not read the adult Hamilton's veneration of Jewry and Judaism backward as all the more proof of a Jewish identity earlier in his life. Rather, Hamilton's Caribbean roots can help us more fully make sense of his subsequent support for Jews and their faith. It is a fundamental truism that we are all shaped by our childhoods. To be sure, a measure of humility is in order when a historian draws connections between a subject's youth and maturity; no biographer can insist with exacting precision how a given element of a figure's upbringing informed decisions made decades afterward. But so too is it folly to think, for instance, that Hamilton's exposure to the brutalities of bondage in the West Indies had no bearing upon his later attitude toward slavery.[9] We would be equally misguided in assuming that his clerkship in adolescence at an import-export firm—which afforded him a real-time education in credit, currency, and trade—was wholly unrelated to his financial acumen as treasury secretary.[10] And surely it is no mere happenstance that among the founders, Hamilton was the only one to attend a Jewish school as a boy and then cultivated the greatest involvement with Jews as an adult.

That Jewry and Judaism are the central themes of this book is *not* meant to imply that they were the central pillars of Hamilton's American years. It would be inaccurate to depict him as engaged in a daily toil on behalf of Jews or perpetually preoccupied with the Jewish religion. Hamilton's affiliations and influences were numerous; other important strands in his story have received extensive treatment elsewhere. This volume seeks to add the relevance of Judaism and its people to our understanding of Hamilton.

————

Among Hamilton's beloved hobbies in New York was the theater, so it is altogether fitting that the Broadway stage has made him the country's favorite founder. His pride of place in American culture at this moment indicates that his story is highly resonant. And yet Hamilton is a profoundly enigmatic character. Here was the treasurer who saved the nation's finances but died in debt, the strikingly decisive leader forever haunted by insecurities, the champion of the rule of law who met his demise in an illicit duel. For all the attention thrust on Hamilton, he eludes us still.

His youth remains the most esoteric of the many mysteries surrounding his life. Hamilton spilled gallons of ink on seemingly every topic but maintained a singular silence about his Caribbean origins. Even with his own children, he was largely mute on the subject. And yet, tantalizingly, he broke from his usual secrecy to share with them a warm memory from boyhood—his time at the Jewish school. If Alexander Hamilton left this clue about his cryptic past, then it is the intent of the pages that follow to explore what larger truths it may suggest.

1

Genesis

AS JEWISH IDENTITY BEGINS with a mother, so must this story. Alexander Hamilton's mother, Rachel Faucette, was born a Christian around 1729 on the island of Nevis in the British Caribbean. Her parents, John and Mary, had a troubled marriage that culminated in a legal separation in 1740. John Faucette died five years later and left the entirety of his estate to Rachel. Determined to begin their lives anew, Mary and Rachel sailed 150 miles northwest to St. Croix, an isle of stunning scenery in the Danish West Indies.[1] An American poet visiting St. Croix in the eighteenth century insisted that "even those that have no taste to admire the beauties of nature would at the view be forced to confess that the valleys of Paradise were now displayed to the eye."[2] St. Croix was part of the Leeward Islands, a string of small isles dotting the eastern Caribbean.

The tropical heat and rich soil of West Indian islands like St. Croix were ideal for producing the era's ultimate cash crop: sugar.[3] European powers often waged bloody battles with one another for control over these lucrative colonies.[4] So profitable was the sugar trade that Britain, for instance, extracted more riches from its collection of Caribbean islands than from the entirety of its territory in North America. During negotiations that ended the Seven Years' War in 1763, the French had to decide between keeping their vast expanse of Canada or the sugar island of Guadeloupe. They chose Guadeloupe.[5] Denmark was among those Old World kingdoms lured by the promise of Caribbean sugarcane. The business-minded Danes preferred to use the purse over the sword, and they peacefully acquired St. Croix from France for 142,000 rigsdalers (Danish rix-dollars) in 1733.[6]

Rachel Faucette and her mother were part of a diverse wave of migrants descending on St. Croix in its early years under Danish rule. Whereas other European nations sought to populate their West Indian islands with their own countrymen, Denmark shrewdly foresaw the benefits of a more inclusive immigration policy. After all, sugar plantations were risky undertakings.[7] The costs of the requisite machinery and slave labor meant significant upfront investment. Droughts, diseases, and hurricanes could summarily wipe out a plantation before a profit was realized.[8] The Danes reasoned that if foreigners wanted to hazard their capital on St. Croix, then Denmark could happily levy its duties on whichever planters managed to win the sugarcane lottery. Relatively few residents of St. Croix were Danish.[9]

Among those who took advantage of St. Croix's open borders were Jews. The Caribbean at large was a magnet for Jewish merchants. Jews had been a stateless people for centuries who lived as outsiders in other lands. Barred by law from many professions, they often assumed the role of cultural intermediaries who served as tradesmen between societies. Jews thus cultivated acumen in commerce and languages not purely by choice but in large part because of their marginality. These very skills proved especially valuable in the early modern era (1500–1800), an age of New World colonization and rising global commerce. Jews became important players in port cities across northern Europe, North and South America, and the West Indies. Not only did Jews boast mercantile expertise and linguistic ability, but they were tapped into transatlantic networks of fellow Jews spread throughout the Atlantic world. Colonial powers willing to accept a Jewish presence stood to profit for their tolerance.[10]

Sephardic Jews of Spanish-Portuguese ancestry composed the bulk of Caribbean Jewry, but some Ashkenazi Jews of German and Polish origin also migrated to the islands.[11] Jewish communities in the West Indies were to be found on British colonies like Barbados, Jamaica, and Nevis; on the Dutch isles of St. Eustatius and Curaçao; and on one of Denmark's other Caribbean territories, St. Thomas.[12] St. Croix never developed the sizable population of Jews that these other islands claimed—in Curaçao, for instance, Jews comprised nearly 40 percent of the free population by 1785[13]—but St. Croix could still tally a handful of Jewish residents.[14]

Amid the polyglot mix of Brits, Germans, Spaniards, Dutch, Danes, and Jews on St. Croix, the largest group by far consisted of African slaves. The sugar trade depended on a steady supply of slave labor. By 1755, St. Croix's slaves would outnumber free people nearly seven to one.[15] Caribbean slavery was particularly barbaric. Interminable hours cutting sugarcane, bouts of tropical disease, and unrelenting heat all exacted a brutal toll on those in bondage. Most slaves perished within just five years.[16] Slaves who faced capital punishment for a given offense often exhibited visible relief that their cruel existence was reaching its end. As one slave owner conceded, "Many who have been hanged or decapitated went to their deaths with the greatest cheerfulness."[17] The picturesque beaches, azure waters, and verdant hills of St. Croix must have made for a perverse beauty in the eyes of slaves, who found themselves in hell amid nature's paradise.

When Rachel Faucette and her mother arrived in St. Croix after a twenty-hour journey,[18] their ship most likely disembarked at the growing port town of Christiansted. The dominant structure along the harbor was Fort Christiansvaern. It housed the colonial governor, the offices of the Danish West India Company, and—as Rachel would personally discover—a prison. The West India Company's warehouse stood opposite the fort and included a courtyard for slave auctions.[19] There prospective buyers would inspect naked slaves, peering into their mouths and checking limbs for defects.[20] Merchants and officials built their houses along King Street, Company Street, and Strand Street, three parallel avenues that began near the water and ran inland. Free blacks were barred from constructing homes in central Christiansted and instead relegated to a separate neighborhood. The Danes demonstrated a unique degree of forethought in urban planning; Christiansted's orderly growth along a grid offered a stark contrast to the hodge-podge development of other West Indian islands. Visitors often marveled at the tidy nature of life on St. Croix.[21]

On this map of St. Croix, the insets show the street layouts for the island's two towns: Frederiksted on the west end and Christiansted on the north shore. *Source*: Kort og tegninger (1600–1920), Rigsarkivet (Danish National Archives, Copenhagen).

For Rachel and Mary Faucette, St. Croix was an obvious choice for the next stage of their lives. Rachel's older sister, Ann, had already moved there with her wealthy husband, James Lytton, who purchased a sugar estate on St. Croix that came to be known as the Grange.[22] Plantations like his were oriented around a "great house," typically European or neoclassical in style. A planter and his family occupied the upper story of a great house while using the ground floor for storage. Such homes were strategically situated on a property to catch ocean drafts, though the breeziest parcel of land was reserved for the windmill. A great house's dense walls and vaulted ceiling were designed to withstand hurricanes, which could strike with little notice and even less mercy.[23]

Guests visiting an estate for a dance would ride their carriages up an imposing tree-lined drive. The host family made use of imported luxuries like porcelain and silver. Under the Caribbean moon, the sound of the minuet, aroma of flowers, and flavor of punch easily mingled. But come daylight, the unforgiving sun beat down on the slaves toiling in the cane fields. These slaves often lived in simple huts on the estate, lined in two rows with a road in between where the women prepared meals amid playing children. In addition to boiling cane juice into sugar, plantations also produced rum and molasses. Oxen then carted these valuable commodities to the wharf for shipment to ports throughout the Atlantic world.[24]

———

James Lytton was probably the one who introduced Rachel Faucette to his business associate—and the man she would marry—Johan Michael Levine.[25] Hamilton himself would describe Levine as a "fortune-hunter" who was "bedizzened with gold, and paid his addresses to my mother, then a handsome young woman."[26] Levine acquired a stake in a sugar plantation in 1744. After seeing his investment come to naught, he redirected his energies toward St. Croix's next most lucrative crop: cotton. While the prime real estate on the western side of the island was designated for sugar, the sloping hills of eastern St. Croix were profitably employed for cotton production.[27] Levine's swanky wardrobe surely gave Rachel the impression he was a planter of substantial means.[28]

The vast body of historical scholarship on Hamilton, often excellent in its analysis of his adult years, has been less thorough in documenting his family history. Levine is a consummate example of an understudied and misconceived figure in Hamilton's past. Many Hamilton biographers fail to mention Levine at all.[29] Others acknowledge his presence in Rachel's story but offer no comment on his religious identity.[30] Those who do engage with the question of Levine's faith often make misguided assumptions. Uncovering Levine's religious background is key to unlocking Hamilton's own.

Levine's name raises the possibility of a Jewish identity, specifically ancestry in the tribe of Levi from ancient Israel. His surname appears in various spellings in the historical record, and several of these formulations ("Levin," "Lewin," "Lavien") correspond to surnames used by Jews of Levitic descent in the eighteenth century.[31] Before coming to

St. Croix, Levine worked as a merchant, a common Jewish profession, and he did so on Nevis, an island with a Jewish community.[32] Jews were especially likely to conduct commerce among themselves,[33] so it is perhaps telling that when Levine decided to sell his plantation on St. Croix in 1753, he secured two Jewish buyers (and the property soon ended up in the hands of still another Jew).[34] The list of plantation owners on St. Croix for that year included over 300 Gentiles and no more than six Jews, so the probability that Levine would have made the sale to any Jew by mere coincidence was one in fifty.[35] As we will see, Levine would fail to have his infant son baptized, which was standard practice for Christians on St. Croix. And Hamilton's own grandson unequivocally identified Levine as a "rich Danish Jew."[36] Conversely, there is no known source in the historical record referring to Levine as Christian.

While some Hamilton scholars accept that Levine was Jewish,[37] many others insist that even if Levine did have Jewish origins, he was not a Jew by the time he met Rachel in 1745. The argument that Levine did not belong to the Jewish faith—at least by 1745—originated in 1903 with Gertrude Atherton, a novelist–turned–amateur historian. She was the first Hamilton biographer to journey to the West Indies in the hopes of uncovering new information about his ancestry. Her resulting book offers this tentative statement: "I am also informed that Levine or Lawien probably was a Jew by birth, but must have changed his religion—perhaps when he married Rachael?—or he would have been written down in the records: 'Levine the Jew.'"[38] In 1978, James Flexner produced a biography focused wholly on Hamilton's early life, which echoes Atherton's findings about Levine in more definitive terms. "He was not legally considered a Jew," Flexner writes, citing Atherton.[39] Robert Hendrickson's 1981 book *The Rise and Fall of Alexander Hamilton* similarly claims, "St. Croix records of the time generally identified Jews as such, but Lavien is not so identified. It may be that he had disavowed Judaism by the time of his marriage to Rachel."[40] Meanwhile, William Cissel, a historian with the National Park Service on St. Croix, issued a report in 2004 that expresses doubt Levine was Jewish and repeats Atherton's reasoning: "He was not identified as a Jew (*Joder*) in annual registers."[41]

Plantagies Nommer		*Capable Ma. Kvin.*	*Ma.*	*Over Aar*	*Under*	
	Transport	554	30	60	103	
1.	Emanuel Aboab	13		3	3	19 Dec: 1743.
1.	Francis Brooks	18	4	5		d= dato
1.	Samuel Dauning					d= dato
2.	Francis Broocks					18 april 1737.
3.	James Boyle	8	5		2	12 dec: 1737.
4.	Edward Evans Arsving	23	2		4	10 Feb: 1740.
5.	Friderich Moths Arsving	61	11	6	14	19 Dec: 1743.
6.	James Koones Enche og Arsinger	12	3	4	10	24 Maij 1738.
7.	Valentin French	33		1	5	d.
8.	Joseph Robbinson					29 octob: 1738.
9.	James Lython	16			8	24 Maij 1738.
10.	Samuel Dauning	23	2		7	29 octob: 1738.
11.	Joseph Jones	37	3	12		20 Junij 1739.
12.	Samuel Dauning					20 Aug: 1739.
12.	Johan Michael Lavien	10			7	d= dato

This land register from St. Croix lists Emanuel Aboab, who was Jewish, in the first entry and Johan Levine (under the spelling "Lavien") in the last. Notably, the Danish term indicating Jewish identity, *Joder*, does not appear for either of them. *Source*: Mandtalslister og matrikler (1741–1755), Rigsarkivet (Danish National Archives, Copenhagen).

However, the notion that the Danish records necessarily identified Jews *as* Jews is erroneous. The names of six other residents of St. Croix who were known Jews appear a total of ninety-eight times in the island's *Matrikler* (land register) and *Mandtalslister* (census list) for 1741–1755. In ninety-seven of those entries, the clerks logged no reference whatsoever to these Jews' religious identity;[42] only in one anomalous instance is *Joder* used.[43] For over a century now, the basis for denying that Levine was Jewish has been the absence of the term *Joder* next to his name. In reality, these Danish records provide no grounds for concluding he was a Gentile by birth or choice.[44]

Cissel also argues that Levine was probably not Jewish because "Jews listed in the annual St. Croix property, population, and head-tax registers . . . bore Sephardic surnames."[45] Yet it does not follow that because many of the colony's Jews were Sephardic, Levine was therefore not Jewish. Caribbean Jews in general and St. Croix's Jews in particular were not exclusively of Spanish-Portuguese descent. Records from the Privy Council of St. Croix during Levine's era explicitly acknowledge the presence of both Sephardic and Ashkenazi Jews on the island.[46]

The precise details of Johan Michael Levine's engagement to Rachel Faucette remain lost to history, but whatever the nature of their courtship, it culminated in a wedding in 1745 that was most likely held at the Grange.[47] Rachel bore Johan a son, Peter, the subsequent year. The circumstances surrounding Peter's religious life harmonize with the notion that he was not Christian by birth or upbringing. Unlike his maternal cousins on the island who were dutifully baptized shortly after their births, Peter was not. Only in adulthood did Peter undertake a baptism in the process of joining the Anglican Church.[48] While Anglican doctrine called for infant baptism, there were three circumstances under which Anglicans would have baptized an adult. The first involved someone who grew up in a Christian denomination that practiced adult rather than infant baptism (such as Mennonites) and who had yet to undergo an adult baptism in his original church. However, this possibility could not have applied to Peter because no such denomination operated on St. Croix at that time.[49] Another potential explanation for an adult baptism in the Anglican Church is that the person in question had been baptized in a non-Trinitarian denomination of Christianity (for instance, Unitarians). Anglicans accepted baptisms from other Christian denominations as valid, except those that reject the Trinity: the belief that God is the Father, the Son, and the Holy Ghost. So the Anglican Church would have rebaptized someone whose initial baptism had not been in the name of the Trinity.[50] Yet Peter could not have fallen under this category either because there were no non-Trinitarian denominations on St. Croix while he lived on the island.[51] A final reason why Anglicans would have baptized an adult—the only one plausibly pertaining to Peter—is that the person was converting to Christianity.

Hamilton scholars, fixed on the assumption that Peter Levine was born Christian, have been confounded by his adult baptism when they do not ignore it altogether. In 1939, the Danish military officer H. U. Ramsing published a study of Hamilton's origins that notes of Peter, "On Nov. 22, 1769 he was on St. Croix where he, strangely enough, was baptized."[52] Ron Chernow's sweeping biography *Alexander Hamilton* (2004) characterizes Peter's adult baptism as "shocking and seemingly inexplicable," and poses a question for which Chernow has no sure answer: "Why had he not been baptized before?"[53] Cissel is also puzzled by Peter's adult baptism, describing it as "most curious."[54]

That Rachel and Johan failed to infant baptize Peter is indeed strange, shocking, inexplicable, and curious if we cling to the presupposition that Peter was Christian throughout his life. But if Rachel converted to Judaism prior to his birth, then the matrilineal nature of Jewish identity would make Peter a Jew, and this long-standing mystery about his need for an adult baptism is easily explained.[55] Still another possibility is that Rachel did not convert to Judaism herself but agreed to raise Peter as a Jew to appease her husband.[56] Yet such a scenario is unlikely owing to the matrilineality of Jewish identity and the fact that, as we will see, Rachel maintained ties to Jewry well after Johan and Peter were no longer part of her life.[57] It is also worth noting that the choice of the name "Peter," which is not conventionally Jewish, does not necessarily indicate a Christian identity. Some Jews at this time gave their children non-Jewish first names such as Mark, James, and Andrew.[58]

There were certainly enough Jews on St. Croix to have convened for Rachel a *beit din*—a Jewish court that could authorize a conversion. The Talmud requires only three adult Jewish males to constitute a *beit din*, and none need be a rabbi. For a woman converting to Judaism, the sole Talmudic obligation is immersion in a ritual bath known as a *mikveh*.[59] A conversion for Rachel would not have been unique in the Atlantic world; other Christian women at the time converted to the faith of their Jewish husbands.[60] Given the paucity of Jews on St. Croix relative to many other islands, it would be unsurprising if Levine sought out a Gentile willing to convert in the absence of a suitable Jewish-born woman to marry.

————

Around five years after their wedding, the marriage between Johan and Rachel Levine deteriorated to the point where he had her imprisoned for adultery. Rachel endured months in a cell usually occupied by petty criminals and disobedient slaves.[61] Johan later said that he had hoped, upon her release, "everything would change to the better and that she, as a wedded wife, [would] change her unholy way of life."[62] Yet once freed from her confinement, Rachel boarded a ship for the island of St. Kitts, abruptly deserting her spiteful husband and their young son.[63]

St. Kitts, like St. Croix, belonged to the Leeward Islands. There the still legally married Rachel met a Christian colonist from Scotland named James Hamilton. Many an enterprising Scotsman moved to St. Kitts hoping to profit from either crops or commerce before returning home. Although James claimed lineage in one of Scotland's aristocratic families, he never met with much success in the West Indies, lacking in talent or luck—or perhaps both. The ill-fated James and Rachel relocated to the neighboring island of Nevis, where Rachel had spent her childhood.[64]

Dominating Nevis's landscape is an extinct volcano, whose peak is perennially kissed by low-hanging clouds. The volcano, thick with green forests, slopes downward into hills, valleys, and beaches before disappearing into the sea. One eighteenth-century observer, approaching

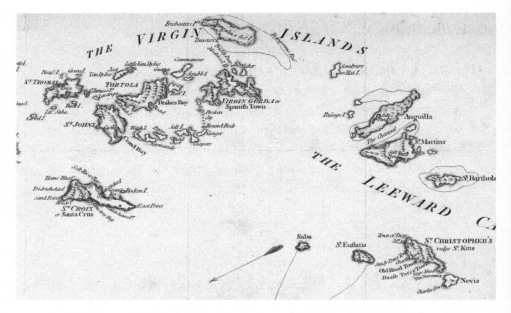

The distance from St. Croix (also known as Santa Cruz) to St. Kitts (St. Christopher) is about 150 miles. Nevis is only two miles from St. Kitts. *Source: A map of the Caribbee, Granadilles and Virgin Isles*. London: Published by M. Richmond; sold by W. Faden & J. Harris, 1779. Library of Congress, Geography and Map Division.

Nevis by boat, described how "some refreshing rains had made the whole face of the earth look so verdant and smiling, that no other part of the Globe, which I have as yet seen, could afford a richer gratification of its kind."[65]

The island brimmed with wildlife, from native pelicans to imported monkeys.[66] One visitor described a "certain monstrous spider" that was larger than "the palm of a man's hand." And the air hummed with birds of "such art and speed that the huntsman's dexterity is not comparable." Nevis boasted all manner of lizard, the longest of which stretched five feet. When European settlers first tried to kill these giant lizards for food, their bullets proved surprisingly ineffective. Indigenous people taught the naive newcomers that a stick shoved up a lizard's nostril was the surest way to bring death to the reptile and dinner to the colonist.[67]

A French geographer created this map of Nevis at the time that Hamilton was living on the island. *Source*: Jacques Nicolas Bellin, *Carte de l'isle de Nieves* [Paris, 1764]. Library of Congress, Geography and Map Division.

As with St. Croix, a slave-based sugarcane economy was the lifeblood of Nevis. A network of paths hewn through the trees connected the various sugar estates.[68] The richest soil was to be found in the valleys, but even the flinty land closer to the volcano's peak was employed for sugarcane.[69] So central was sugar to island life that it substituted for currency. "Pounds of sugar and not pounds of sterling is the balance of all their accounts," noted an Englishman.[70] Because nearly every inch of arable terrain was reserved for sugar, islanders imported most of their food rather than making it fresh. Their diet suffered accordingly. In the words of one disappointed diner, the butter was "bad and the cheese worse."[71]

Upwards of fifty vessels a year departed Nevis for England, their hulls full of sugar.[72] Each shipment was a tacit testament to the slaves whose lives were sacrificed to produce what the British called "white gold." Due to the island's acute demand for slave labor, blacks outnumbered whites by more than seven to one. The insufferable workday of a slave could stretch to eighteen hours during boiling season in late winter and early spring.[73] At night, the fires from the boiling houses illuminated Nevis in a fantastic display of light.[74]

———

It was on Nevis where Alexander Hamilton was born out of wedlock to Rachel Levine and James Hamilton in 1754. They already had one son together, named James Jr.[75] According to island lore, the boys grew up in Nevis's port village, Charlestown.[76] Facing west from the shoreline, Alexander would have seen an endless stretch of Caribbean waters; turning east, Charlestown's maze of winding streets and wooden homes.

Island life was gritty. Slave auctions and public whippings were common sights.[77] In the pointedly named Gallows Bay, captured pirates marked their final moments with the tightening grip of the hangman's noose.[78] A clergyman who lived in Charlestown for nine months described a bizarre habit among the townspeople that was thought to detoxify their bodies. The river water was "operated both by stool and urine" and the locals "would drink of it till they puked, and say they found great benefit by so doing." The clergyman opted not to join them, explaining, "As I have an aversion to puking, I never cared to use it in that way."[79] If Alexander Hamilton ever partook in this curious tradition in his youth, it was not a practice known to have continued into his adulthood.

Charlestown was home to a Jewish community. In the seventeenth century, Sephardic Jews facing expulsion from Portuguese Brazil had found refuge on various Dutch and British islands in the West Indies, including Nevis.[80] Jews arrived in Nevis no later than the 1670s, and within fifty years they comprised fully one-quarter of Charlestown's white population. The town featured the trappings of an established Jewish neighborhood, complete with a synagogue, cemetery, and pathway in between known as "Jew's Alley." This kind of walkable distance between a synagogue and burial ground was standard Jewish practice. There was also "Jew Street," where many Jews resided.[81]

The Jews of Nevis, like their Christian neighbors, were implicated in the institution of slavery. While it appears that these Jews were not especially involved in the slave trade,[82] some notable portion did own slaves. An eighteenth-century priest reported that "with the respect to the Jews" on Nevis and St. Kitts, "many [were] owners of numbers of slaves." He also observed that throughout the Leeward Islands, slaves operated markets on Sundays when they would "traffick with the Jews in colonies where Jews live, and with the looser sort of Christians."[83] Although Jews were second-class citizens relative to white Christians, their marginality was of course negligible compared to the subjugation of slaves.

Today the last surviving remnant of the Jewish presence on Nevis is the cemetery. Typical of Sephardic tradition, the horizontal tombstones are partially elevated from the ground. Their inscriptions mix Hebrew, Portuguese, and English, reflecting the linguistic acumen that made Jews so valuable as merchants. Several tombstones bear the same verse from the book of Samuel: "May his soul be bound up in the bond of everlasting life." The image of open hands on the grave of one Daniel Cohen is symbolic of a priestly blessing.[84] All the graves were dug facing east toward Jerusalem, as per Jewish custom, so that upon resurrection during the Messianic Age, the deceased could walk to the Holy Land.[85]

———

Jewish identity is complex and can assume at least eight forms. *Personal identity* means that an individual sees herself as Jewish. *Communal identity* signifies that someone is accepted as a Jew by his local Jewish community. *Public identity* relates to a person who is considered Jewish by her Gentile neighbors. *Universal identity* pertains to an individual whom any Jewish congregation in the world would acknowledge as a member of the faith. *Legal identity* denotes that someone meets the requirements of Jewish law—that is, he is either the child of a Jewish woman or himself a convert to Judaism. *Ethnic identity* applies to a person who is descended from the ancient Israelites. *Religious identity* concerns adherence to the devotional obligations of Judaism. *Cultural identity* entails an association with the customs, lifestyle, ethics, art, and/or heritage of the Jewish people.

These varieties can overlap but may not necessarily. For instance, the children of a Jewish woman who sheds her faith and hides her past are still legally Jews despite their having no knowledge of their true religious background and thus no personal Jewish identity. A crypto-Jew practicing the faith only in secret to stave off persecution could have a personal Jewish identity, and even a communal one within a subculture of fellow crypto-Jews, but no public identity as a Jew. An individual who converts to Judaism under the auspices of a meager Jewish community— one on the fringes of the diaspora with unrigorous requirements for conversion—might find acceptance communally but not universally. Someone whose father's lineage traces back to the ancient Israelites and whose mother is a Gentile has some Jewish ethnicity but no claim to a legal identity as a Jew.

The eighteenth-century Atlantic world throws into high relief the idiosyncrasies of Jewish identity. Under the Inquisition in Spain and Portugal, for example, Jews had been forced to flee or convert to Catholicism, and many of the conversos' descendants revived their Jewish heritage after migrating to more tolerant territories on both sides of the ocean.[86] Meanwhile, crypto-Judaism persisted in lands under Spanish or Portuguese rule, including New World colonies like New Mexico and

Brazil.[87] Further testament to the diversity of Jewish identities was the sizable population of black Jews in the Dutch colony of Suriname that resulted from relations between Jews and slaves.[88] And, as mentioned earlier, there are several known instances of Christian women who converted to Judaism for marriage.

In a world where Jewishness had a multiplicity of dimensions and assumed a variety of forms, the question of Alexander Hamilton's religious identity cannot be reduced to a simple Jew/Gentile binary. Instead, we must consider the likelihood that Hamilton had a Jewish identity in one or more of its many senses for any span of his life. With respect to Jewish law, the Talmud specifies that Jewish identity is matrilineal and, even for converts, permanent.[89] Therefore, if Rachel converted to Judaism to marry John Levine, then Alexander Hamilton legally would be a Jew—at least by the standards of those who oversaw his mother's conversion—regardless of whether she still presented herself as Jewish at the time of Alexander's birth. And the case for Alexander's Jewish identity does not rest on Talmudic technicalities alone. There is compelling evidence that Rachel passed on some communal Jewish identity to her son (and if so, his communal identity likely coincided with other forms of Jewish identity, such as public and personal).

It must first be noted, however, that there is little historical documentation concerning Alexander's birth that is instructive here. If Alexander were born a Jew, he would have been circumcised consistent with Jewish tradition, and if born a Christian, baptized. Yet no records survive from the synagogue in Charlestown, and so if Alexander were indeed circumcised, any source attesting to such a ritual has been lost.[90] Meanwhile, extant church registers from Nevis for the 1750s show no baptismal entry for Alexander (or for his brother, James Jr.). These parish records, however, are fragmentary and thus cannot provide definitive conclusions.[91]

The best evidence of Alexander's Jewish identity is that he attended a Jewish school on Nevis. While he was not known in adulthood for divulging much about his origins, even to his family, one happy memory he did share with his children was his Jewish education. "Rarely as he alluded to his personal history," Hamilton's son recalled, "he mentioned with a smile, his having been taught to repeat the Decalogue [i.e., the Ten Commandments] in Hebrew, at the school of a Jewess, when so small that he was placed standing by her side upon a table."[92] (It remains unknown whether James Jr. also attended this school.)

Many Hamilton biographers make no mention of his Jewish instruction.[93] Those who reference this peculiar detail typically do so in passing without any reflection on why a supposedly Christian child attended a school for Jews.[94] The few scholars who try to make sense of this curiosity point to his illegitimacy. In her 1970 history of St. Croix, Florence Lewisohn maintains without evidence, "Schooling for the boys had been one of the problems in Nevis, since they were held ineligible for church school there because the parents were unmarried. Alexander had gone for a time to the Jewish school."[95] Chernow uses more measured language in speculating along similar lines: "His illegitimate birth may well have barred him from Anglican instruction."[96] There is, in fact, no basis for concluding that Alexander's out-of-wedlock birth raised an obstacle to his attending a church school on Nevis, and good cause to think otherwise. Church records from around the Caribbean—including the very church to which Rachel's parents had belonged on Nevis—list infants who were "bastards" yet baptized.[97] We have no grounds for assuming that a church willing to baptize children *despite* their illegitimacy would at the same time refuse to educate those very children *because* of their illegitimacy.[98]

Moreover, there is ample reason to expect that Alexander would have only attended the Jewish school if the community's Jews accepted him as a coreligionist. Although no records still exist from Hamilton's school, we can glean much about the nature of contemporary Jewish education from other schools in that era.[99] As with Christian schools, Jewish educational institutions existed to impart religious precepts. And because Jews were a dispersed minority, their schools took on the added mission of cultivating a shared sense of Jewish peoplehood that bound Jews together across the diaspora. In sum, students gained the knowledge, customs, and identity necessary for adult lives as observant Jews.[100] Jewish schooling for any given child in this era is, therefore, a strong indicator that the local Jewish community considered the

Parish Register of St. George's, Nebis.*

1738 August 12th Baptized Daniel Son of Sarah Harris. Illegitimate
     Septemʳ 5th Baptized Frances D. of Simon Browne Deceased & Sarah
        his Widow
     Septemʳ 9th Buried Anne Herbert W. of Thomas Herbert
     Do.   Married Thomas Parry & Frances Kelly

The entry for August 12 shows that Daniel Harris was baptized despite his classification as "illegitimate." *Source*: Vere Langford Oliver, ed., *Caribbeana: Being Miscellaneous Papers Relating to the History, Genealogy, Topography, and Antiquities of the British West Indies*. Vol. 3. London: Mitchell Hughes and Clarke, 1914.

student a Jew. What's more, the Talmud prohibits Jews from teaching the Torah to Gentiles (and Hamilton made clear to his children that he undertook, at the very least, rudimentary study of the Torah in its original Hebrew), furnishing yet another reason for Hamilton's school on Nevis to admit Jewish students exclusively.[101]

The fraught nature of Jewish-Christian relations on Nevis further suggests that the Jewish school would likely have educated Hamilton only if local Jews saw him as one of their own. Britain's quest to populate its Caribbean colonies with settlers led to laxer restrictions on religious minorities than those applied in Britain proper. Jews, along with other out-groups such as Quakers and Catholics, gained a foothold on islands like Nevis. But religious diversity was not a principle that the British celebrated; it was, instead, a reality that required begrudging acceptance in the name of cash crop cultivation. Tolerance for minority faiths had its limits, especially as islands reached peak productivity and, accordingly, the imperative for additional immigration waned. By 1701, Nevis had banned both Catholics and Quakers. When the Leeward Islands General Assembly—a federated legislature with representatives from Britain's various Leeward colonies—sought to repeal restrictions on Catholics in 1752, the local Nevis legislature erupted in protest.[102]

Nevis's Jews fared better than Quakers and Catholics but still faced civic inequality and cultural stigma. Members of the Jewish faith were disallowed from casting ballots, serving as jurors, joining the militia, becoming justices of the peace, or holding elected office.[103] In 1694, the Leeward Islands General Assembly barred Jews from trading commodities. Although that prohibition would later be lifted, there was still plenty of cause for anxiety among Jews on Nevis and throughout the British West Indies. They were prominent as merchants, and Jewish success in commerce was perceived to come at the expense of Christians. On Barbados, English merchants complained to the Crown that Jews were crafty swindlers who threatened to rob the island of its wealth: "The Jews are a people so subtle in matters of trade that in a short time they will not only engross trade among themselves, but will be able to direct the benefit hereof to other places."[104] Aggrieved Gentile merchants in Jamaica used more dire terms, lamenting, "The Jews eat us and our children out of all trade. . . . This is a great and growing evil, and had we not warning from other colonies, we should see our streets filled and the ships hither crowded with them. This means taking our children's bread and giving it to Jews."[105] Confronted with this kind of bigotry, Jamaican Jews sought to curry favor with local officials by gifting them "Jew pies," which were baked pies with coins inside.[106]

Nevis was scarcely immune to the antisemitism infecting the British West Indies at large. Nevisian Jews were pegged by the local legislature as "evil-minded persons, intending nothing but their own private gain, and the ruin of the poor." It was further alleged that these Jews tended to "buy whole cargoes of provisions at a cheap rate" and "retail them again at excessive prices, thereby forestalling the market."[107] The Jewish community may have been especially vulnerable to prejudice after a series of misfortunes bedeviled Nevis. Although anointed "the Queen of the Caribbees" in its early colonial history,[108] the island's condition steadily deteriorated. Antigua replaced Nevis as the capital of the Leeward Islands in 1687. Soon after, the Nevis-based Royal African Company lost its monopoly on trafficking slaves. The most devastating blow came in 1706, when an invading French force ransacked the island for eighteen days. With crops ravaged, homes reduced to rubble, and the courthouse set aflame, Nevis managed only a partial recovery in the decades to follow.[109] The governor of neighboring St. Kitts relayed to London in 1728 that "Nevis has quite lost its trade and is a desert island to what it was

thirty years ago."[110] Hurricanes, soil erosion, and slave rebellions com-
pounded Nevis's decline throughout the eighteenth century.[111]

In troubled times, Jews could become easy scapegoats. A reverend
conveyed to the bishop of London that among the free population on
Nevis, "one 4th are Jews, who have a synagogue here, and are said to be
very acceptable to the country part of the island, but are far from being
so to the town [i.e., Charlestown], by whom they are charged with taking the bread out of Christians' mouths." Charlestown's Jews were "by
many thought to be the true cause of the strange decay of this place."[112]
That fellow Jews had been expelled from the French West Indies likely
stoked anxieties for Jews on Nevis that a similar fate could befall
them.[113]

The geography of Jewish life in Charlestown reflects how the Jews
occupied a separate, and subordinate, rung on the island hierarchy. Jews
were not dispersed evenly throughout the town but rather concentrated
in a Jewish quarter. And this Jewish neighborhood was hardly the island's most prized real estate. Situated in south Charlestown, the Jewish
quarter was sandwiched between the jail on one side and a mosquito-
infested backwater called "the bogs" on the other.[114] Jews in many European nations similarly dwelled in their own, less desirable districts. In
other words, Jews and Christians did not move to Nevis and create a
new set of spatial and social dynamics with each other. Rather, they re-
created patterns of Jewish-Christian relations from the Old World—
patterns designed to ensure a degree of distance, both physical and cultural, between the two faith groups.[115] The clustered nature of Jewish
life on Nevis characterized other Jewish communities throughout the
Caribbean.[116] (We do not know where Rachel Levine lived on Nevis.
Island legend has it that she inhabited a waterfront property that she
inherited from her father, but the claim remains unsupported by historical evidence.)

The site of the official parish church in Charlestown further illustrates how the European practice of religious segregation migrated with
the colonists to Nevis. Known as St. Paul's, the church resided on the
northern corner of town, far from the synagogue. Throughout much of
Europe, church regulations called for maximal distance between Jewish

and Christian houses of worship. No such rule existed in Nevis, and yet the island's Christians chose to adhere to this convention anyway, testifying to the endurance of Old World religious customs.[117]

When Nevis's Christians made reference to someone who happened to be Jewish, that Jewish identity was often noted, underscoring that Jews' religious difference was a salient feature in the eyes of their Christian neighbors. One Gentile recorded after a fishing expedition, "In the month of July, 1719, one Mr. Moses Pinheiro, a Jew, and myself went to angle in Black Rock Pond."[118] A planter similarly remarked that a local woman compensated "Sampson the Jew for repairing an earring." The use of language like "the Jew" speaks to a mentality among island Christians that Jewish residents were fundamentally different.[119]

———

Given the role of Jewish schools in cultivating Jewish identity, the Talmudic prohibition on Jews teaching the Torah to Gentiles, and the segregation of Jewish and Christian life on Nevis, there is substantial cause to believe that the Jewish school would have educated Alexander Hamilton only if the local Jewish community recognized him as a fellow Jew. Alexander's attendance at the Jewish school is also the most compelling indication that his mother had converted to Judaism back on St. Croix. Under the tenets of Jewish law, recognition of Rachel as a Jew would have been a precondition for Alexander's own Jewish status. If we proceed from the conventional wisdom that Rachel lacked prior ties to Judaism, it becomes difficult to explain why she would, or how she even could, enroll her child in a Jewish school.

One wonders what the place of Alexander's father, a Christian, means for making sense of Alexander's religious identity. Alas, the record is silent; it is impossible to state the extent of James's involvement in Alexander's life. We do know that Rachel Levine never married James, which may have made it easier for the Jews of Nevis to accept her.

If Rachel did profess a Jewish identity even after fleeing St. Croix, her motivations for doing so remain a matter for speculation—and may have been more strategic than spiritual. Perhaps Rachel found it convenient on Nevis to trade on an earlier conversion to Judaism to secure some measure of acceptance in the Jewish community. And although that community constituted a sizable proportion of Nevis's free population, in absolute numbers the Jewish population there was far smaller than many sister congregations on other islands,[120] and so Nevis's Jews would have had little incentive to rebuff a woman willing to both claim a Jewish identity and contribute tuition payments to the school's coffers. Rachel and Alexander were marginal people; it would be altogether unsurprising if they found themselves on the margins of different faiths at different times in their lives. Indeed, the theory that they were Jewish—in at least some senses of the term and for at least some stretch of time—accounts for more evidence in the historical record than the long-standing assumption they were cradle-to-grave Christians.[121]

2

Exodus

AROUND THE TIME of Alexander Hamilton's eleventh birthday, in 1765, his family relocated to the site of Rachel Levine's past imprisonment: Christiansted, St. Croix. Notably, Rachel appears in the Danish tax rolls under her married name and sometimes under her maiden name but not as Rachel Hamilton, demonstrating that she made no pretense to be James Hamilton Sr.'s wife. James Sr. did move to Christiansted around the same time, but the fact that he is not mentioned at all in the rolls indicates that Rachel and her sons did not even live with him. He abandoned St. Croix altogether not long after his arrival, further suggesting a lack of engagement in the lives of his boys and their mother.[1] Johan Levine, for his part, had secured a divorce from a local court years earlier during Rachel's lengthy absence from St. Croix. She need not have worried about daily run-ins with her ex-husband, as he was now living in the town of Frederiksted on the other side of the island.[2]

St. Croix had come to vie with Jamaica and Barbados as a premier sugar producer in the West Indies.[3] Christiansted was home to a gradually growing population of some 2,200 residents[4] and featured all the varied imports typical of a Caribbean port city. Islanders could purchase flour from New York, oats from Denmark, wine from Madeira—and from the Gold Coast of West Africa, slaves. The local newspaper featured advertisements from craftsmen who journeyed to St. Croix to offer their services. A jeweler from Copenhagen who "flatters himself with giving the utmost satisfaction" promoted his goldsmithing talents,

The harbor in Christiansted, St. Croix. *Source*: Kort og tegninger (1600–1920), Rigsarkivet (Danish National Archives, Copenhagen).

while a Bostonian skilled in "the sailmaker's business in all its branches" sought a market among the seafaring.[5]

Life on the island did not center solely on sugar and commerce, at least for whites who could afford to partake in festivities and cultural pursuits. Celebratory balls and St. Patrick's Day merriment added color to the social calendar. For those partial to the literary arts, the printing office on Queen Street sold German poetry and English treatises. Planters and merchants hoping to impart some measure of erudition to their children could send them to a private school, which touted a curriculum in "spelling, reading, and writing, together with that truly laudable and excellent accomplishment, the noble science of arithmetic." (There is no evidence that Alexander attended any Caribbean school other than the Jewish one on Nevis.) Rival theater companies put on Shakespearean classics, catering to the tastes of an island where the gentry class had far more Brits than colonists of any other European nationality. Twelve shillings purchased a ticket to a performance of *Hamlet* or *King Lear*.[6]

Rachel Levine and her two sons took up residence at 34 Company Street in Christiansted. They resided on the second story, while Rachel ran a store on the ground floor that sold provisions like beef, apples, and rice.[7] Her library held nearly three dozen books, which likely fed Alexander's hunger for knowledge that would characterize him throughout his life.[8] Rachel's mother, now deceased, had bequeathed to her several slaves. One of those slave's children, Ajax, was enlisted to attend to Alexander.[9]

———

In February 1768, both Rachel and Alexander were struck with a mysterious illness. A doctor was summoned to the fevered mother and son, who suffered together in a single bed. Thirteen-year-old Alexander pulled back from the brink, but on February 19, Rachel Levine drew her dying breath.[10]

Rachel's passing was marked in the St. John's church register, a fact that would seem on its face to signal that she identified as a Christian, at least at the end of her life. However, the recording of a death in a church register may not necessarily indicate that the deceased was a member of that church or even an adherent of the Christian faith generally. At the time, many governments that did not yet keep civil records of births and deaths instead relied on religious institutions to log such details, not just for their respective parishioners but for those outside the flock as well. Jewish people were especially likely to appear in church registers in areas where there were not enough Jews to have a synagogue with its own records.[11]

The details of Rachel's burial may be telling of her religious identity. A plot in a Jewish burial ground would not have been an option for Rachel or anyone else on the island at that time; the earliest epitaph in St. Croix's Jewish cemetery dates from 1779, eleven years after her death.[12] An island Jew in 1768 could therefore only be laid to rest at a family home, and in fact Rachel was buried at the Grange, the estate that her sister's husband had purchased. To be sure, plantations like the

Grange often had graveyards, so such a burial was not unusual for an islander of any faith.[13] Still, the fact that Rachel was not interred in the church cemetery would at least conform with the theory that she had a Jewish identity until her death. She also bore her ex-husband's surname even at the end of her life—eighteen years after leaving him—another possible indication of an enduring link to Judaism. Her death was recorded under Johan's last name and a slightly varied spelling of her given name: "Rachael Levine."[14]

A stubborn myth among Hamilton scholars is that a local reverend presided over her funeral. H. U. Ramsing's *Alexander Hamilton's Birth and Parentage* describes how "the English minister, the Rev. Cecil Wray Goodchild, performed the ceremony of casting earth upon the coffin."[15] In a work that is otherwise exhaustively documented, Ramsing conspicuously cites no source to substantiate this statement. Presumably, he uses the fact that Rachel's death appears in the St. John's register to infer that the Reverend Goodchild of St. John's must have officiated. Broadus Mitchell's study of the first half of Hamilton's life proceeds along similar lines: "Rachael's body was taken in a hearse to the family plot of James Lytton on Grange plantation and was buried there, February 20, by the English minister, the Reverend Cecil Wray Goodchild." Mitchell adds that the "particulars of Rachael's illness and death are from claims presented to the probate court" as well as from "the burial register of St. John's."[16] Yet neither the probate court record nor the burial register make any mention of the Reverend Goodchild's attendance at the interment.[17] Robert Hendrickson's biography of Hamilton follows Mitchell nearly word for word—"Rachel's body was taken in a hearse to James Lytton's family plot on Grange plantation and buried there on February 20 by the English minister, the Reverend Cecil Wray Goodchild"—while providing no evidence for the assertion.[18] Meanwhile, Willard Sterne Randall's *Alexander Hamilton: A Life* takes poetic license in imagining that "under ancient mahogany trees in the burial yard overlooking the azure Caribbean, Alexander heard the local Church of England curate intone the matter-of-fact Anglican formula."[19] And in *Odd Destiny*, author Marie B. Hecht mistakenly writes that Rachel "was buried in the churchyard of St. John's Anglican church."[20]

These biographers' sundry assumptions notwithstanding, there is no source in the historical record documenting the presence of the Reverend Goodchild at Rachel Levine's funeral.[21]

———

In the aftermath of his father's flight and mother's burial, Alexander confronted life as an orphan. The tragedies of his childhood only multiplied from there. His vengeful stepfather, Johan Levine, legally challenged the right of Alexander and his brother, James Jr., to their inheritance on account of their illegitimacy. The local probate court awarded Levine's son, Peter—Rachel's only child born in wedlock—the entirety of the estate.[22] Alexander and James Jr. were left in the custody of a cousin named Peter Lytton, and within a matter of months Peter committed suicide. According to the St. Croix records, he "stabbed or shot himself to death."[23] Alexander Hamilton's achievements in America are all the more impressive when considered in light of the calamities that befell him in childhood.[24] His contemporaries in the United States would fail to fully appreciate his rise from these harrowing origins partly because of his lifelong silence about his Caribbean past.

Any identity as a Jew that Hamilton may have had almost certainly died with his mother. A plucky youth like him would have been disinclined to compound his troubles as a dispossessed orphan with a second-class religious status. Had Hamilton still resided on Nevis at this point—with its Jewish community and the Jewish school that educated him—perhaps Rachel's passing would have been less likely to occasion her son's disaffiliation from the Jewish faith. But St. Croix was home to far fewer Jews than Nevis. If Hamilton ever laid claim to a Jewish identity, he was now bereft of a family or community that might have kept it alive.

While James Jr. began an apprenticeship with a carpenter, Alexander finally had a moment of luck that allayed his seemingly endless succession of hardships—an affluent merchant named Thomas Stevens agreed to house him. Stevens's son Edward was, like Hamilton, a precocious youth, and the two boys became lifelong friends. In fact, they looked so similar in appearance that commentators from Hamilton's day to our own have speculated that Thomas Stevens might have been Hamilton's biological father.[25]

Hamilton worked as a clerk at the import-export firm of Beekman and Cruger, a job he had begun even before his mother's death.[26] Although he did not personally travel off St. Croix, Hamilton was now immersed in vast trading networks and exposed to seafaring merchants from across the Atlantic. Given the prominence of Jewish traders in the Caribbean, it is all but certain that Hamilton came into contact with the kinds of Jewish merchants with whom he would later collaborate in America. His time at Beekman and Cruger offered him a practical education in global markets that informed his later stewardship of the Treasury Department. While many other founders of the United States grew up on farms and plantations, and hence were schooled in agrarian life, Hamilton was uniquely prepared to become the visionary of America's financial future.

The Beekman and Cruger firm trafficked in a wide variety of goods, from rope and rice to brick and bread—and occasionally slaves.[27] Hamilton learned the nuances of accounting, pricing, and inventory. He gained mastery over exchange rates between numerous national currencies. And perhaps most significantly for his later endeavors, he cultivated an advanced understanding of credit.[28]

One of the firm's partners, Nicholas Cruger, recognized Hamilton's extraordinary acumen for commerce. When poor health prompted Cruger to return to his native city of New York for five months in 1771, he entrusted the firm to his teenage clerk.[29] Hamilton proved equal to the task, managing the firm's affairs with remarkable poise for someone so young. After one Captain William Newton arrived with a shipment of subpar mules from South America, Hamilton described to Cruger's brother "41 mules in such order that I have been obliged to send all of them to pasture, and of which I expect at least a third will die."[30] Hamilton chastised Captain Newton in unequivocal terms: "Reflect continually on the unfortunate voyage you have just made and endeavor to make up for the considerable loss therefrom."[31] Even in correspondence with his employer, Hamilton could be blunt. As he once told Cruger, "Your

Philadelphia flour is really very bad, being of a most swarthy complexion and withal very untractable."[32] The confident judgment, swift decision-making, and unvarnished candor that would all define Hamilton's life in America were already on full display at this early stage.

A newly unearthed court transcript from 1771 concerning Cruger's firm demonstrates that Hamilton unquestionably identified as a Christian by this point in his life. But it also raises questions about the recency and extent of Hamilton's church affiliation. He was called as a witness to testify about the delivery of goods in a legal dispute. To determine Hamilton's competence to take an oath on the Bible before testifying, he was asked "how old he was and of what religion, and if he had received the sacrament of the altar [i.e., communion], as well as if he understood the meaning of the oath." Hamilton said that he was seventeen and assured the court that he was "brought up in the Reformed religion as it was observed in the English Established Church [i.e., the Anglican Church]." He conceded, however, that "he had not yet received communion." The lawyers debated whether Hamilton could take the oath; in the end, the court forbade him from so doing. He was permitted to share what he knew about the delivery of the goods in question, albeit in a statement lacking the greater credibility that the oath would have provided.[33]

While there is no reason to doubt Hamilton's claim that he was an Anglican in 1771, his failure to have taken communion suggests that his relationship with the church had not been lifelong. The text governing Anglican rituals—*The Book of Common Prayer*—specified that the related rites of confirmation and communion were to take place in childhood. Those eligible for confirmation were "children being now come to the years of discretion," defined as youngsters capable of reciting "the Creed, the Lord's Prayer, and the Ten Commandments" and answering some basic questions about Anglican theology. Once confirmed, a child could then take communion. As *The Book of Common Prayer* stipulated, "there shall none be admitted to the holy Communion, until such time as he be confirmed."[34]

It seems, then, that Hamilton's comment about being "brought up" Anglican had shades of both truth and exaggeration. In all likelihood he *was* brought up Anglican, at least nominally, in the years that he lived with Thomas Stevens. But Hamilton's choice of words must also be read in the context of the legal case. Seeking to give testimony for the benefit of the man who paid his salary, Hamilton had a clear incentive to puff up his Christian credentials in court. And the fact that Hamilton had not received a sacrament by age seventeen that was expected of Anglican children is consistent with the theory that he came late to Christianity. As we will see, his relationship with Christianity in his American adulthood would be largely ambivalent. Even at the twilight of his life, when a bleeding Hamilton was laid down on his deathbed, he still had never taken communion.

———

Although Hamilton was of considerable use to his trading firm, he did not thrill to the life of a clerk. Island hierarchy positioned European planters at the top rung, African slaves at the bottom, and clerks somewhere in between. Hamilton bristled at the strictures of a stratified society that afforded little hope for advancement. In a revealing letter to his childhood friend Edward "Ned" Stevens, who was then studying in New York, Hamilton expressed an intense hunger to rise above his modest circumstances: "To confess my weakness, Ned, my ambition is [so] prevalent that I condemn the groveling conditions of a clerk . . . and would willingly risk my life, though not my character, to exalt my station." He added, "I wish there was a war." Hamilton believed that for someone like him—without an esteemed father or extensive fortune—martial glory was the surest path to respectability.[35]

At the time that he penned these sentiments, in 1769, colonists in both North America and the West Indies were agitating against taxes levied by the British Parliament, but the prospect of a military revolt by any of these colonies against the motherland was not yet imaginable. War was more of an abstract hope rather than a concrete likelihood for Hamilton. Yet war would indeed break out the following decade and present Hamilton with the opportunity for battlefield heroics.

If commerce was a new subject for Hamilton in his St. Croix years, then Hebrew may have been an old one that he revived. Some scholars go so far as to claim that Hamilton was fluent in Hebrew.[36] While his level of proficiency is impossible to ascertain, if he did in fact achieve fluency, the Reverend Hugh Knox may have played some part. Hamilton became friendly with Knox,[37] who not only mastered Hebrew but insisted that it was a "duty" to study the Hebrew Bible in its "mother tongue." In one "discourse" that Knox published, he lamented the failure of English translations to adequately capture the majesty of the Psalms. "Words are too feeble," Knox reflected, "to express that sublimity of sentiment, that grandeur of figure and style, and that pure flame of ardent and rapturous devotion which animate almost every line of these wonderful compositions in the original Hebrew."[38] As a Christian interested in Hebrew, he was not alone. Christian Hebraists on both sides of the Atlantic were keen to read their Old Testament in its original language.[39]

———

After sundown on August 31, 1772, a catastrophic hurricane brutalized the Leeward Islands. Its eye passed directly over Christiansted. Amid gale-force winds and seventy-foot waves, homes were destroyed, ships hurled inland, and the lives of hundreds of islanders summarily extinguished. Survivors assessed the damage the next morning, uncovering the corpses of their neighbors strewn about the rubble.[40]

The best contemporary description of the storm came from the pen of an eighteen-year-old Alexander Hamilton, whose baroque letter detailing the calamity appeared in the local island paper. "It seemed as if a total dissolution of nature was taking place," he recounted. "The roaring of the sea and wind, fiery meteors flying about it in the air, the prodigious glare of almost perpetual lightning, the crash of the falling houses, and the ear-piercing shrieks of the distressed, were sufficient to strike astonishment into Angels." Hamilton's depiction of the hurricane included the line, "Jesus be merciful!" which is notable for its aberrancy— the name "Jesus" appears nowhere else in the voluminous writings and correspondence that he produced throughout his life.[41]

According to legend, the publication of Hamilton's letter in the news-paper suddenly and profoundly changed his life's trajectory because his precocious eloquence inspired islanders to raise money so that he could receive a college education in America.[42] In truth, Hamilton's patrons almost certainly were already acquainted with his intellectual prowess, and his letter about the hurricane likely confirmed—rather than created—their impression that he merited advanced schooling on the mainland.[43] Soon Hamilton was boarding a ship bound for Boston, with most accounts placing his arrival in the fall of 1772. From there, he jour-neyed south to the city that would one day be nicknamed Hamilton-opolis: New York.[44]

This initial stay in New York was brief. Although brilliant, Hamilton lacked formal schooling on St. Croix and was not yet ready for college. He used Hugh Knox's connections to secure a place at the Elizabeth-town Academy in New Jersey, where he quickly absorbed the prepara-tory curriculum.[45] His notebook from the time demonstrates that what-ever study of the Hebrew Bible he had begun in Nevis continued in America. Over several pages, Hamilton recorded a verse-by-verse para-phrase of the book of Genesis. He wrote in one column, "1. God created heaven and Earth 2. The earth shapeless and without light/spirit moved on the face of the waters," and then he scribbled in a second column, "inference that Earth and Sea were mingled together."[46]

When Hamilton set about to choose a college, he looked for an in-stitution that would allow him to accelerate through the curriculum according to his aptitude rather than force him to follow the standard academic calendar. His eagerness to hurdle through his studies was typi-cal of the constant sense of urgency that would characterize the rest of his life. The College of New Jersey (later Princeton) denied his request, but King's College (later Columbia) in New York was amenable to Hamilton's plan.[47]

Hamilton peddled the fiction that he was younger than his real age by some two-and-a-half years, claiming January 11, 1757 as his birthday.[48] Numerous biographers accept at face value the date of birth that Ham-ilton offered once he appeared in America.[49] Yet all the relevant evi-dence from the Caribbean debunks this myth and instead aligns with a

1754 birth year. In August of 1771, Hamilton testified in the previously mentioned legal case on St. Croix that he was seventeen years old.[50] Four months earlier, a poem published in the St. Croix newspaper in 1771 by "A. H."—widely believed to be Hamilton—included a note from the author describing himself as "a youth about seventeen."[51] This language suggests a sixteen-year-old with an imminent birthday. We can thus infer that Hamilton likely turned seventeen as early as April but no later than August 1771. This timeline accords with the record of the probate court that handled Rachel Levine's estate, which identified Hamilton as thirteen years old in February 1768.[52] It also harmonizes with documentation from Johan Levine's divorce proceedings from 1759. In that case, a witness recalled that back in 1757, Rachel's youngest child (i.e., Alexander) had been "about" three years old.[53] In sum, every relevant piece of evidence from the West Indies is consistent with a birth date between April and August 1754.

It is unsurprising that Hamilton disguised his true age. King's College skewed younger than other institutions of higher learning; the average incoming student at King's was only fifteen.[54] Aware of his outsider status, Hamilton was surely anxious to fit in with students who were a few years his junior. His small size and boyish face would have made the deception easy to carry out.[55] Having committed himself to a 1757 birth year after he arrived in America, Hamilton then had to maintain this fiction throughout his life for consistency's sake. And he did so without any Caribbean acquaintance ever exposing his falsehood. That Hamilton was able to misrepresent the date of his birth so successfully makes it all the more likely that he could obscure any Jewish origins for the duration of his adulthood without a West Indian contemporary correcting him.

———

Founded in 1754, King's College was situated in a stately three-story building with a cupola adorning its roof. The college sat atop a hill that gradually descended to the Hudson River.[56] A visiting Scotsman remarked that the setting was "one of the finest situations perhaps of any

King's College was renamed Columbia after the Revolution. *Source: View of Columbia College in the City of New York*. Miriam and Ira D. Wallach Division of Art, Prints and Photographs: Print Collection, New York Public Library.

college in the world."[57] The library, staircases, and student accommodations were all designed on the model of Oxford and Cambridge. A typical day for an undergraduate began with morning prayers in the chapel shortly after dawn, academic study until noon, a ninety-minute break for lunch, additional study until evening prayers, and then time to himself until curfew. Academic gowns were to be worn at all times, even when students ventured into town. The campus was encircled by a fence that (usually) reined in students after nightfall.[58]

The student body at King's was small, consisting of merely thirty-six pupils.[59] Undergraduates were exclusively white and male, and typically from well-to-do Protestant families (although there was a lone Jewish student in the 1770s named Isaac Abrahams). While the students were demographically similar to each other, they shared no common education prior to their arrival at King's. Some had received independent tutoring as children; others, like Hamilton, had attended preparatory academies. All that the college required for admission was sufficient ability in Latin and Greek, and even that standard was leniently applied.[60]

The King's College curriculum, following Oxbridge, emphasized classical civilization. The poetry, history, and philosophy of ancient Greece and Rome were seen as vital fodder for a student's intellectual development. Indeed, classical thought would deeply inform Hamilton's approach to the modern world throughout his career. Students also studied ethics, logic, rhetoric, mathematics, and metaphysics. When not attending lectures, undergraduates kept busy with assigned readings and by memorizing declamations—passages to be read aloud from either classical texts or their own essays.[61]

Given that much of Hamilton's college education was administered in private tutoring, we do not know which subjects he undertook. He may well have resumed his study of Hebrew while an undergraduate. This much is clear—Hamilton's intellect did not tire from the demanding curriculum. He was part of a quintet of classmates who gathered weekly of their own volition to hone their writing and speaking skills.[62]

A King's College education was intended to impart not just knowledge but virtue, and to that end the college banned all sorts of juvenile buffoonery. During Hamilton's time, the college president made use of a notorious "Black Book" that recorded indiscretions. Transgressive behavior ranged from the predictable (skipping classes) to the mischievous (teacup theft) to the downright unseemly (cockfighting). Punishment often entailed paying a fine or translating Latin texts.[63] In his later capacity as a trustee of the college, Hamilton would advise with moderation that a college president should "be of a disposition to maintain discipline without undue austerity."[64]

The academic year began in July and ran for four terms, each concluding with examinations. At the end of their fourth year, seniors had to pass a final evaluation covering the totality of the curriculum to earn the bachelor of arts degree. Routinely graduates then pursued one of the three learned professions of the day: law, medicine, or ministry. Given that King's was in a city rather than the countryside, it is little surprise that just as many alumni took up careers in commerce, finance, or manufacturing.[65]

The matter of Hamilton's relationship to Christianity during his undergraduate days was addressed after his death in a remembrance penned by his former roommate, Robert Troup. According to Troup, Hamilton "was a zealous believer in the fundamental doctrines of Christianity."[66] But there is cause enough to question the credibility of this account. In the only study to date focused exclusively on the topic of Hamilton and the Christian faith, historians Douglass Adair and Marvin Harvey write that his "manifestation of public piety" at King's was merely "skin-deep" given his postcollege "lapse into complete indifference" toward Christianity. They continue, "One suspects, too, a strong element of opportunism in the early display of conventional orthodoxy. Hamilton was probably paying his devout patrons for his college education with spiritual coin of less than sterling value."[67] Perhaps the same desire for belonging that led Hamilton to falsify his age also prompted him to make pretenses to religiosity in a college with an avowed Anglican affiliation.

Hamilton biographer Nathan Schachner challenges the accuracy of Troup's description by pointing out that Troup wrote this testimonial at the request of a clergyman, the Reverend Dr. John Mason. In Schachner's words, "The whole business has too much the air of having been thrown into the narrative for Dr. Mason's especial benefit."[68] That Troup's account contains other statements about Hamilton's past that are incorrect lends further doubt to this picture of religious fervor. And aside from Troup's remembrance, no evidence indicates that Hamilton enthusiastically embraced the Christian faith in his early adulthood. Regardless of Hamilton's religious practices at King's, he was largely disengaged from Christianity in the years that followed.

———

Hamilton's matriculation at King's made him not just a college man but, more importantly, a New Yorker. Depending on one's perspective, visitors to this bustling port encountered either a lively bastion of opportunity or a repugnant pit of vice. Thomas Jefferson condemned the city as a cesspool of "all the depravities of human nature."[69] John Adams found New York superficially impressive but substantively impoverished. "With all the opulence and splendor of this city, there is very little good breeding to be found," he griped. "At their entertainments there is no conversation that is agreeable. There is no modesty—no attention to one another. They talk very loud, very fast, and all together. If they ask you a question, before you can utter three words of your answer, they will break out upon you again—and talk away."[70] While New York may have repelled the genteel southerner and irascible New Englander, it was the ideal stage for a Caribbean orphan with boundless ambition. That city—a magnet for immigrants and transplants, merchants and lawyers, traders and financiers—would prove not merely background scenery but foundational to Hamilton's meteoric rise.

New York's population numbered around 25,000 when Hamilton arrived, making it the second-largest urban center in America after Philadelphia, with its 40,000 residents.[71] Little more than the southernmost mile of Manhattan was then settled. Amid the labyrinth of narrow streets were government buildings, houses of worship, and merchant homes.[72] King's was situated toward the northwestern corner of town. A block to the college's east was a triangular green expanse called the Common.[73]

Broadway was the widest avenue in the city, originating off Bowling Green park near the island's southern tip and running northward. Bowling Green featured a recently erected statue of King George III on horseback. The other noteworthy statue in town, on Wall Street, was of William Pitt in honor of his outspoken resistance to the Stamp Act, a 1765 piece of parliamentary legislation that had taxed a wide array of colonial goods and provoked riotous opposition from Americans. That New York commissioned both statues in 1770—the one, a symbol of British authority; the other, a celebration of American autonomy— aptly reflects the torn loyalties that characterized the city's political culture. Neither statue would survive the coming revolution intact. The king was ripped apart and remade into bullets by the Americans, while Pitt was decapitated by British soldiers.[74]

Among the churches lining Broadway was St. Paul's, known less for the salvation within its walls than for the sins just beyond them—the neighboring lot was home to 500 prostitutes and subversively called the "Holy Ground." King's College was only two short blocks away. As a visitor remarked, "The entrance to this college is through one of the

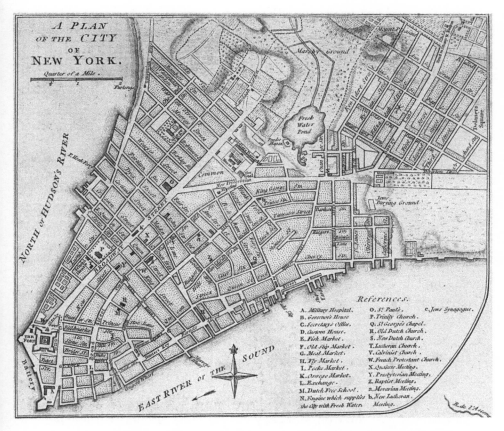

Map of New York. *Source*: Thomas Pownall and Samuel Holland, *The provinces of New York and New Jersey; with part of Pensilvania, and the province of Quebec.* London: Robt. Sayer & John Bennett, 1776. Library of Congress, Geography and Map Division.

streets where the most noted prostitutes live. This is certainly a temptation to the youth that have occasion to pass so often that way."[75] It remains unknown whether Hamilton, who had a weakness for women, ever indulged in such carnal pleasures. John Adams, for one, would show limited faith in Hamilton's self-restraint, describing him after his death as a "superabundance of secretions which he could not find whores enough to draw off."[76]

Near the corner of Broadway and Wall Street was City Hall. It housed the collections of the Union Library Society; for thirty shillings in dues,

patrons could peruse nearly a thousand volumes.[77] Farther east, at the
river's edge, the marketplaces alongside the wharves brimmed with all
manner of provisions. A pound of beef ran four pence, the same of butter sixteen pence, and a "good hen" no more than a shilling. Rum, cider,
and wine were all affordably priced. Only beer from London, at a steep
two shillings a bottle, was relatively costly.[78]

Although New York claimed only 3 percent of the population of London, it still faced the various problems of urban life. The New Gaol
prison, at the eastern corner of the Common, was deluged with con-
victed felons. The city took a number of measures to address rising
crime rates, from hiring patrolmen to installing street lamps. Disease ran
rampant as well, and a new hospital was under development on the
northern fringe of town.[79] Another hazard of a condensed population
was that an uncontained fire in a single home could threaten the entire
community. To mitigate the risk of a widespread outbreak, the city appointed a number of fire captains and offered a financial reward to who-
ever among them most promptly summoned his team of men to the
flames. Water pumps were also placed at regular intervals throughout
the city, although water potable enough for tea had to be hauled in from
the suburbs on carts.[80]

If Alexander Hamilton were to head through the college gates, down
Broadway past the Common, beyond the Holy Ground, turning left
onto Wall Street, then right at City Hall, and left again onto a cramped
lane called Mill Street, there he would have beheld a sight he had first
encountered as a child in Nevis—a synagogue.

3

Revolution

WHEN THE JEWS OF NEW YORK first formed a congregation, they chose a name rife with messianic significance: "Shearith Israel." These Hebrew words translate to "remnants of Israel," reflecting a prophecy that the scattering of the Jewish people was a necessary precondition for the coming of the Messiah and the ultimate reuniting of the dispersed Jewish tribes.[1] Jews had been present on the island of Manhattan since the days of Dutch rule in the seventeenth century, when the city was known as New Amsterdam.[2] The Dutch imposed significant restrictions on Jewish colonists, barring them from running for office, casting ballots, buying land, or worshipping publicly.[3] After the British took control of the city in 1664 and renamed it New York, Jews came to enjoy greater religious and economic freedom.[4] Small concentrations of Jews also appeared in Newport, Philadelphia, Charleston, and Savannah during the era of British colonial rule.[5]

New York Jewry tallied around 250 souls by the late colonial period.[6] With a vibrant congregation and commercial opportunity, the city's Jewish community highlights the rich possibilities for Jewish life in the New World even before the advent of a revolution waged in the name of equality. Still, European bigotries migrated westward across the Atlantic. New York may have been the most inclusive toward Jews of the thirteen colonies, but toleration there had its limits.

The hub of New York's Jewish community was the brick synagogue on Mill Street. Jewish donors from as far afield as Boston, Barbados, and Britain had helped fund its construction in 1730. All local Jews were expected to participate in synagogue life, and most lived in close proximity to the house of worship. At the heart of the building was the sanctuary where the congregants prayed. The ark was at the sanctuary's east end—that is, in the direction of Jerusalem—and housed the Torah scrolls on which the Five Books of Moses were inscribed. A glowing lamp above the ark symbolized the eternal light that had burned in the holy temples of Jerusalem in ancient times. During worship, the men took up the sanctuary's lower level while the women occupied a balcony. The president and vice president of the congregation enjoyed the best seating by the ark. Those who failed to pay sufficient dues were relegated to the least desirable seats.[7]

A Gentile physician who once observed a religious service at Shearith Israel noticed that the men were donning skull caps and prayer shawls—known as *kippot* and *tallitot* in Hebrew—but he had only a vague sense of what he was witnessing: "The men wore their hats in the synagogue and had a veil of some white stuff which they sometimes threw over their heads in their devotion." He also remarked that "the women, of whom some were very pretty, stood up in a gallery like a hen coop."[8]

Although Ashkenazi Jews had outnumbered their Sephardic counterparts at Shearith Israel since the 1720s, the congregation's customs continued to bear the distinctive mark of its Sephardic origins. In accordance with Sephardic practice, the leader of the religious services was positioned at the center, rather than the front, of the sanctuary. Hebrew prayers were intoned in the Sephardic style (as they still are to this day at Shearith Israel). And in a tradition that would end with the Revolution, the congregants offered a prayer in Spanish for King George III.[9]

A board of elders selected and counseled the president, a lay leader who received no compensation for his services. Sometimes there were two copresidents. A president's duties included management of the synagogue's finances and arbitration of conflicts between congregants. He also supervised Shearith Israel's salaried employees. Among them was the *hazzan*, whose function was akin to that of a rabbi. (The synagogue would not have an official rabbi until the 1840s.) He ran religious services twice daily and thrice on the sabbath, *Shabbat*. The *hazzan* also circumcised baby boys, trained congregants' sons for their bar mitzvahs, and addressed theological inquiries as they arose. The *shamash* was the second paid officer and attended to the maintenance of the sanctuary. A third staffer, the *shochet*, ensured that the meat was kosher. The *shochet's* diligence in his duties was of concern far beyond Shearith Israel because the kosher meat that he oversaw in New York was exported to Jewish communities throughout North America and the Caribbean. The synagogue also ran a school in a separate building where students learned Hebrew as well as secular subjects.[10] In one congregant's will, £50 annually were bequeathed "for the support of our Hebrew School at said New York to teach poor children the Hebrew tongue."[11]

Tradition formed the bedrock of community life. Observance of *Shabbat* was paramount, a sacred time of rest from sundown Friday to sundown Saturday. Working and even writing were forbidden.[12] Circumcision of boys was also an important religious tradition, taking place eight days from birth. The infant was given his name after a specially trained *mohel* performed the circumcision. In a set of instructions for the medical and ritualistic aspects of circumcision, a New York *mohel* wrote to Rhode Island's Moses Seixas in 1772, "The first and principal thing is, to have a good heart, to perform the operation with courage intermixed with tenderness."[13] As we will see, this was the same Moses Seixas to whom George Washington would address his famous Newport letter of 1790.

Yet another tradition was the bar mitzvah, a rite of passage wherein a thirteen-year-old boy chanted from the Torah. Weddings, too, were important events. If a man sought to wed a woman, his father first approached her family for permission. The presumptive groom then solicited the blessing of the congregation at large, underscoring the collective nature of Jewish life in colonial New York. A wedding contract was drafted consistent with Jewish custom. In the absence of rain, the ceremony took place outdoors; otherwise, the bride's family hosted the affair. Jewish couples tended to enjoy long marriages and averaged five children.[14]

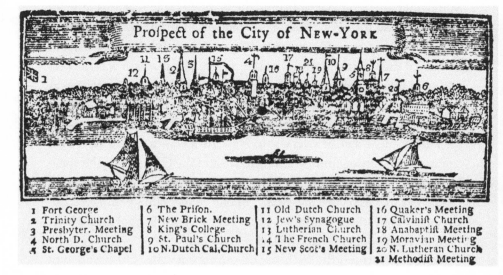

Prospect of the City of NEW-YORK

1 Fort George	6 The Prison.	11 Old Dutch Church	16 Quaker's Meeting
2 Trinity Church	7 New Brick Meeting	12 Jew's Synagogue	17 Calvinist Church
3 Presbyter. Meeting	8 King's College	13 Lutherian Church	18 Anabaptist Meeting
4 North D. Church	9 St. Paul's Church	14 The French Church	19 Moravian Meeting
5 St. George's Chapel	10 N.Dutch Cal.Church	15 New Scot's Meeting	20 N. Lutheran Church
			21 Methodist Meeting

This illustration from a 1771 almanac shows the religious diversity of Manhattan in the late colonial period. The synagogue is identified as #12. *Source: The New-York Pocket Almanack, for the year 1771 . . . by Thomas Moore, Philo.* New York: Hugh Gaine, 1770.

Although Jews made up less than 1 percent of New York's population, they played an outsized role in the city's economic life. At the top of the Jewish hierarchy was the mercantile elite, comprising businessmen whose success in trade placed them among the colony's most prosperous merchants. They tended to sport fashionable British apparel and enjoyed working relationships with Christians. Beneath this gentry was a middle class of Jewish shopkeepers, vendors, and craftsmen. An underclass of impoverished Jews—including some who spent time in debtors' prison—survived on charity administered through the synagogue.[15]

In percentages consistent with New Yorkers at large, Jews were slave owners. Slavery was less central to life in urban New York than to the agrarian economies of the American South or West Indies. Still, New York had more slaves than any other city in the northern colonies. An affluent merchant—Jew or Gentile—might have claimed upwards of five slaves who cooked, cleaned, and cared for children. Artisans owned fewer slaves, using them to assist in workshops. Numerous other colonists did not own slaves themselves but would rent a given slave's labor from his or her owner. Slaves, of course, occupied the lowest stratum of New York society and offer a grisly reminder of the far superior position of contemporary Jews.[16]

Jewish life in New York had its share of internal conflict. Intermarriage between Sephardic and Ashkenazi Jews sometimes generated tensions at Shearith Israel. Whereas London and Amsterdam boasted large enough Jewish populations to have separate Sephardic and Ashkenazi synagogues, New York Jewry was too small for that kind of segregation.[17] Another fault line at Shearith Israel divided wealthier, established Jews from poorer newcomers. The former feared that their own status in the eyes of Gentiles might be imperiled by the meager appearance and broken English of recent Jewish immigrants.[18]

Sometimes high drama within the Jewish community emerged simply from personality clashes. When an elder rose to read from the Torah on one occasion, a younger man laughed at his unkempt prayer shawl—and a lawsuit was filed. In another disturbance, an aggressive congregant was forcibly escorted from the synagogue as he prepared to brawl with an adversary. And after the synagogue president refused a congregant's request to sermonize at a funeral service, the rejected congregant began to openly curse the president while a second unruly attendee offered a rogue "amen."[19]

Shared traditions and commercial ties bound the Jews of the New World with those in the Old, but American Jewry nevertheless claimed its own unique features. Jews in New York and other American cities came from a diverse array of European countries and Caribbean colonies, and so marriage between Jews of different geographic backgrounds fused together discrete Jewish subcultures and produced children who were a new type of Jew—the American Jew. Back in Europe, religious authority pervaded all realms of Jewish life. Synagogues levied taxes on their members' business dealings, and Jewish courts adjudicated various disputes among congregants. By way of contrast, in New York and elsewhere in the American colonies, Jews partook in commercial and civic affairs without the intervention of synagogue patriarchs. The American

Jew kept one foot in the congregational community and another in the outside world. Sometimes these two spheres came into tension; eating kosher and observing *Shabbat* were especially difficult when traveling on business. Levels of religious adherence could vary widely even within a single Jewish family.[20]

American Jews also enjoyed more security and liberty than their European coreligionists.[21] Jews in British North America never faced banishment or state-sanctioned violence as they had in the Old World. And they found greater ability to achieve prosperity as merchants and shopkeepers than many European nations allowed.[22] New York Jews were the freest of any in the British Empire, and the property-owning among them were nearly on equal legal footing with their Christian neighbors by the eve of the Revolution.[23] The American Jewish community, moreover, confronted less discrimination than other religious minorities, partly because Jews were too few in number to generate as much notice as larger maligned groups. The total Jewish population in the thirteen colonies was around 2,000 in 1776, compared to 25,000 Catholics, who were more conspicuous and thus more likely to encounter intolerance.[24]

For all the advantages Jews in colonial America enjoyed relative to European Jewry, to American Catholics, and of course to slaves, acceptance only went so far. Most of the thirteen colonies barred Jews at various times from all manner of civic life—running for office, electing officials, practicing law, testifying in court, sitting on juries.[25] Even relatively tolerant New York saw its share of prejudice against Jews.

The most egregious incident in colonial New York involved mob violence directed at a Jewish funeral procession in 1743. A throng seized the corpse and subjected it to a mock conversion to Christianity.[26] One Gentile eyewitness, aghast at the spectacle, wrote into the *New York Weekly Journal* to deplore the "rude unthinking wretches" who formed a "rabble." These agitators were "lost to shame and humanity" as they "insulted the dead in such a vile manner that to mention all would shock a human ear." The bystander lamented, "I've only reason to abhor and despise many who (oh impudence!) dare style themselves Christians."[27]

New York Jewry worried about the desecration of its cemetery. Situated on the northeastern edge of Manhattan's settlement—some twenty minutes by foot from the synagogue—the burial ground was ringed by a wall to thwart intruders. Sister congregations in Newport, Philadelphia, Charleston, and Savannah likewise built walls or fences around their graveyards. Despite these precautions, all five Jewish cemeteries were vandalized.[28]

Old World caricatures of the conniving Jewish merchant resurfaced in New York. In 1765, a visitor from Massachusetts observed that in New York most businessmen "are observed to deal very much upon honor, excepting some Jews." These Jews "sustain no very good character, being many of them selfish and knavish, (and where they have an opportunity), an oppressive and cruel people."[29] Even a compliment about a Jew could unwittingly reveal the extent of antisemitic prejudice. When a respected Gentile lawyer praised a New Yorker as "the honestest Jew that has been in this place," he intimated much about the perceived integrity of Jews in general. The very word "Jew" carried pejorative connotations.[30] As a Gentile trader wrote in a letter, he had been so relentless in his efforts to sell his inventory of sugar that he had "almost turned Jew."[31]

The stubborn stereotype of the deceitful Jewish merchant was not without irony. In reality, Jews in New York and elsewhere achieved prosperity in large part because they could depend on the integrity of their fellow Jews. They cultivated an ethos of collective support among themselves in reaction to the discrimination that they encountered as a group. Jews prospered not because they duped their Gentile counterparts, as was so often alleged, but because they tapped into trusted networks of their coreligionists.[32] But Jewish probity in business was lost on bigots.

———

It was against this mixed backdrop—religious and economic freedom on the one hand, lingering antisemitism on the other—that New York Jewry questioned its fealty to the Crown as tensions flared between the mother country and her New World colonies. Political tumult in the 1760s and 1770s led many colonists of all faiths, Jews included, to reconsider their allegiance to Britain. A series of unwelcome taxes from Parliament sparked unrest across British North America. Colonists regarded these taxes as tyrannical encroachments on their liberty. After the Townshend Acts of 1767 levied duties on a variety of goods shipped from Britain to America—paper, glass, tea, paint, lead—ten respected Jewish merchants joined their names to a nonimportation agreement against British goods subject to these new duties.[33]

By 1775, colonial resistance to the British had become organized and violent. The first shots of the Revolution were fired in Lexington and Concord in April of that year. The following spring, the Continental Army stunned the British by seizing Boston, and the redcoats then turned their attention to capturing New York. As the British planned their invasion of the city, General George Washington convened his troops at the Common in Manhattan on July 9, 1776, for a public reading of the Declaration of Independence, signed by the Continental Congress five days prior.[34]

The members of the Jewish community in New York now faced a difficult choice. They could side with the Patriots and flee the city before it fell into British hands, or stay and pledge their loyalty to the Crown. Some feared that their exodus from New York would irreversibly dissolve the oldest Jewish congregation in America, one that had taken generations to develop. Others wanted to leave the city in solidarity with the Patriots.[35] In the end, most of New York's Jews abandoned their homes and aligned themselves with the cause of independence.[36] Their motivations for doing so were a combination of high-minded principles and hard-nosed practicalities. For many Jews, a revolution animated by the radical promise of equality understandably inspired stronger fidelity than did a mother country that relegated its Jews to second-class citizenship.[37] What's more, Jews were heavily involved in the mercantile life of America's port cities and thus had felt the effects of British interference in the colonial economy as directly as any group.[38]

A majority of those Jews who deserted New York that summer fled to Connecticut and later found refuge in Philadelphia. A fair number of

New Yorkers counted among the nearly one hundred Jews nationwide who fought the redcoats. Several Jews became officers in the Continental Army, in contrast to the British forces, which limited their officer ranks to professing Christians. And there is at least one known case of a Jewish soldier on the Patriot side who was afforded leave from his sentinel duties on Friday nights so that he could observe *Shabbat*.[39]

––––––

Although Alexander Hamilton did not identify as a Jew at this point in life and his relationships with American Jews would form in earnest only after the Revolution, he shared much in common with New York Jewry in the late colonial era. Like many of the city's Jews, Hamilton was an immigrant who had to rely on his wits, not family fortune, to survive. He too gravitated toward an urban environment that was more receptive than the countryside to cosmopolitan outsiders. And in parallel with the majority of the New York Jewish community, Hamilton cast his lot with the Patriots.

When the conflict in America turned bloody, Hamilton wasted no time in joining the fray. Word of the skirmishes at Lexington and Concord incited a fervor in New York. Hamilton enlisted in a local militia alongside other King's College classmates who ran drills before morning classes. In March 1776, Hamilton was appointed an artillery captain and commanded sixty-eight men. When the British finally did invade New York that September, Hamilton was among the last of the Patriots to retreat. The twenty-two-year-old Hamilton then led his troops into battle in pivotal American victories at Trenton and Princeton.[40]

In these early days of the war, General Washington struggled to keep pace with the volume of his incoming correspondence—Congress, state governments, and, of course, the Continental Army all required his attention. "At present, my time is so much taken up at my desk, that I am obliged to neglect many other essential parts of my duty," he wrote to a lieutenant colonel under his command. "It is absolutely necessary therefore for me to have persons that can think for me, as well as execute orders."[41] In other words, Washington needed a talented ghostwriter, and

British forces invade Manhattan in September 1776. *Source*: Franz Xaver Habermann, *Debarquement des troupes engloises a nouvelle Yorck* [ca. 1775–1796]. Miriam and Ira D. Wallach Division of Art, Prints and Photographs: Print Collection, New York Public Library.

he soon found one in Hamilton. In early 1777, Hamilton accepted an invitation from Washington to join the general as an aide-de-camp. The new role came with an elevation in rank for Hamilton to lieutenant colonel.[42]

Contemporaries attested to the autonomy that Washington afforded his astute assistant. "Hamilton had to *think* as well as *write* for him," an adjutant general wrote of the Hamilton-Washington dynamic.[43] Another officer offered a similar assessment: "The pen of our army was held by Hamilton and for dignity of manner, pith of matter, and elegance of style, General Washington's letters are unrivaled in military annals."[44] Thus began a relationship that would forever alter the trajectory of Hamilton's life.

———

The American quest to become the first colonies in the hemisphere to successfully secede from a mother country was a blood-soaked crucible—but not so hazardous as to prevent Hamilton from courting various young women in between battles. He put his talent at flirtation to use during elegant balls where military officers mingled with stylish ladies. Although short in stature and slight in frame, Hamilton had a handsome face with magnetic blue eyes. The arrival of Elizabeth Schuyler near the army's encampment in February 1780 brought a hasty end to Hamilton's dalliances with other romantic interests. Known as "Eliza," or sometimes "Betsey," she belonged to the illustrious Schuyler family of Albany. Her father, Philip, was a wealthy statesman who had served as a representative in the New York State Assembly, delegate in the Continental Congress, and general in the Continental Army. An orphan of limited means like Hamilton might not have typically expected to court a daughter of an aristocratic clan. But the turmoil of war shifted the usual course of social relations, and Hamilton's position as Washington's aide-de-camp elevated him to an acceptable standing.[45] Hamilton had mused eleven years earlier as a teenage clerk in St. Croix that military service in wartime could provide him upward mobility in an otherwise stratified world—and his prediction was proving strikingly prescient. He would later remark generally about "great revolutions" that they "serve to bring to light talents and virtues which might otherwise have languished in obscurity."[46]

The twenty-five-year-old Hamilton charmed the twenty-two-year-old object of his affection and her parents. After a two-month courtship, the Schuyler family consented to a marriage. Eliza was intelligent if not quite brilliant, attractive if not quite stunning—it was her virtuous character that set her apart. Her unassuming integrity went hand-in-hand with her religious devotion. One of Hamilton's fellow aides on Washington's military staff called Eliza "the little saint." Her family had Dutch origins and so naturally belonged to the Dutch Reformed Church.[47]

It is somewhat surprising that Hamilton chose a devout wife given his general apathy toward Christianity. Alexander and Eliza would move on divergent tracks in the realm of faith, with the husband keeping a distance from church life that the wife fully embraced. Hamilton, to be sure, was not the sole husband of the era who showed less commitment to Christian piety than did his wife. Still, most other founders had more

Elizabeth Hamilton. *Source*: Ralph Earl, *Portrait of Mrs. Alexander Hamilton* [ca. 1787].
Museum of the City of New York. Image courtesy of the Athenaeum.

engagement with Christianity relative to Hamilton.[48] Only Benjamin
Franklin appears to have rivaled Hamilton in ambivalence toward the
Christian faith. Franklin acknowledged in his autobiography that he
"seldom attended any public worship" and complained that church services were "dry, uninteresting, and unedifying."[49] Maybe church liturgy
similarly struck Hamilton as stale. Or perhaps a Jewish upbringing
made him resistant to little more than a nominal Christian identity.

As the now betrothed Hamilton awaited his wedding, he crossed paths with a prominent Jewish officer, Major David Salisbury Franks, amid the most scandalous moment of the Revolution. Franks was born in Philadelphia around 1740. He relocated in 1774 to Montreal, where he worked as a merchant and assumed the presidency of the local synagogue. Canada was then under British control but retained a significant Francophone population from an earlier day of French colonial rule. Like many fellow Anglophones, Franks felt betrayed by the British in 1774 when Parliament, in a bid to appease French Canadians, instituted French law in civil matters in the province of Quebec. Anglophones bristled at this concession, which they considered an affront to their fundamental liberties. One disaffected Montrealer draped a garland of potatoes around a statue of King George III in the town square. When a French Canadian suggested that the potato culprit should face death, Franks offered a barbed reply. The verbal spat gave way to a fistfight, with Franks besting his opponent. Franks subsequently spent a week in jail for the brawl, affording him plenty of time to ruminate on his animus toward the British.[50]

After American forces captured Montreal early in the war, Franks provided the revolutionaries with supplies and funds. The Americans were later forced to retreat from Canada, and Franks decided to enlist in the Continental Army. Staying in British-occupied Canada would have been dangerous for him given his treason against the Crown.[51] Franks was soon appointed aide-de-camp to General Benedict Arnold.[52] Although Arnold fought valiantly against the British at first, he grew increasingly pessimistic about America's chances of success and struck a secret bargain with the enemy. In exchange for money and the promise of a high rank in the British Army in the future, Arnold would remain in the Continental Army as a spy and furtively notify the redcoats of American troop movements.[53]

Hamilton, Franks, and Arnold all converged on a fateful September day in 1780. Arnold was then the commanding officer at West Point's fort, perched above the Hudson River some fifty miles north of New

York City. He dispatched a spy to relay covert information about the fort to the British. Meanwhile, George Washington and a coterie of aides, including Hamilton, were journeying to West Point to see Arnold. Hamilton was sent ahead to the Robinson House—which served as Arnold's headquarters near the fort—to prepare for Washington's arrival later that day.[54] David Franks was on hand when Hamilton appeared.[55]

As Hamilton ate breakfast with Arnold, the traitorous general received a note from a colonel on the Patriot side. The note explained that Patriot soldiers had intercepted a spy and recovered from the spy's boot the secret plans for West Point's fortifications. The colonel who had authored the note was not complicit in the subterfuge; he was informing his superior Arnold of the spy merely as a matter of course. The note had the unintended effect of tipping off Arnold that his scheme had been foiled. Although Arnold himself was not yet implicated, he surmised that his own role in the espionage would likely come to light in short order. Arnold suddenly announced that he needed to check on the fort and would return in an hour. In reality, Arnold made a hasty escape to a British warship.[56]

Washington soon appeared on the scene at the Robinson House, and not long after a messenger came with materials documenting Arnold's treason. The crestfallen Washington lamented, "Arnold has betrayed me. Whom can we trust now?"[57] Not surprisingly, suspicion fell on Franks as well as another Arnold aide, Richard Varick. But exoneration for both men would come almost immediately. On the very day that Arnold absconded, he penned a letter to Washington taking sole responsibility for his treason. Arnold wrote that, "In justice to the gentlemen of my [military] family, Colonel Varick and Major Franks, I think myself in honor bound to declare that they" were "totally ignorant of any transactions of mine" that "were injurious to the public."[58]

Although Washington was wholly convinced of Franks's rectitude, nevertheless Franks pressed for a military tribunal to undertake a full probe so that no one could entertain the slightest misgiving about his commitment to the Patriot cause. Washington acceded to the request. As the case was pending, Franks wrote to Washington to ask that the tribunal expand its purview to include not just the recent treason but also an earlier, unrelated episode in 1779. At that time Arnold had been court-martialed for numerous infractions, including financial malfeasance. Franks—who had given testimony in those proceedings refuting the notion that Arnold was guilty of improper expenditures—was convinced that rumors abounded he had perjured himself to protect Arnold. If the imminent military tribunal would investigate perjury as well as treason, then Franks could clear his names on both counts. In his letter to Washington, Franks bemoaned that they lived in a "world too easily misled by first reports and prejudices."[59]

Hamilton, ghostwriting for Washington, replied to a nervous Franks. He told Franks that while the military tribunal would adjudicate the matter of treason, the question of perjury "is so much of a civil nature that I think you had best procure some sort of civil examination."[60] It is unclear why Hamilton thought an inquiry into possible perjury in a court-martial would be a civil matter. His suggestion may have been a tactical one to spare the pending military tribunal the burden of an investigation beyond its original remit. In any event, the tribunal convened shortly thereafter to consider the question of treason alone. Its final determination was unequivocal: "Every part of Major D. S. Franks' conduct . . . reflects the highest honor on him as an officer, distinguishes him as a zealous friend to the independence of America, and justly entitles him to the attention and confidence of his countrymen."[61]

Yet Franks was still uneasy. He requested that Washington make public the tribunal's report, fearing that "many people are to this hour inclined to think that my connection with Arnold could not be void of criminality."[62] There is no extant reply from Washington, but he surely did allow for the report's release, as he had already done the same for Varick, who underwent a similar investigation. Franks also took up Hamilton's advice to undergo a civil inquiry, which further acquitted him of wrongdoing.[63]

Given that no army generals ever doubted Franks's innocence, his hypersensitivity about his reputation is telling. A common antisemitic trope, salient in novels of the time, was the Jew as a shifty operative engaged in espionage.[64] So it would be unsurprising if Franks felt that he, as a Jew, had to take particular care to demonstrate his patriotism. His complaint about a world rife with "prejudices" probably stemmed from a belief that undercurrents of antisemitism were feeding rumors of his alleged treachery.[65] After the war, Franks was rewarded for his loyalty with the opportunity to represent the United States as an envoy to France and Morocco, thereby becoming the first Jewish diplomat in American history.[66]

Once Washington became president, Franks solicited him for a post in the new administration. The president opted not to appoint Franks to a full-time role. Washington did, however, name the Jewish veteran as secretary to a trio of federal commissioners embarking on a two-month assignment in Georgia where they were to negotiate a peace treaty with the Creek Indians. At the conclusion of the undertaking, the entourage returned to the capital—then New York—and shared a meal with Washington.[67] The president recorded in his diary, "The commissioners . . . dined with me today, as did their secretary Colo. Franks."[68] This was, perhaps, Washington's first and only instance dining with a professing Jew.[69]

As the coda to his long career in public service, Franks took a position in the early 1790s at the Bank of the United States, one of Hamilton's signature endeavors during the Washington administration.[70] But soon thereafter a yellow fever epidemic claimed Franks's life. Washington counted "Colo. Franks" among those "acquaintances [who] have fallen victims to the prevailing malignant fever."[71] This choice of language seems to hint at more than just tangential familiarity, if not quite friendship, between the two men.[72] In all his dealings with Franks, Washington showed a total absence of antisemitic bias, which is in itself notable by the standards of the day. Washington's lack of prejudice against Jews was of a piece with Hamilton's, although the former never developed the extensive ties to Jews that the latter would.

———

Hamilton also had an important, albeit indirect, connection to the most renowned Jew of the Revolution: Haym Salomon. During the war, the new nation suffered from depreciating currency and ballooning debt.[73] Hamilton set forth a bold proposal for how the embattled United States could bring the war to an end through financial maneuvers—and Salomon's unique skills would prove pivotal in realizing that vision.

Insatiable in his quest for knowledge, Hamilton somehow found time to study economics amid the duress of war. He had first honed his mercantile acumen as a clerk in the Caribbean. Now Hamilton read widely about European financial affairs, taking note that Jews featured prominently in the markets of the Old World. "Prague is the principal city of Bohemia," he recorded in a notebook, "the principal part of the commerce of which is carried on by the Jews."[74]

Hamilton's survey of various financial systems culminated in a lengthy letter to Robert Morris in the spring of 1781. Born in Liverpool, Morris came to America as a fourteen-year-old in the 1740s.[75] He found success as a merchant and, notably, was derided by a critic for being "rich as a Jew."[76] It is unlikely that his wealth would have provoked an antisemitic slur had Morris been the heir to a large plantation in the countryside (in the manner of a Christian aristocrat) instead of a self-made businessman (in the mold of a Jew). Morris served in the Continental Congress, signed the Declaration of Independence, and—with the nation mired in economic crisis during the Revolution—was nominated by Congress to the newly created position of superintendent of finance of the United States.[77] On the eve of assuming office and inheriting a financial emergency, he received a forty-five-page handwritten letter from the twenty-six-year-old Hamilton, who was never shy about exhibiting his talents to older men in power.[78]

Hamilton's message conveyed the crucial insight that British credit buttressed the enemy's army while America's insufficient credit beleaguered its own. Bolstering American credit could obviate protracted fighting. As he told Morris, "Tis by introducing order into our finances—by restoring public credit—not by gaining battles, that we are finally to gain our object." Hamilton believed that the best means to address the ongoing "catastrophe" was a national bank that alone could provide the substantial credit required. He then offered a highly detailed blueprint for such a bank. Hamilton's plan reflected an impressive depth of financial knowledge for someone who had never before worked as a banker, much less designed a national economic strategy.[79]

Morris was humble enough to appreciate Hamilton's letter, replying, "I have read it with that attention which it justly deserves" and "I esteem myself much your debtor for this piece." He signaled to Hamilton that future suggestions would be most welcome: "My office is new and I am young in the execution of it. Communications from men of genius and abilities will always be acceptable."[80] Morris's words were more than just empty flattery. Less than three weeks after receiving Hamilton's correspondence, Morris submitted to Congress a plan for a national bank that reflected many of the younger man's ideas.[81] The success of the endeavor—called the Bank of North America—would hinge not just on financial capital but also human talent. As Hamilton had explained to Morris, "The game we play is a sure game, if we play it with skill."[82] And Morris managed to find the most skilled player of the era: Haym Salomon.

Born in Poland in 1740, Salomon wandered through Europe as a young man—picking up six foreign tongues along the way—before settling in New York. He was working as a merchant in 1776 when stories filtered down to the city about the troubled American military campaign against the British in Quebec. The revolutionaries were lacking vital supplies, and so the enterprising Salomon headed north with provisions. While en route he encountered a Patriot leader who agreed to furnish him with a letter of introduction to General Philip Schuyler, Hamilton's future father-in-law. Salomon soon crossed paths with Schuyler himself, whose battered troops had retreated southward from Canada. The letter of introduction endorsed Salomon as a trustworthy businessman, assuring Schuyler, "Mr. Salomon has hitherto sustained the character of being warmly attached to America." Schuyler gladly accepted Salomon's services.[83]

Salomon returned to New York just before the redcoats seized the city in September 1776. He was imprisoned by the British on account of his American sympathies but managed to exploit his German-language skills to win over the Hessian guards who monitored the prison. Following his release, Salomon trafficked in goods for these guards, all the while smuggling out American and French prisoners of war. When a fire erupted in New York, he immediately came under suspicion of arson by British soldiers. They chased him through the city streets, but Salomon evaded capture. Once safely settled in Philadelphia, he wrote to the Continental Congress describing his "great service to the French and American prisoners." Salomon recounted how he had "assisted them with money and helped them off to make their escape." He was "so obnoxious to the British Headquarters" that he had been "pursued by the guards" but "made his happy escape."[84]

After Robert Morris received congressional approval for establishing the Bank of North America in Philadelphia, he quickly tapped Salomon to join the endeavor. Salomon combined a talent for languages with an intimate understanding of foreign currencies. As Morris's broker, he facilitated the exchange of Spanish, French, and Dutch money for American bonds. Salomon himself was among the early investors in the Bank of North America. The willingness of the country's foremost bill broker to dedicate his own resources to the bank prompted other men of means to do the same.[85]

The challenge of stabilizing the nation's finances required not just Salomon's knowledge base but his persuasive abilities as well. Rival brokers, unlike Salomon, did not work for the U.S. government and were thus free to sell bonds below the government's rates. Yet Salomon prevailed upon them to raise their prices to match his own. This would admittedly cost Salomon's rivals some business, but the boon to the country's financial health would lead to victory in the war, he assured them. Salomon also devised a scheme to ensure that banks in London would accept American currency. He convinced British officers that they had to legitimize American bills by signing them in order to aid British prisoners of war who were reliant on the stability of American legal tender for their supplies.[86]

As Salomon generated public funds for the nation, he donated personal funds to the Jewish community. In the early 1780s, he made the largest contribution of any individual to the construction of a synagogue in Philadelphia and paid for a Torah scroll. His generosity was not limited to his coreligionists. Salomon gave loans for little or no interest to several prominent statesmen, and apparently Hamilton was among them. Hamilton's ledger book shows that he repaid Salomon £150 in Pennsylvania currency shortly after the war.[87]

Salomon contracted tuberculosis—known at the time as "consumption"—and died in 1785 at the age of forty-five. He was survived by his young wife, Rachel, and their three children. Although Salomon's estate included large holdings in government securities, they were significantly depreciated, and Rachel was left destitute.[88] Still, his legacy of a national bank, one that Hamilton had envisioned, endured well beyond Salomon's premature demise. Both men illustrate how the financial world of the early republic was particularly accessible to talented outsiders.

As Hamilton handled Washington's correspondence and studied finance in his quieter hours, he hungered to return to the battlefield. His desk work for the general was vital to the war effort, but Hamilton sensed that the musket rather than the pen would earn him the esteem he craved. The headstrong Hamilton was not shy about reminding Washington of his preference for combat, prodding his boss, "I explained to you candidly my feeling with respect to military reputation and how much it was my object to act a conspicuous part in some enterprise that might perhaps raise my character as a soldier above mediocrity." Washington, for his part, had little inclination to risk his gifted aide in the field. A disaffected Hamilton eventually left the general's staff in frustration. But the rupture proved temporary as Washington eventually acceded to Hamilton's request for command of a battalion in the summer of 1781. That October, Hamilton led the charge against the British in the Battle of Yorktown in eastern Virginia. The battle proved decisive in ensuring America's independence and making Hamilton a bona fide military hero. Yorktown would not be the final time that Hamilton hazarded death for honor.[89]

When the guns of the Revolutionary War fell silent, Hamilton set off for his father-in-law's mansion in Albany, where Eliza awaited him, now pregnant with their first child.[90] Just as Hamilton was settling into family life, a ghost from his Caribbean boyhood intruded on his domestic idyll. Recall that after Rachel Levine's death, the Danish probate court on St. Croix awarded the entirety of her estate to her one son born in wedlock, Peter Levine. Alexander and his full brother, James Jr., were left destitute. Now, fourteen years later, Hamilton received word that Peter had died and bequeathed to him little more than a pittance. Hamilton relayed to Eliza the news of "the death of my brother Levine" and the "disagreeable piece of intelligence" that "he dies rich, but has disposed of the bulk of his fortune to strangers."[91] For the second time in his life, Hamilton had been effectively robbed of his mother's estate. This festering wound from his woeful adolescence is just one example of how the adult Hamilton was inescapably informed by his earliest years. His advanced understanding of international trade and preoccupation with military glory were also rooted in his West Indian upbringing. And as we will see, Hamilton would forge relationships with Jews in yet one more illustration of how his Caribbean past echoed in his American adulthood.

4

New York

WITH THE COUNTRY FINALLY AT PEACE, Alexander Hamilton embarked on a legal career that furnished some of his most important links to New York Jewry. The war had prematurely ended Hamilton's collegiate education in 1776 before he and his fellow classmates could graduate. Now, at age twenty-seven, he was far too old to pick up his undergraduate studies, and in any event a bachelor's degree was not a prerequisite for professional success at that time. Hamilton even bypassed the usual clerkship in a law office that most lawyers-in-training undertook. Instead, he delved into a legal curriculum of his own device. There were two kinds of credentials for practicing law in New York at the time—one to become an attorney who prepared cases and another to qualify as a counselor who litigated them in court. After several months of solitary study in Albany, Hamilton earned both credentials by October 1782.[1]

The redcoats, meanwhile, continued to occupy New York until the United States and Britain agreed to the final terms of a peace treaty. Finally, in late 1783, British troops evacuated the city, leaving the triumphant Americans to peacefully reclaim what was violently lost seven years earlier. The war had exacted a severe toll on New York. Homes were in ruins, the streets strewn with garbage, and the wharves corroding with rot. Nevertheless, Hamilton resolved for the second time in his life to make the city his adopted home. Alexander, Eliza, and their baby, Philip, took up residence on the road that would become forever associated with Hamilton: Wall Street.[2]

Evacuation Day. *Source: "Evacuation Day" and Washington's Triumphal Entry in New York City, Nov. 25th, 1783.* Philadelphia: E. P. & L. Restein. Library of Congress, Prints and Photographs Division.

Hamilton was hardly the only displaced New Yorker to find his way back. Thousands returned to rebuild their lives and their city, including many Jews. They found the synagogue still intact; it had been maintained throughout the war by the Loyalist bloc within the Jewish community that stayed in New York. To the credit of the British Army, two redcoats who desecrated the synagogue during the war were harshly disciplined. Now in peacetime, the Patriot and Loyalist factions of Shearith Israel managed to reunite with minimal discord.[3]

The 1780s were tumultuous for New York's mercantile class as it confronted a new era of Atlantic commerce. The Revolution had upended long-established trade networks, presenting merchants with unprecedented opportunities and novel challenges. On the one hand, they were freed from royal authority; on the other, Britain barred Americans from lucrative business with its Caribbean colonies. Alongside these upheavals in the market were new developments in the legal arena. America had become a sovereign nation, unencumbered by the judicial precedents and legislative statutes of its former mother country. The quickly shifting terrain of both commerce and law meant that the nexus of the two—commercial law—was particularly ripe for a versatile mind like Hamilton's.[4]

He began work as an energetic young lawyer with a client roster that included the city's leading Jewish merchants. Among the first Jews whom Hamilton represented was a prominent figure within Shearith Israel, Solomon Simson. He was the son of Joseph Simson, a Frankfurt native who had come to New York at the age of thirty-two in 1718. In Hamilton's day, Joseph enjoyed status as a revered elder known for recounting firsthand memories of New York as it had existed in the early 1700s, when lower Manhattan consisted largely of orchards.[5] Before the Revolution, Solomon Simson and his brother, Samson—apparently their father had a taste for alliteration—teamed with three other Jews in a candle business. In a bid to co-opt competition, a New England–based candle conglomerate persuaded the Simson brothers and their partners to merge into the combine.[6]

The Simsons were Patriots whose fidelity to the Revolution prompted them to join the Jewish exile from New York as the British prepared to invade Manhattan in 1776. Joseph had been obligated to wear a "Jew badge" in his youth in Frankfurt, a bitter memory that drew him to the American revolutionaries' promise of equality.[7] When Solomon returned to New York after the war, he resumed his professional endeavors as a merchant and his religious leadership in the community. Solomon was elected president of Shearith Israel on multiple occasions. He also corresponded with the far reaches of the Jewish diaspora, penning letters to Jewish congregations in India and China.[8]

Solomon Simson turned to the thirty-year-old Hamilton for help in 1784 in a suit against Ebenezer Jones that was filed in the New York Supreme Court. Hamilton sought for his client compensation of £4,000 in New York currency after Jones had seized "with force and arms" a variety of goods from Simson, including clothing, furniture, and 1,454 bushels of salt. Jones argued that the merchandise had been lawfully taken as the spoils of war because the goods in question were confiscated behind enemy lines before Britain and America negotiated a peace.[9] (The litigation between Simson and Jones would continue into the 1790s, by which point Hamilton had left private legal practice to serve in the Washington administration.)

The case is noteworthy because the lawyer whom Hamilton opposed in the courtroom was the same man he would one day face on the dueling grounds—Aaron Burr. The commonalities between Hamilton and Burr are striking. Born within just two years of each other, both were orphaned as children. Each joined the Patriot cause during the Revolution and served on General Washington's staff. Though diminutive in stature, Burr and Hamilton alike were handsome and flirtatious. They passed the bar in quick succession after the war and moved with their wives to homes on Wall Street. Hamilton and Burr would become giants of the legal profession in New York and ultimately major figures in American politics.[10]

Yet for all the similarities between these two men, their disparities are even more conspicuous. While Hamilton was begotten out of wedlock on a Caribbean island and left a penniless child upon his mother's tragic death, Burr claimed lineage in one of America's most aristocratic families. Whereas Hamilton forged a close relationship with Washington during the war, Burr irritated Washington and remained forever at a remove from the celebrated general. If Hamilton was a man of deeply held principles, then Burr had few convictions. And in contrast to Hamilton's propensity for publicly airing his views, Burr's penchant was for strategic silence.[11]

It was in court that their differences were at their most pronounced. Hamilton delivered grandiose performances that stretched for hours; Burr was at once less evocative and more concise. A New York congressman remarked, "When they were rivals at the bar . . . Burr would say as much in half an hour as Hamilton in two hours. Burr was terse and convincing, while Hamilton was flowing and rapturous."[12] Their contrasts in the legal arena went beyond style to their most fundamental beliefs about law. Burr held no special reverence for the law, defining it as "whatever is boldly asserted, and plausibly maintained."[13] Hamilton, conversely, celebrated the majesty of the law. For him, devotion to the rule of law was the only means by which America's experiment in self-government could endure. As Hamilton once wrote in an essay, "If it were to be asked, What is the most sacred duty and greatest source of security in a Republic? The answer would be, An inviolable respect for the Constitution and Laws."[14] That which Hamilton held sacrosanct was for Burr merely a game to be won.

Burr and Hamilton faced off against one another in court more often than they collaborated for the same client,[15] but even in the latter instances, their rivalry could flare up. Early in their careers, for example, they were cocounsels in a trial, and protocol dictated that the lead lawyer give the closing argument. The self-assured Hamilton, fashioning himself the lead, proposed that Burr give the opening and he the closing. Piqued at Hamilton's suggestion, Burr slyly acquiesced—only to make all of the points that Hamilton intended to cover. Hamilton was left with nothing to say, and Burr alone received the accolades for the case.[16]

———

It was in these early years of Hamilton's legal practice that he began a decades-long role as lawyer and trustee for the Jewish trading firm of Moses and Company. The head of the firm was Isaac Moses, one of Shearith Israel's great patriarchs. He was known for his charitable donations to indigent Jews, involvement in synagogue life, and taste for European art.[17] Firmly allied with the revolutionaries, he fled the city in 1776 as the British invaded Manhattan. According to legend, Moses received word of the imminent arrival of redcoats on *Shabbat* and insisted on escaping by foot rather than wagon so as to adhere to the Sabbath's prohibition on riding. He joined other Jewish Patriots who eventually settled in Philadelphia until the war's conclusion.[18]

Moses's contributions to the fight for independence were substantial. To establish the credibility of the Continental Congress's paper currency, he helped raise $20,000 in coins that were exchanged for Continental dollars, a service that won him the appreciation of the congressional president, John Hancock. Moses also furnished a £3,000 bond to fund supplies for the army and personally ensured that soldiers had access to scarce commodities.[19] When the Bank of North America was struggling, Haym Salomon sought the aid of Moses (who was related to Salomon through marriage). Moses understood that the Revolution hinged not just on cannons but on currency, and so he drew from his considerable fortune to purchase promissory notes from the bank, which stimulated its cash flow.[20]

Isaac Moses's greatest involvement in the American cause was his role as a privateer—that is, someone whom the government deputized to arm private ships that would attack British vessels on the high seas. He provisioned eight boats, some quite large, like the *Marbois* with its crew of eighty-five.[21] Among Moses's partners in privateering was the nation's superintendent of finance, Robert Morris.[22] When Moses was unable to secure sufficient gunpowder for a schooner, he petitioned Congress for help. He explained that his search for gunpowder left him "everywhere disappointed" and he was "now under the disagreeable necessity of troubling Your Honors, and to pray that you would be pleased to spare . . . out of the public stores, two or three hundred weight of powder." Moses touted his "principles as a true Whig [i.e., Patriot] and friend to the liberties of his country" and was confident that it was "needless" to "remind your body of the assistance" he had thus far extended to the Revolution.[23]

While in wartime Philadelphia, Moses assumed the presidency of the local congregation, Mikveh Israel (meaning "Hope of Israel"), a position he had held previously at Shearith Israel in New York. He understood the importance of diplomacy with Philadelphia's Christians. As his congregation prepared to build a synagogue on a particular plot of land, a local church expressed its displeasure at the location, and Moses, in turn, sent a conciliatory note. "Our intention was to build a synagogue and a school-house thereon, for the use of our congregation, not conceiving that we would in the least disturb you," he explained. "To our great surprise we are told that it will." Moses informed the church that although a different location for the synagogue would be both more expensive and less accessible, his congregation would make that sacrifice because "we wish to live in friendship with our neighbors." When construction on the synagogue finally began, Moses was one of four congregants conferred the honor of laying a cornerstone. He may have exhibited tactful deference to Christians but was less measured with his own congregants, chastising them for chatting during religious services. "We now bind ourselves by the strictest ties of honor to behave with decency and decorum," Moses demanded.[24]

Following the British evacuation, Isaac Moses was among those who returned to New York. He became president of Shearith Israel once again and continued to represent the Jewish community to the outside world. Moses counted among three Jews who sent a letter to the governor of New York on behalf of "the Ancient Congregation of Israelites." They claimed that among the various "religious societies," none had "manifested a more zealous attachment to the sacred cause of America in the late war with Great Britain" than the Jews. The governor could rest assured that Jewish law required Jews to "obey our rulers" and that the Jewish community in New York would diligently fulfill "the duties of good citizens." The letter praised the state constitution of 1777, which in its guarantee of the free exercise of faith was "wisely framed to preserve the inestimable blessings of civil and religious liberty."[25] Amid the Revolution, as American colonies-turned-states had set about drafting constitutions for themselves, New York's constitutional convention was the only one in which the question of equality for Jews had been assumed rather than debated.[26] It is notable that the letter sent to the governor referred to Jews as a religious "society." In Europe, Jews were considered a foreign "race" or "nation" unto themselves, whereas Christian denominations were called "societies." Isaac Moses and his cosignatories were thus rejecting the prejudicial language of the Old World and indicating their intent to be counted as equals with their Christian counterparts.[27]

Beyond Isaac Moses's leadership in Shearith Israel, he was also a founding member of the Bank of New York, a thoroughly Hamiltonian institution. Postwar New York was a city with no bank. Several merchants were keen to collectively establish one; they were equally keen to avail themselves of Hamilton's services when he agreed in 1784 to help launch

The Bank of New York occupied the Walton House in its early years. *Source:* Abraham Hosier, *The Walton House, Pearl Street. Large Tree on Walk to Left; Garden Wall, Trees, and Shrubs to Right.* Miriam and Ira D. Wallach Division of Art, Prints and Photographs: Print Collection, New York Public Library.

the endeavor. Hamilton wrote the Bank of New York's constitution unilaterally, served as a director, and represented the bank as its lawyer. He was motivated in part by concerns about the volatility of the currency markets. Despite the existence of the dollar as national currency, businesses still advertised goods in pounds, shillings, and pence. Complicating matters further was the fact that individual states printed their own paper money. Meanwhile, foreign bills from European countries circulated widely in New York City. And exchange rates were far from uniform. Hamilton knew that a bank could stabilize the currency market by disseminating its own money and publishing exchange rates. Support from reputable merchants such as Moses was central to the success of the bank, which helped make New York a hub for global finance.[28]

At the time that Hamilton became involved in Isaac Moses's shipping firm in 1785, Moses had two business partners who were also Jewish merchants: Moses Myers and Samuel Myers. The two Myerses were unrelated but warm friends who shared much in common besides their surname. Both were New York–born and had served in the Virginia militia.[29] Virginia was one of several states that, despite having almost no Jews prior to the Revolution, boasted a number of Jewish soldiers in their militias during the war.[30] This dispersal of Jews is unsurprising given that British troops managed to occupy for some stretch of time each of the five American port cities that claimed a Jewish community.[31]

Moses and Company ran offices in New York and Amsterdam. The partners exported materials such as lumber, grain, and fur, while importing liquors, spices, and teas. At a time when overland travel was difficult, a given partner in the firm would sometimes journey a grueling 500 miles throughout America in a nine-day span to transact with far-flung clientele.[32]

The 1780s were trying years for merchant shippers like Moses, Myers, and Myers. Not only had Britain cut off Americans from profitable business with its Caribbean islands, but other European powers—including France, Spain, and Portugal—resisted commercial treaties with the United States, which they viewed as a trading rival to be bested. Without foreign markets for their produce, American farmers lacked funds with which to purchase goods from domestic merchants. Oversupplied merchants, in turn, were forced to flood local markets with underpriced wares. Bankruptcy loomed for soil tillers and traders alike.[33]

Compounding these difficulties was the fragmentary nature of economic life under the Articles of Confederation, which had governed America since 1781. The United States was more of a loose collection of thirteen mini-nations than a unified country with a single-minded economic policy. Every state in the Union levied its own tariffs on foreign goods and sometimes even on imports from other American states. Moses Myers spoke for many when he voiced his concern that economic disorder would breed political disorder. Writing to his partner Samuel, he remarked, "For my part, [I] should not be surprised at a civil war taking place on this continent."[34]

Isaac Moses's firm was vulnerable in these troubled times. As its American debtors failed to make payment, Moses and his partners were unable to meet their own debt obligations to creditors in Holland and England. Moses, Myers, and Myers soon owed upwards of £150,000. That they had managed to accrue such a staggering debt betokens their prominence in transatlantic trade.[35]

In April 1785, one of the firm's American creditors, Jeremiah Wadsworth, asked his lawyer—Hamilton—if he and his business partner should be concerned. "I have received very unfavorable accounts respecting Isaac Moses and Co," he reported to Hamilton, expressing his fear that "we shall be liable to any loss in case of his ruin."[36] Hamilton replied that he was aware of the firm's difficulties, as he had already met with Moses personally. "Mr. Moses, who is one of the partners, called upon me to consult me professionally as to the measures I should think it advisable for him to pursue," Hamilton shared. "I told him . . . that as I did not think your interest incompatible with his, I should freely give him my counsel." Hamilton knew that if creditors grew anxious and began demanding payment, the insolvent Moses would face financial downfall. Creditors such as Wadsworth would in turn receive little of what they were owed. So Hamilton urged patience on Wadsworth's part, and vouched for Moses: "He is very enterprising."[37]

Wadsworth had good reason to trust Hamilton's integrity on this count. Wadsworth's business partner, John Church, was married to Hamilton's beloved sister-in-law. Church had wedded Eliza's older sister, Angelica, in 1777 shortly before Hamilton entered the Schuyler family orbit. Angelica and Alexander shared a deep friendship that sometimes edged into flirtation. Whereas Eliza attracted Alexander with her character, Angelica enchanted him with her charisma. The elder sister was whimsical in demeanor, sharp in intellect, and astute in politics.[38] Alexander's fascination with Angelica was fully reciprocated. As she once needled Eliza, "If you were as generous as the old Romans, you would lend him to me for a little while. . . . You were a lucky girl to get so clever and so good a companion."[39] With respect to the debts that Moses owed Jeremiah Wadsworth and John Church, Hamilton surely would not have offered advice that could have harmed the financial stability of his dear Angelica.

Moses and the Myerses could not, in the end, stave off financial collapse amid dire market conditions. On November 25, 1785, their remaining assets were entrusted to the supervision of Hamilton and two businessmen; together these three would serve as trustees for the partners as they proceeded through bankruptcy. Moses and the Myerses—obliged to pay off half their debts—were reduced to selling their furniture and silver. At the behest of Hamilton and the other two trustees, Samuel Myers made an arduous wintertime journey through Pennsylvania, Maryland, and Virginia to collect what monies he could from the firm's debtors in early 1786. Meanwhile, Hamilton and his cotrustees held a public auction for property that Moses owned in lower Manhattan's Dock Ward, a district where many of the city's Jews lived because of its proximity to the synagogue. Some of Moses's land was purchased at auction by Hamilton's college roommate.[40]

As might be expected, bankruptcy did little to foster warm relations among the firm's partners. The Myerses managed to stay close with one another, but Isaac Moses grew estranged from them both. Moses Myers, with little more than £50 to his name and overcome with distress, paid a visit to the home of Shearith Israel's *hazzan*. "I laid on the sofa . . . most of the night reflecting on my situation, bereft of almost everything dear to me," he recounted in a letter to Samuel. The devout Moses Myers relied on his faith to sustain him, assuring Samuel, "God is great and in him [is] all my trust." The partners could at least take solace that they had lost only their money and not their reputations. After all, many great trading houses were then failing due to economic circumstances beyond anyone's control. One of the Myerses wrote, "Our firm has been very unfortunate" but "our characters as men of honor remain unsullied." They certainly garnered the respect of the county sheriff; when a creditor initiated a lawsuit against the firm, the sheriff tipped off the Myerses in advance so they could preemptively secure funds for bail and avoid any time in debtors' prison.[41]

Samuel and Moses Myers soon returned to Virginia, where they launched new ventures that met with success. Isaac Moses, for his part, proved just as "enterprising" as Hamilton had promised; he too reversed his misfortunes in the fullness of time.[42] John Church was pleased that he had deferred to the discretion of Angelica's brother-in-law, telling Hamilton, "I think you have done the best with respect to Moses's matters."[43] Hamilton's relationship with Moses, Myers, and Myers prefigured a much deeper involvement with the Jewish merchant class to come in the 1790s.

———

As Hamilton was establishing himself as one of New York's most skilled lawyers, a missing figure from his enigmatic childhood sent him a letter: his brother, James Hamilton Jr. Recall that James, like Alexander, is unlisted in the surviving baptismal records from Nevis.[44] Whether James too attended the Jewish school on the island is unknown. All that can be said with certainty about James's earliest years is that he apprenticed with a carpenter on St. Croix after his mother's death.[45] Then, in 1785, James wrote to Alexander from the Caribbean island of St. Thomas to solicit money.[46]

Alexander's reply indicates that he was hurt by James's lack of interest in maintaining a relationship, noting, "Your letter of the 31st of May . . . and one other, are the only letters I have received from you in many years." Still, the orphaned Alexander was so eager to bring James back into his life that he took his brother's self-serving correspondence as an occasion to demonstrate his own fraternal devotion. "Nothing will make me happier than, as far as may be in my power, to contribute to your relief," Alexander informed James. "I will cheerfully pay your draft upon me for fifty pounds sterling." If money was the means by which Alexander could hold on to some vestige of his family of origin, then he would be grateful for even that much. He added, "My affection for you . . . will not permit me to be inattentive to your welfare, and I hope time will prove to you that I feel all the sentiment of a brother." Alexander then offered to arrange for James to immigrate to the United States and secure him farmland.[47] But James never came to America. He disappears from the historical record for good at that point, leaving behind no hint of his future destiny or religious identity.[48]

By 1787, Hamilton had built a reputation not only as one of the great talents of the New York bar but also as a civic leader. He took an active role in the affairs of his alma mater and served in the New York State Assembly. At the nexus of these two roles, Hamilton partook in the drafting of a new charter for the college that had to meet with the approval of his fellow legislators. The contents of the charter reflect Hamilton's commitment to religious liberty in general and to Jewry in particular.

During the British occupation of New York, King's College had shut down and been repurposed by the redcoats as a military hospital. The state legislature reopened the college in 1784 under the name Columbia; in the wake of a successful revolution against a monarch, the old name would no longer do. But the success of the college was in doubt because of certain "defects" in its charter.[49] Before Alexander Hamilton and John Jay collaborated on the joint endeavor for which they would long be remembered—their defense of the U.S. Constitution in the Federalist Papers—they first served together on a committee in March 1787 to rewrite the charter of their shared alma mater. (Jay had graduated in 1764, ten years before Hamilton matriculated.)[50]

The new charter revived the college's founding charter from 1754 but with several important modifications in the name of religious freedom. Originally, students were obliged to practice Anglican modes of worship. The 1754 charter had mandated that the twice-daily religious services be "constantly performed" in adherence to "the liturgy of the Church of England." In a repudiation of sectarian conformity, the 1787 charter explicitly revoked the power of the administration to "prescribe a form of public prayer to be used in the said college." Moreover, the initial charter had imposed a religious test on the president: "The President of the said College . . . shall forever hereafter be a member of and in communion with the Church of England." The new charter now abolished any requirements "which render a person ineligible to the office of president of the college on account of his religious tenets."[51] This was no minor reform. By way of contrast, other colleges with colonial roots, such as Brown and Rutgers, did not ban religious tests for their presidencies until the twentieth century.[52] And in a gesture of great significance to New York Jewry, Columbia's 1787 charter also named as a trustee of the college the *hazzan* of Shearith Israel, Gershom Seixas.[53]

But the new charter was meaningless without a favorable vote from the state legislature, and approval was not a foregone conclusion. The charter provoked opposition from upstate assemblymen who wanted the college under the control of the state rather than its own board of trustees. It was Hamilton, more than any other legislator, who took up the charter's cause and secured its passage in April 1787.[54] Seixas and Hamilton had previously sat together on a board of regents that oversaw education writ large in the state of New York, but now—for the first time since higher education began in America with the founding of Harvard in 1636—a Jew would serve as a trustee of a specific college.[55] Columbia would not have another Jew on its board until 1928.[56] Seixas's appointment at Columbia put him into contact with fellow board members who counted among the city's foremost citizens, including a future U.S. Supreme Court justice, the mayor of New York, and of course the ubiquitous Hamilton.[57] For seventeen years, Seixas and Hamilton would serve alongside one another as trustees.[58]

A Jewish leader of steadfast dignity, the forty-one-year-old Seixas was the ideal choice to represent Jews in this seminal role at Columbia. He was born in New York in 1746 to a Sephardic father from Lisbon and an Ashkenazi mother from London, thus personifying how American Jewry became a melting pot for different European-Jewish subcultures. At the age of twenty-two, Seixas became the first American-born *hazzan* anywhere in the thirteen colonies. One of his first duties was to travel to Pennsylvania to officiate a Jewish wedding.[59] Seixas's father had doubts if his novice of a son was up to the task and wrote a letter to the bride's father in a bid to manage expectations: "He has never been so far from home, and if you find anything amiss in his behavior, impute it favorably to his want of experience and kindly admonish him for it."[60]

Within a few years, the young *hazzan* confronted a far more daunting duty than presiding over nuptials: he would have to lead a Jewish community through the hazards of war. Seixas fled New York with many of his congregants in the summer of 1776 as British troops prepared to invade Manhattan. He carried with him Torah scrolls from the synagogue as both a practical matter of ensuring their safety and a symbolic gesture of his belief in the providential blessing for the Patriot cause. Seixas absconded first to Connecticut and then in 1780 to Philadelphia, where he became the *hazzan* of the local congregation, Mikveh Israel.[61]

He viewed the Revolution as a divine mission and prayed fervently that God would protect George Washington, the members of Congress, and any foreign power allied with America. "May the supreme King of Kings through his infinite mercies, save and prosper the men of these United States, who are gone forth to war," Seixas proclaimed in a sermon.[62] He sent a copy of the address to Hamilton's future client, Isaac Moses. Seixas's commitment to the Patriot cause did not, however, lead him to shun those Jews who stayed in New York and sided with the British. More than once during the war, Seixas risked capture by stealing into New York to conduct weddings for Loyalist Jews (including that of Samuel Lazarus, whose great-granddaughter Emma would write the famous words that appear on the Statue of Liberty: "Give me your tired, your poor, your huddled masses, yearning to breathe free").[63]

As war gave way to peace, and many exiled Jews returned to New York, Seixas was unsure where to build his future. Isaac Moses—whose £115,000 fortune made him the richest Jew in Philadelphia—had bankrolled Seixas's salary during the war. But when Moses left Philadelphia for New York in 1783, Seixas's financial stability went with him. In a letter to the board of Mikveh Israel, Seixas expressed his hope that "your honors will not take it amiss in me applying for some individual security" given Moses' absence.[64]

Meanwhile, the Shearith Israel congregants were keen to see Seixas move back to New York. Seixas, however, had reservations. In a letter written to a friend in December 1783, he voiced several concerns about the prospect of resuming his old post. Despite his Sephardic ancestry, Seixas was "unacquainted with the Spanish and Portuguese languages" used in the synagogue. (It is unclear why this was not an issue for him when he led Shearith Israel prior to the war.) He was also worried about "disunion" among members of the congregation, which he felt undermined their ability "to serve the Deity consonant to our holy law." Finally, the question of sufficient remuneration weighed heavily on him. "As I now have a family to provide for," Seixas explained, "I cannot think of giving up this place till I meet with some encouragement" that "my salary will be made equivalent to what I receive here."[65] His desire for a sound wage was understandable considering that Seixas's growing family was in the process of ballooning to no fewer than sixteen children.[66] In the end, Shearith Israel lured Seixas back to New York in 1784 with the promise of £200 annually, an allotment of hickory wood, and an unspecified amount of matzah.[67]

He delivered a sermon to Shearith Israel in 1784 to mark his return to the congregation. After praising "Almighty Providence" for his "manifold mercies" amid "the course of a perilous and most distressing war," Seixas turned to matters particular to the synagogue. Congregants were engaged in disrespectful behavior, "such as leaving the synagogue in times of prayer" or "talking and laughing" during services.[68] In his role as *hazzan*, Seixas not only led worship (and scolded babblers) but also raised funds for the synagogue and taught children in the Jewish school. Congregants further called upon him to attend to the milestones of their lives—bar mitzvahs, weddings, funerals. Seixas relied on his skill with a knife to supplement his income, conducting circumcisions and slaughtering animals.[69]

While Jews of the Old World were often relegated to their own ghettos, Seixas mingled easily with Gentiles in New York.[70] His predilection for cultivating relationships beyond Jewish circles positioned him well to sit on the Columbia board alongside Christian leaders. Notably, Seixas used his perch at the college to make the case for Jewish belonging in the United States. He authored a commencement address that touted the role of Jews in the Revolution; the speech was delivered by Sampson Simson, the son of Hamilton's legal client and one of the only Jewish students to attend Columbia in the eighteenth century. "In the year 1776," Seixas wrote, "at the time when the people of this country stood up like one man in the cause of liberty and independence, every

Israelite that was among them rose up likewise and united in their efforts to promote the country's peace and prosperity."[71] Seixas was overstating the case, for he well knew that many of his own congregants had stayed loyal to the Crown. But his rendition of Jewish fidelity to the Patriot cause had more truth in it than falsehood, and betokened his fervent desire to write Jews into the American story.

That Seixas—thanks in large part to Hamilton—had been elevated to the Columbia board is rather remarkable given the marginal relationship of Jews to eighteenth-century colleges. Almost every college was originally founded by some Christian denomination. Columbia had enrolled only one Jewish student by the time Seixas was tapped as a trustee. Most American colleges had not graduated any.[72] Because colleges were important institutions whose alumni disproportionately supplied the ranks of the political elite, Jews' limited access to higher education is one indication of their relative subordination to Christians. Seixas's appointment at Columbia thus marked an important, if incremental, step toward the leveling of traditional hierarchies. In a young country caught between egalitarian promises and enduring prejudices, Hamilton's reforms at his alma mater demonstrate his commitment to the revolutionary ideal of equality.

———

Hamilton's labors in the spring of 1787 to win passage of the college charter met with success, but a much grander challenge lay ahead. During the very same legislative session in which the New York assemblymen approved Columbia's new charter, they chose Hamilton as a delegate to the imminent Constitutional Convention in Philadelphia. In fact, it had been Hamilton himself—with an apparent gift for surfacing at the center of world-historical events—who several months earlier had drafted the official call for a national convention to address the defective Articles of Confederation.[73]

Approved by the Continental Congress in 1777 and ratified by the states in 1781, the Articles of Confederation governed America. And they were failing. They bound together the thirteen states only tenuously. An impotent Congress could neither levy taxes nor compel individual states to abide by treaties it had negotiated with foreign powers. The Articles did not provide for an executive branch to enforce laws or a federal judiciary to adjudicate legal disputes between citizens of different states. What's more, amendments required unanimity among the states to take effect, giving veto power to any one state over the rest of the country. In 1781, for instance, twelve states agreed to an amendment providing for a 5 percent import duty to be funneled directly to the federal government, but tiny Rhode Island withheld approval and unilaterally sank the measure.[74]

These structural problems with the government exacerbated the economic challenges then bedeviling the nation. By 1786, frustration gave way to political violence in what became known as Shays' Rebellion. A Revolutionary War veteran named Daniel Shays formed a ragtag militia in western Massachusetts in response to the imprisonment of farmers who could not afford to pay their debts. Although creditors eventually hired a mercenary army that quelled the insurrection, the inability of the federal government to help maintain the rule of law in Massachusetts threw into high relief the failures of the Articles of Confederation.[75] The colonial experience under British rule had bred a mistrust of centralized power, but Americans overcorrected—their national government was too weak to function. Hamilton and delegates from across the country now embarked for Philadelphia to salvage a republic whose continued existence was mired in doubt. Jews did not likely imagine that these delegates would propose a radical advance for religious liberty, one that would thrust upon the country the fundamental question of whether adherents to Judaism and other marginal faiths should claim the full prerogatives of national citizenship.

5

Constitutions

THE COMMONWEALTH OF PENNSYLVANIA was a fitting tableau in which the delegates to the Constitutional Convention were to shape, among other matters, the course of religious freedom—the state had witnessed fervent antisemitism as well as a remarkable bid by its Jewish residents to grasp for civic equality. Prejudice against Pennsylvania's Jews had first surfaced in the colonial era. Their cemetery in Philadelphia was desecrated in 1751 when some "sportsmen" used it for target practice. A local Jew lamented that they "set up marks, and fired several shots against the fence of the Jewish burying-ground, which not only destroyed the said fence, but also a tomb-stone."[1] It is unclear whether the offenders deliberately sought to vandalize the cemetery or were simply reckless, but the fact remains that no Christian graveyard in colonial times was treated with comparable disrespect.[2] Meanwhile, a woman from an elite Quaker family in Philadelphia concluded in 1759 that Jews were "the scum of the earth" after attending a Jewish religious service.[3] The town of Lancaster, home to a sizable Jewish community, saw its share of shopworn stereotypes about Jews as swindlers. One resident in 1766 derided "the Jew landlords" as "terrible people" who "make false claims."[4] A Lancaster clergyman similarly griped in 1772 that Jews "hesitate not to defraud, when opportunity presents."[5]

It might be tempting to dismiss these comments as anomalous. After all, Jews belonged to Philadelphia's various cultural institutions, like the lending library and the Chestnut Street Theater.[6] Yet when the start of the Revolution prompted Pennsylvanians to write a state constitution, the specter of a Jew or other non-Christian in elected office proved broadly threatening. Pennsylvania's colonial charter had required "faith in Jesus Christ" to vote and run for office.[7] In the summer of 1776, a proposed draft of the state constitution tried moving in a more tolerant direction, only to provoke a backlash. The draft included no religious restriction on suffrage and made monotheism, rather than a belief in Christianity, a prerequisite for legislative office. Under this plan, inductees to the state legislature would have taken an oath that included the phrase: "I do believe in one God, the Creator and Governor of the universe." While falling short of religious liberty for atheists or polytheists, this approach was still relatively enlightened—too much so for many Pennsylvanians.[8]

A contributor to the *Pennsylvania Evening Post* suggested that if a mere "belief in God" was all that the constitution mandated for state officials, then undesirable religious minorities could seize power and turn the machinery of government against Christians. "Jews or Turks [i.e., Muslims] may become in time not only our greatest landholders," he predicted, "but principal officers in the legislative or executive parts of our government, so as to render it not only uncomfortable but unsafe for Christians." Such fears amounted to unfounded paranoia—Jews constituted a miniscule fraction of Pennsylvania's population and had shown no desire to oppress their Christian neighbors (and any Muslim presence would have comprised enslaved Africans who posed even less of a plausible threat). The editorialist was willing to concede that religious dissenters should be allowed to live in the Commonwealth but maintained that a Christian oath of office would "prevent, as far as possible, our acting as a state contrary to or in opposition to the general doctrines and laws of Christianity in the New Testament."[9]

A still more heated essay appeared in the same newspaper two days later. It cautioned that the proposed constitution's opening of legislative office to "deists, Jews, Mohamedans [i.e., Muslims], and other enemies of Christ" might summon the "Anti-Christ." The writer shuddered at the anticipated reaction of "the Christian states in Europe" if Pennsylvanians were to approve a "frame of government for themselves, by a Convention, by which Jews, Turks, and Heathens may not only be free men of that land but are eligible for Assemblymen." He was, moreover, appalled that "this new constitution mentions not a word of the Bible, Christ or the Christian religion, much less Protestantism." The author invoked the horror of "a mosque, a synagogue, or heathen temple" enjoying "equal privileges" with a "Presbyterian meeting house."[10] Meanwhile, the founding pastor of the local Lutheran church warned in a fit of hyperbole, "It now seems as if a Christian people were [to be] ruled by Jews, Turks, Spinozists, Deists, [and] perverted naturalists."[11] The term "Spinozist" was a double insult, for Baruch Spinoza—the Dutch philosopher—was both a Jew and an alleged atheist.[12]

Despite the democratic promise of the Revolution, these voices of bigotry ultimately triumphed in Pennsylvania. The state constitution in its final form incorporated the following exclusionary language in the oath of office for members of the legislature: "I do acknowledge the Scriptures of the Old and New Testament to be given by Divine inspiration."[13] Only in a place where prejudice against Jews and other minorities was prevalent would opponents of the test clause have ceded such ground.[14] An eminent lawyer living in Philadelphia during these years later recalled that "the Jews were yet a hated and a despised race."[15]

Benjamin Franklin, chair of the state constitutional convention, at first opposed the foregoing religious test. But ultimately he sided with those who favored it. Indeed, it was Franklin himself, at the behest of a Lutheran minister, who introduced the motion for the discriminatory oath to the convention. The historian William Pencak argues that Franklin had sympathy for Jews but "sacrificed the state's tiny Jewish minority to what he considered the more urgent need of Christians to tolerate each other." Moreover, Pencak interprets Franklin's decision to support the oath as a self-serving bid to shore up his credibility with Pennsylvania's antisemitic majority.[16] Yet even this rendition—in which an instinctively pluralistic Franklin sold out his convictions for the sake of political expediency—is too generous.

Franklin's initial (and short-lived) resistance to the religious test in the state constitution was hardly rooted in any notion of religious equality for Jews. He was instead motivated by his skepticism about the Jewish faith. In a letter to an English theologian, Franklin explained that his aversion to the oath stemmed from its description of the Hebrew Bible as inspired by God. "There are several things in the Old Testament impossible to be given by divine inspiration," he insisted. Franklin preferred that the Hebrew Bible be acknowledged as earthly in its origins and consequently disavowed. As he put it, "I should rather suppose it given by inspiration from another quarter, and renounce the whole." Franklin's letter raised no objections to the New Testament appearing in the oath.[17]

His concerns about Judaism as a faith were of a piece with his limited regard for Jewry as a people. Franklin repeatedly trafficked in tropes about Jews as money-hungry grifters. He lived in London in the 1760s and there gained membership to the Royal Society, which advanced scientific knowledge. Franklin lamented to a family member that an employee at the Royal Society had been stealing funds. Tellingly, Franklin felt compelled to mention the clerk's religion. "We have had an ugly affair at the Royal Society lately," he divulged. "One Dacosta, a Jew, who, as our clerk, was entrusted with collecting our monies, has been so unfaithful as to embezzle near £1300 in four years."[18] In a letter to a French physicist three months later, Franklin was still bemoaning the clerk's duplicity while highlighting his Jewish background. "A wicked Jew, entrusted as our clerk and collector, has unobserved run away with our money upon Earth, to the amount of near 1500 pounds," he reported.[19]

Franklin exhibited similarly stereotypical attitudes toward Jews while serving as a diplomat in Europe in the early 1780s. He was then engaged in negotiations on behalf of the U.S. government with a Dutch Jewish banker named Jean de Neufville. The United States had ordered £50,000 of goods from Neufville and his associates, but they were refusing to convey the goods until they received "the payment of a petty demand for damages," Franklin relayed in a letter to John Adams. From Franklin's perspective, the goods should first be delivered and then damages discussed. He derided Neufville's demand as "not only ungenteel and dishonorable treatment but a monstrous injustice." Franklin's letter exclaimed that this disreputable behavior was surprising—even for a Jew—since Neufville had a history of making warm remarks about America. In Franklin's words, "Though I believe him to be as much a Jew

as any in Jerusalem, I did not expect that with so many and such constant professions of friendship for the United States, with which he lards
all his letters, he would have attempted to enforce his demands (which
I doubt not will be extravagant enough) by a proceeding so abominable."[20] Neufville's Jewish proclivities had won out over his amiable rhetoric, according to Franklin.

Despite Franklin's wishes to be rid of Neufville, there was still other
business to be transacted between the two men—the arrangement of a
loan for the United States totaling two million Dutch guilders. Neufville
drafted an agreement that would require the U.S. government to pledge
all of America's land as collateral. While he assured Franklin that such
language was entirely "usual" for Dutch loans given to foreign countries,
Franklin deemed it "an extravagant security for a trifling sum." Franklin
was especially outraged that Neufville had floated the idea that Congress should pass a law, in gratitude to Neufville, making him the exclusive consignee of American produce to be sold in Europe.[21]

Neufville's English was mediocre, so there were language barriers,
and likely cultural ones as well, in these negotiations. Yet in Franklin's
eyes, it was Neufville's Judaism that accounted for his supposed avarice.
Franklin sarcastically suggested to Adams that Neufville was not quite
as Jewish as he could be, since the Dutchman had not gone so far as to
outright steal American property or take American lives. "I was wrong
in supposing J. de Neufville as much a Jew as any in Jerusalem," Franklin
sneered, "since Jacob was not content with any percents, but took the
whole of his brother Esau's birthright; and his posterity did the same by
the Canaanites, and cut their throats [in] the bargain, which in my conscience I do not think Mr. J. de Neufville has the least inclination to do
by us,—while he can get anything by our being alive."[22] To Franklin,
greed was an inveterate characteristic of Jews.

He was not unconditionally prejudicial toward Jewry. Whenever any
religious denomination raised money for the construction of a house of
worship in Philadelphia, Franklin donated, including for the local synagogue.[23] And he displayed some esteem for the heritage of biblical Judaism when, as a member of the Continental Congress, he was tasked with
designing the Great Seal of the United States in 1776. Franklin chose to

depict Moses summoning the waters of the Red Sea to drown Pharaoh (an image that Congress ultimately rejected).[24] Franklin's inconsistent mix of bias and tolerance toward Jews and their faith made him typical of several other founders—and distinct from Alexander Hamilton, whose writings and correspondence reflect no animus against Jewry and Judaism.

———

Many of Franklin's fellow Pennsylvanians simply saw no conflict between the egalitarian rhetoric of the Revolution and religious discrimination against Jews. In a 1782 issue of the *Pennsylvania Gazette*, a signer of the Declaration of Independence disparaged Jewish merchants for allegedly rigging their scales: "Is not the gravity which retains Jupiter in his orbit, the same gravity which operates on a grain in the scales of a Jew?"[25] A piece appearing soon thereafter in Philadelphia's *Independent Gazetteer* called Jews "despisers of Christianity" who were "the bane of all countries wherever they are countenanced." The writer gleefully shared an absurd rumor that an "air balloon" had been arranged to transport "all the Jew brokers to New Scotland [i.e., Nova Scotia], where they will be abundantly more thought of than in Pennsylvania."[26] This allusion to New Scotland was ripe with political meaning. The Canadian province was a haven for Loyalists who had deserted America. Contemporary readers would have readily understood the author's implication that Pennsylvania's Jews were faithful to the British rather than to the Patriots. (In reality, the state's Jewish community had overwhelmingly supported the Revolution.)[27]

Doubts about the commercial integrity and political allegiance of Jews were not new—but the willingness of Jews to challenge their opponents was. Many Jews had abandoned their homes, invested their savings, and even risked their lives to defend a revolution that was waged in the name of equality. They would not now passively accept second-class citizenship. Resistance to antisemitism was arguably more pronounced in Pennsylvania than in any other state during the founding era, and with good reason. New York and Virginia had no religious

limitations on elected office, so Jews there did not have specific constitutional clauses to protest. Other states, such as Delaware and Maryland, employed religious tests for public officials but lacked concentrated Jewish populations to take umbrage. And because Jews in
Pennsylvania had sided with the Patriot cause almost uniformly, the
state's failure to reward Jews' loyalty with equality made its discrimination particularly pernicious.

In 1783, Philadelphia Jewry formed a committee to advocate repeal
of the state's religious test for legislative office. Among the committee's
five members were Jews who would come into Hamilton's circle, including Haym Salomon and Gershom Seixas. The committee petitioned the
Council of Censors, an elected body invested with the power to com-
mence a new state constitutional convention for Pennsylvania. The Jewish "memorialists," as they referred to themselves, pointed out the fundamental hypocrisy of a state constitution that paid lip service to
religious liberty but then imposed a civil disability on Jews for exercis-
ing that very liberty. On the one hand, the constitution's bill of rights
stated without ambiguity, "No man who acknowledges the being of a
God can be justly deprived or abridged of any civil rights as a citizen on
account of his religious sentiments." On the other, the constitution
made a belief in the New Testament a prerequisite for service in the
state legislature. The memorialists lamented that "this religious test de-
prives the Jews of the most eminent rights of free men." The constitution
thereby imposed a "stigma" upon the Jewish people.[28]

The petition further assured the Council of Censors that citizens of
the Commonwealth had nothing to fear from the prospect of Jews in
elected office. "In the religious books of the Jews" were to be found "no
such doctrines or principles" that "are inconsistent with the safety and
happiness of the people of Pennsylvania." The memorialists also cited
the manifold contributions of Jewish Patriots to the war as evidence that
Jews would be trustworthy public servants, insisting, "The conduct and
behavior of the Jews in this and the neighboring states has always tallied
with the great design of the Revolution." They made a practical appeal
as well, one that Hamilton himself would echo in later years: religious
freedom would help increase immigration, as "men who live under

restraints in another country" would find Pennsylvania "attractive." In concluding their petition, the memorialists requested that the council convene a constitutional convention for the purpose of untethering the oath of office from Christianity.[29] But the council was unmoved by this bid for full civic equality.[30]

The fight against antisemitism in Pennsylvania continued in 1784 after a Quaker lawyer named Miers Fisher recommended to the state legislature the termination of the Bank of North America, which was based in Philadelphia. The bank—a brainchild of Hamilton—had intimate associations with prominent Jews such as Haym Salomon, who served as the bank's official broker, and Isaac Moses, who used his fortune to help keep the bank afloat. While Fisher's speech in its entirety is lost, a surviving excerpt reveals that he resorted to stereotypes about usurious Jews. Fisher declared that "the Jews were the authors of high and unusual interest" at the bank.[31]

In the pages of Philadelphia's *Independent Gazetteer*, a contributor under the name "A Jew Broker" (quite likely Salomon himself) issued a scathing castigation of Fisher. The editorial was addressed directly to Fisher and repudiated "the indecent, unjust, inhumane aspersions you cast so indiscriminately on the Jews of this city at large." According to the author, Fisher's antisemitism was evidence of his corrupt character: "The attack on the Jews seemed wanton and could only have been premeditated by such a base and degenerate mind as yours."[32]

During the war, Fisher's refusal to serve the Patriot cause had led to his expulsion from Pennsylvania to a detention center in Virginia. He may have had genuinely Loyalist sympathies or, like many fellow Quakers, was simply a pacifist who refused to take up arms. In either case, the "Jew Broker" delighted in reminding readers that Fisher was "once exiled and excommunicated by the state." Jews, in contrast, had sided with the revolutionaries from the war's inception and "were second to none in our patriotism and attachment to our country!" This vigorous defense of Jews tried to deflect accusations of Jewish disloyalty by suggesting that Quakers rather than Jews were guilty of "avarice" by charging high interest on loans.[33]

The piece is notable not only for its derisive tone but also for its author's belief that the birth of the United States was a signal moment for Jewry, which had suffered oppression for centuries. "I exult and glory in reflecting that we have the honor to reside in a free country, where, as a people, we have met with the most generous countenance and protection," gushed the "Jew Broker." And although the attempt to expunge the language about the New Testament from the state constitution had not yet met with success, he optimistically predicted, "We shall still obtain every other privilege that we aspire to enjoy along with our fellow citizens."[34] It is telling that in an editorial defending Jewish financiers, the "Jew Broker" saw fit to allude to the exclusionary oath of office; he surely feared that negative stereotypes about Jews in the marketplace were hamstringing Jewish efforts to access the State House.

Pennsylvania was not the only state where Jews challenged their Christian neighbors to realize the Revolution's promise of equality. In 1785, the circulation of an antisemitic pamphlet in Georgia prompted a local Jew to issue a direct rebuke. The pamphlet, entitled *Cursory Remarks on Men & Manners in Georgia*, invoked the usual clichés about Jews. Under the pen name "Citizen," the author denounced Jews as a greedy people whose "pecuniary interests" were "the life and soul of all their actions." He questioned their fealty to both the country and its republican system, alleging, "If indeed they have any choice as to governments, it must be in favor of a monarchy." He also undertook a survey of Jewish history and concluded, "The Jews always insinuate themselves most into favor among those nations who remain in darkness and in the shadows of death."[35]

At the time, Jews were not on equal footing with a majority of Christians in Georgia—the state constitution limited eligibility for the legislature to Protestants—but the "Citizen" was aghast at the notion of Jewish participation in *any* form of civic life.[36] His impetus for writing the pamphlet had been a ruling from a state judge that a Jew, Mordecai Sheftall, could not be denied the right to file a lawsuit simply because he was Jewish.[37] The "Citizen" warned that the Jews' quest for civil rights would culminate in their seizing power and crushing Christians: "What are we to expect but to have Christianity enacted into a capital heresy, the synagogue become the established church, and the mildness of the New Testament compelled to give place to the rigor and severity of the Old."[38] There was, of course, no evidence that Georgia's Jewish community aspired to persecute Christians. That Jews constituted less than one-tenth of 1 percent of the state's population makes the author's histrionics that much more absurd.[39]

In the pages of the *Georgia Gazette*, Mordecai Sheftall's brother, Levi, admonished the prejudiced pamphleteer in a concise response. Levi remarked that the pamphlet had afforded its author little more than "an opportunity to show his hatred" and advised that "he might have employed his time to some better purpose." Referring to Mordecai, whose right to sue was upheld, Levi asked why "the Jew particularly alluded to . . . should not also be entitled to the rights of citizenship." He concluded the piece by questioning the patriotism of the self-described "Citizen" and signed off, "A Real Citizen." Georgia's Jews had supported the Revolution with near unanimity—and none more fervently than Mordecai Sheftall—providing Levi Sheftall a strong basis for affirming Jewish claims to the prerogatives of full-fledged citizenship.[40]

That Jews in America would petition for their rights and shame their antagonists set them apart from European Jews, who had more to fear from speaking out. While numerous European countries had banished Jews, none of the thirteen states in the Union had done so, either before or after the Revolution. Moreover, European prejudice was often directed squarely at Jews because they commonly comprised the sole religious minority in a given place. In America, by contrast, Jews were joined by the likes of Quakers and Catholics as dissenters; bigots in the United States usually grouped Jews together with these other undesirables.[41] And perhaps most importantly, Jews in Europe—unlike their American coreligionists—had not hazarded death to establish a republic whose founding document championed equality.[42]

British Jewry offers an instructive counterpoint to the Jewish-American experience. In 1753, Parliament passed the "Jew Bill," which lifted certain economic restrictions on foreign-born Jews living in Britain. Although the Jew Bill was modest in its reforms, it provoked a fiercely antisemitic reaction and was quickly repealed.[43] British Jews had learned the dangers of seeking even a marginal advance in their rights. Thirty years later, the Jewish Board of Deputies—which formally represented Britain's Jews to the Crown—considered sending a letter of congratulations to King George III upon Britain's successful negotiation of a peace treaty with the United States in 1783. Tellingly, the board in the end abstained. As one Jewish deputy explained, "Peace or war being political concerns, addressing [them] would be taking a part in matters we ought to avoid."[44] So at the very historical moment when Philadelphia Jewry was protesting the discriminatory clause in the Pennsylvania constitution, the Jewish Board in London was fearful of sending even a laudatory message to the king.

———

Although America was less antisemitic than Europe, the Jewish pursuit of equality in the United States still faced significant opposition. Pennsylvania and Georgia were not alone in codifying prejudice into law. Most of the early state constitutions similarly imposed civil limitations on Jews and other defamed religious groups. Delaware mandated for state officials a belief in the Trinity, which left out some Christians and, of course, all non-Christians. New Jersey was less inclusive still, reserving elected office for Protestants solely. One New Jersey newspaper celebrated that the state constitution "justly restricts your votes to persons professing a belief in the faith of any Protestant sect." The governor of New Jersey unironically praised the oath as a "beautiful" expression of religious freedom, presumably because it did not privilege any particular Protestant denomination over the others. Both Carolinas followed New Jersey's lead and made elected office the exclusive preserve of Protestants. Maryland limited not only public office but religious freedom itself to Christians. It took Connecticut more than forty years to replace its colonial charter with a new constitution; in the interim, the state passed "acts of toleration," but none of them granted equal rights to Jews. Rhode Island did not extend civic equality to its Jewish residents until 1843, and New Hampshire failed to do so until 1877. Several states in the early republic had government-subsidized churches that used tax dollars from Jews and Gentiles alike to fund Christian clergy. And most states barred Jews from practicing law.[45]

Even in New York—which had arguably the most enlightened state constitution in the Union and did not ban Jews from elected office—toleration only went so far. The state considered language for its constitution of 1777 that would have promised "free toleration" to "all the denominations of Christians" as well as "all Jews, Turks, and Infidels."[46] However, this phrasing was ultimately replaced by a less specific clause: "The free exercise and enjoyment of religious profession and worship, without discrimination or preference, shall forever hereafter be allowed."[47] Jews were to enjoy freedom of worship by tacit default, not explicit affirmation.

Moreover, New York (like many other states) adopted a blue law that disallowed all business activity on the Christian Sabbath. These laws disproportionately burdened Jews, who were compelled to abstain from work on Saturdays by their faith and on Sundays by their state. Accordingly, Jews had one less day each week to earn a living than did Christians. When the New York state legislature considered resurrecting a colonial-era blue law in 1788, one assemblyman warned that it "would lead to intolerance and persecution." He observed that "a Jew, to be consistent with himself, is obliged to keep holy the 7th day of the week," and so a blue law would be tantamount to "taxing" him for being Jewish. "This was not equal liberty, one of the boasted blessings of our government," the assemblyman lamented. But he did not reflect majority sentiment, and the bill passed.[48] New York's Jews were still better off than Catholics in at least one respect. The same year that New York revived its blue law, the state legislature also banned from public office any Catholic who refused to forswear the pope as a religious authority.[49]

Hamilton's fellow New Yorker John Jay was typical of most other founding fathers in that he showed some support for Jewry while also harboring antisemitic views. He was among the principal architects of the state constitution, which afforded the free exercise of faith to Jews and other nonconformists.[50] As mentioned in the prior chapter, Jay teamed with Hamilton to implement pluralistic reforms at Columbia. And, we will see, he lobbied Congress on behalf of the Jewish merchant

Solomon Simson, a Hamilton legal client, when Simson sought the establishment of a national mint. Jay's inclusive sensibilities were rooted in his family history. His grandfather was a Huguenot who faced exile from France when he refused to convert from Protestantism to Catholicism. Jay was thus born into a family alive to the perils of religious oppression.[51]

But Jay nevertheless exhibited bias against Jewry. Although Jews could run for office in New York under the constitution he had helped draft, Jay still hoped voters would reject Jewish candidates. "It is the duty as well as the privilege and interest of our Christian nation to select and prefer Christians for their rulers," he told a fellow politician.[52] Jay's greatest aspiration for Jews was that they would abandon their faith. As president of the American Bible Society, he remarked in a speech that "individual Jews have, from time to time, been relieved from their blindness, and become Christians." Jay further explained that for Jews to convert en masse, they must first resume control of the Holy Land—a belief rooted in a Christian prophecy that Jewish reclamation of Judea and conversion to Christianity were critical steps in the return of Jesus. He anticipated that "a time will come when all the twelve tribes [of Israel] shall be restored to their country, and be a praise in the earth," but until then "their blindness will not be sooner removed" and thus "their conversion is not to be sooner expected."[53] These views were popular not just with Jay but a number of contemporary Christians.

A pamphlet of the era entitled *Israel Vindicated* denounced this kind of thinking as antisemitic. Its anonymous author sought to rebuke the idea that Jews were a benighted people, dwelling in a Christian America, who might yet embrace the light of Christianity. The pamphleteer inveighed against any depiction of Jews as "degraded and uncultivated" in contrast to their Christian compatriots who fashioned themselves "completely civilized." Such a mentality erroneously proceeded from "the impolitic principle" that the United States was a Christian, rather than nonsectarian, nation. *Israel Vindicated* acknowledged that such Christians were acting on a prophecy, and scoffed at how "they think they pay us [i.e., Jews] a compliment" when they see a role for Jews, as converts, in Jesus's return.[54] Jay's comments about the necessity of

Christian rulers and the defects of Judaism—common enough in his day—never flowed from the pen of Hamilton.

John Adams is yet another founder who assumed a key role in drafting a state constitution and whose liberality toward Jews had its limits. He wrote the Massachusetts constitution, which promised religious liberty in the abstract but discriminated against non-Christians in practice. Prefiguring the Free Exercise Clause in the federal Bill of Rights, the constitution in Massachusetts stipulated that "no subject shall be hurt, molested, or restrained, in his person, liberty, or estate, for worshipping God in the manner and season most agreeable to the dictates of his own conscience." Adams, however, included a religious test for governors and legislators in the form of an exclusionary oath: "I, A.B., do declare that I believe the Christian religion, and have a firm persuasion of its truth." Jews found mere toleration, not civic equality, in Adams's commonwealth.[55]

The mixed picture that Massachusetts's constitution presents was of a piece with Adams's varied views on both Judaism and its adherents. At times, Adams belittled the Jewish faith. He suggested to Thomas Jefferson that the study of Jewish law and Jewish mysticism would take nearly a millennium, time that "would be wasted to very little purpose." Jewish law was worse than just an exercise in squandered effort, Adams claimed—it was demonic. Referring to the two components comprising the Talmud, he lamented, "The demon of hierarchical despotism has been at work both with the Mishna and Gemara."[56] And in a wartime letter to the president of the Continental Congress, Adams unfavorably alluded to biblical Jews. He reported that the British in their arrogance mistakenly assumed that "the People of America will dethrone the Congress and like the Israelites demand a King."[57]

In several instances, Adams derided someone or some group by analogizing them to Jews. He employed the word "Jew" as an insult to demean a Gentile. "Tom is a perfect Viper—a Fiend—a Jew—a Devil," Adams remarked about a disliked relative.[58] During the Revolution, he drew disparaging parallels between Brits and Jews. "Quite as selfish and as blind as the Jews," Adams said of the British, "there is no present probability of their opening their eyes to their true interest and safety."[59]

He served as the U.S. minister in the 1780s to the Netherlands, where he bemoaned the greed of Dutch creditors by likening them to Jews. As he grumbled to John Jay, "Five or six people have all the money under their command, and they are as avaricious as any Jews in Jews Quarter."[60] Adams soon issued a similar complaint that Jews and Jew-like Christians throughout Europe were speculating on American currency. "My indignation is roused beyond all patience," he wrote to Jefferson from London, as Americans fell "prey to every robber, pirate and cheat in Europe. Jews and Judaizing Christians are now scheming to buy up all our Continental notes at two or three shillings in a pound, in order to oblige us to pay them at twenty shillings a pound."[61] In casting such aspersions, Adams was trading in well-worn stereotypes about Jewish moneylenders.

He could also be critical of his own country, and once again found in Jewry a useful point of pejorative comparison. As Adams told a fellow signer of the Declaration of Independence, "We are not a chosen people that I know of, or if we are, we deserve it as little as the Jews."[62] His penchant for antisemitic smears even combined with his hatred for Hamilton. Reviving an old canard that Hamilton's true loyalties lied with the Tories (that is, Loyalists) rather than with the Patriots, Adams insisted, "He was followed, by all the Tories on the continent, as false messiahs were always followed by the Jews."[63] Because Jews were often condemned as globetrotting cosmopolitans whose allegiance to the United States was dubious, they constituted a particularly useful group for Adams to invoke as he cast doubt on the fidelity of Hamilton and his supporters to America.

Just like John Jay, Adams endorsed the Jewish reclamation of the Holy Land. "I really wish the Jews [to be] again, in Judea, an independent nation," Adams wrote to the Jewish leader Mordecai Noah. His motivations for the creation of a Jewish state in the Holy Land did not likely resonate with Noah—Adams believed it would help cure Jews of their shortcomings and hasten their conversion to the Christian faith. As he explained, "Once restored to an independent government and no longer persecuted, they would soon wear away some of the asperities and peculiarities of their character and possibly in time become liberal Unitarian Christians."[64] That Adams had been taught Hebrew at

Harvard by a Jewish convert to Christianity perhaps informed his hope about the prospects for widespread conversion.[65]

Adams did, however, convey appreciation for Jewry at times. In another letter to Noah, he praised Jewish people as upstanding members of society. The Jews whom Adams had encountered were "men of as liberal minds, [and] as much honor, probity, generosity and good breeding, as any I have known in any sect of religion." Given these commendable traits, he reasoned, Jews were worthy of full-fledged citizenship anywhere on the globe: "I wish your nation may be admitted to all the privileges of citizens in every country of the world."[66] Adams's letter failed to mention that he himself had drafted a constitution for Massachusetts that banned Jews from elected office.

Still, his positive appraisal of the Jewish people was not exclusive to correspondence with a Jew. Writing to a Christian friend, Adams criticized the French philosopher Voltaire for his antisemitic take on Jews. "How is it possible this old fellow should represent the Hebrews in such a contemptible light?" he inquired. "They are the most glorious Nation that ever inhabited this Earth. The Romans and their Empire were but a bauble in comparison of the Jews." Adams also exalted Judaism for being the first of the three Abrahamic faiths, observing of Jews, "They have given religion to three quarters of the Globe." His esteem extended to Jews from antiquity to the present, for throughout history Jews "have influenced the affairs of mankind more, and more happily, than any other nation ancient or modern."[67]

Overall, then, Adams's attitude toward Jews and their religion was inconsistent. As with other founders, he offers a useful benchmark by which to measure Hamilton. Like Adams, Hamilton expressed admiration for the people and faith of Judaism but, unlike Adams, Hamilton did not mitigate that admiration with bigoted comments. In a world where prejudice toward Jews was commonplace, Hamilton is almost as noteworthy for what he did *not* say as for what he did.

————

Exclusionary constitutions, discriminatory statutes, and cultural antisemitism throughout the various states would have been strong reason for Jews to experience anxiety on the eve of the federal Constitutional Convention. In the eleven years since the colonies declared their independence, Americans showed a willingness to tolerate Jewry but resisted fulfilling the promise of equality enshrined in the Declaration of Independence. Precedent would now seem to suggest that a national constitution, to be drafted behind closed doors by an entirely Gentile body of delegates, would likely infringe on Jewish rights. Just a year before the convention, a French diplomat in New York reported back to Paris that the high ideals of the American Revolution had failed to vanquish antisemitism in the United States. "It would be very remarkable if this people, after having suffered the contempt of all ages and nations, should succeed in America in taking part in the affairs of government," he wrote. "But this revolution is not yet ripe . . . prejudices are still too strong to enable the Jews to enjoy the privileges accorded to all their fellow-citizens."[68] It was in the midst of this paradox—a new nation conceived in the name of equality yet riddled with old bigotries—that Hamilton and his fellow delegates convened in Philadelphia in May 1787.

———

Philadelphia was an energetic but tidy urban center. A Scottish military officer praised "the great and noble city of Philadelphia" as "perhaps one of the wonders of the world."[69] A traveler from Germany was equally impressed: "The city, if not greatly beyond others in America in wealth and number of houses, far surpasses them all in learning, in the arts, and public spirit." Indeed, Philadelphia was home to numerous cultural institutions, printing shops, and the University of Pennsylvania.[70]

Stretching west from the Delaware River, Philadelphia had been organized along a grid by William Penn when he founded the colony of Pennsylvania in 1681.[71] Roads parallel to the river that ran north-south were numbered—Second Street, Third Street, and so forth—while east-west avenues typically bore the names of trees such as Chestnut, Spruce, and Pine. In Hamilton's day, the streets were often well maintained by the locals,[72] although one resident griped that "dead animals—horses and cows—are left to putrify on vacant lots."[73] Pedestrians strolling down lamplit sidewalks in the evenings could hear night watchmen announcing the time and weather. Church bells were commonly rung, occasionally thirteen times in a row to honor the states of the Union. "At Philadelphia there is always something to be chimed," remarked a visitor, "so that it seems almost as if it was an Imperial or Popish city."[74]

Houses lining the roads were largely uniform: brick architecture on the outside and English-style décor within. Rooms usually featured a fireplace and, for those able to afford it, mahogany furniture. A garden or courtyard could be found behind each home; during the Constitutional Convention, Benjamin Franklin was known for chatting with Hamilton among other delegates in his courtyard under a mulberry tree. In the eyes of one observer, Philadelphians managed their residences with an ideal balance between the austerity of Amsterdam and pomposity of Paris: "The taste generally is for living in a cleanly and orderly manner, without the continual scrubbing of the Hollanders or the frippery and gilt of the French."[75]

How newcomers experienced Philadelphia often suggested more about the origins of the traveler than about the local inhabitants. A planter from the Virginia countryside found Philadelphians to be pretentious and complained that he was "heartily tired of the etiquette and nonsense so fashionable in this city."[76] But a European visitor, accustomed to the social hierarchies of the Old World, saw in Philadelphia a remarkable spirit of equality: "People think, act, and speak here precisely as it prompts them; the poorest day-laborer on the bank of the Delaware holds it his right to advance his opinion, in religious as well as political matters, with as much freedom as the gentleman or the scholar."[77]

To be sure, Philadelphia had its problems. Crime was a concern; eighteen convicts escaped the municipal prison just two months before the Constitutional Convention. Disease also posed a recurrent threat. The city had already endured several yellow fever epidemics mid-century and would suffer its worst outbreak yet just a few years after the convention.[78] Because doctors and laymen alike mistakenly believed that unpleasant smells caused disease, Philadelphians who lived near the dock, with its noxious odors, were particularly distressed.[79] A petition they submitted to the Pennsylvania General Assembly bemoaned "the stench of mud and putrifying filth" that wafted from the dock, which was not only "offensive to the senses" but supposedly "dangerous and injurious to the health of neighboring inhabitants."[80]

Philadelphia's numerous taverns offered lodging, food, and of course alcohol. These taverns were also important meeting places for political and commercial discussion.[81] When Hamilton first arrived in the city, he congregated with other delegates to dine at the Indian Queen Tavern around the corner from Fourth Street and Chestnut.[82] Upon entering its luxurious premises, Hamilton may have regretted that he had arranged for a bed elsewhere. One patron described having his bags handled by a servant in extravagant attire, complete with a "blue coat, sleeves and cape red, and buff waistcoat and breeches, the bosom of his shirt ruffled, and hair powdered." Needs were dutifully met at the Indian Queen, whether the guest desired tea, magazines, or even a haircut.[83]

Two blocks away, just off Second Street and Walnut, was another locale popular with convention delegates, City Tavern. It was less glamorous than the Indian Queen. A British antique dealer described having "slept at this house two nights, and met with my old tormentors, the bugs." While the bugs paid this Brit too much attention, the hotel staff gave him too little: "We could get hardly any attendance from the waiters, though we rang the bell incessantly." Nevertheless, City Tavern was a focal point for business in Philadelphia. The tavern kept records of incoming and departing ships, and merchants frequented its coffee house daily.[84] At the summer's end, the convention delegates would have their farewell supper there.[85]

Hamilton lodged at Mrs. Dailey's boardinghouse at the intersection of Third Street and Market Street. Mrs. Dailey's stood at the end of an alfresco market abuzz with shoppers. People poured in from the countryside to hawk their wares and purchase provisions. Among the meats to be found at the market were cuts unknown to European taste buds, from raccoon to possum.[86]

During the convention, Hamilton had a short walk to the State House on Chestnut Street for the delegates' daily deliberations. It was there, eleven years earlier, that the Declaration of Independence had been signed, and the building would in time become known as Independence Hall. The State House was elegant in its simplicity. As a contemporary recorded, "The façade is of tiled brick, with no particular decoration, but in comparison regular and handsome."[87] In the East Room, the delegates sat in rows of wooden chairs facing the president of the convention, George Washington.[88]

Two blocks due east from the State House, and another three up Third Street, on a small lane called Cherry, was the center of Philadelphia Jewry: the Mikveh Israel synagogue.[89] It is a striking fact about the Constitutional Convention that among the nation's more than three million people, the only one to petition the delegates on the topic of religious freedom was a member of Mikveh Israel, Jonas Phillips. A war veteran and former president of the synagogue, Phillips submitted a letter to the convention in its waning days.[90] He described himself as "being one of the people called Jews" and noted with consternation that the Pennsylvania oath of office was "absolutely against the religious principle of a Jew." Phillips decried the distance between the democratic promise of the Revolution and the prejudicial reality of the early republic: "It is well known among all the citizens of the 13 United States that the Jews have been true and faithful Whigs, and during the late contest with England they have been foremost in aiding and assisting the states with their lives and fortunes. They have supported the cause, have bravely fought and bled for liberty which they cannot enjoy." Phillips emphasized that if the delegates instituted an oath that was free of the kind of exclusionary clause found in the Pennsylvania constitution, "then the Israelites will think themselves happy to live under a government where all religious societies are on equal footing." In closing, he offered a prayer for George Washington, the convention delegates, and the American people.[91]

Phillips's petition was unnecessary, as it turns out. Because the convention's proceedings were strictly confidential, Phillips was unaware that eight days earlier the delegates had already decided to make federal office blind to religion.[92] Article VI, Section 3 of the Constitution contained this radical clause: "No religious test shall ever be required as a qualification to any office or public trust under the United States." In light of the discriminatory state constitutions, the decision to open federal posts—both elected and appointed—to people of all religious backgrounds was extraordinary. This clause was arguably more significant in expanding religious liberty than would be the First Amendment's guarantee of free exercise (which was not part of the original Constitution). After all, many state constitutions nominally granted religious freedom yet still imposed civil disabilities on members of minority faiths, thereby demonstrating how an abstract promise of religious liberty could mean very little in practice. The U.S. Constitution's ban on religious tests was a concrete provision in a way that the Free Exercise Clause was not; the ban extended substantive equality to Jews and other dissenters in the most important realm of American civic life.[93]

While the prohibition on religious tests found favor with most delegates, support was not universal at the convention. North Carolina's delegates resisted the clause; the delegations from Maryland and Connecticut were both split. The other states approved Article VI, Section 3.[94] One delegate who advocated the ban on religious tests recalled those who did not: "There were some members so unfashionable as to think . . . in a Christian country, it would be at least decent to hold out some distinction between the professors of Christianity and downright infidelity or paganism."[95] Little else is known about what the delegates said concerning the merits of Article VI, Section 3 in the summer of 1787. James Madison's notes make clear that it was Charles Pinckney, a delegate from South Carolina, who moved to bar religious tests. But the historical record is otherwise sparse. Despite the clause's profound advance for religious freedom, it appears to have prompted scant commentary among the delegates during the convention.[96]

Hamilton did not partake in the discussion about Article VI, Section 3, as he was away in New York on business that week.[97] Nor, if present, would he have been eligible to vote on the measure. His two fellow delegates from New York—aghast at the convention's push for a stronger national government—had abandoned the proceedings nearly two

In this rendering of the 1787 Constitutional Convention, Hamilton and Franklin in the foreground appear to be sharing a private word. *Source*: Howard Chandler Christy, *Scene at the Signing of the Constitution of the United States*, 1940.

months earlier, and quorum rules disallowed Hamilton from unilaterally casting New York's vote on any individual provision of the Constitution. He was, however, afforded the opportunity to lend his signature to the final document that exalted religious equality as a paramount principle, much as the Columbia college charter had done thanks to Hamilton's help earlier that year. With Rhode Island boycotting the convention and Hamilton the sole delegate representing his state, the Constitution was approved by "11 States and Col. Hamilton," as George Washington put it.[98]

On the very day that the delegates to the Constitutional Convention completed their final draft, three vandals desecrated Charleston's synagogue.[99] Antisemitism soon found new expression after the Constitution was made public and came under the consideration of the states for ratification. Proponents of ratification called themselves Federalists and branded their adversaries Anti-Federalists; many in the latter camp abhorred the prospect of Jews and other religious minorities serving in federal office. Madison remarked to Thomas Jefferson that Article VI, Section 3 provided for a measure of equality that some found disconcerting: "One of the objections in New England was that the Constitution, by prohibiting religious tests, opened a door for Jews, Turks and infidels."[100] Indeed, a number of voices in New England did speak out in opposition to the clause. The *Worcester Magazine* in Massachusetts published an essay that argued "this new constitution is deficient" in part because "there is a door opened for the Jews, Turks and Heathen [*sic*] to enter into public office and be seated at the head of the government of the United States."[101] At the Massachusetts ratifying convention, one delegate voiced exasperation that "a Turk, a Jew, a Roman Catholic, and what is worse than all, a Universalist, may be the President of the United States."[102] A fellow Massachusetts delegate insisted that "a person could not be a good man without being a good Christian."[103] Meanwhile, the *Newport Mercury* recorded how an opponent of the Constitution "had observed something in it truly abominable, which was, that they had so contrived the doors that a Turk or a Jew might go in and out like a Christian."[104]

Antisemitic hostility to the Constitution was not limited to New England. At North Carolina's ratifying convention, a delegate cautioned that the Constitution was "an invitation for Jews and pagans of every kind to come among us," which "might endanger the character of the United States."[105] Even in relatively tolerant New York, a local newspaper warned that the military could become a tool of Jewish interests, for the Constitution "gives the command of the whole militia to the President—should he hereafter be a Jew our dear posterity may be ordered to rebuild Jerusalem."[106] Alarm at the possibility of a Jewish president was sufficiently widespread that newspapers in Connecticut, Massachusetts, and New Hampshire saw fit to reprint the foregoing piece from New York.[107] It is difficult to know the extent to which anti-Jewish fearmongering stemmed from sincere bigotry versus a calculation that arousing the bigotry of others would help derail ratification. Both motives were surely at play in many cases.

In proposing a historic expansion of religious liberty, the framers of the Constitution had unwittingly provoked a torrent of vitriol about Jews and other out-groups. To be sure, Anti-Federalists did not predicate their resistance primarily on eligibility for office. They were more concerned about centralized power in general. Still, a pattern had emerged wherein the forces of antisemitism and Anti-Federalism overlapped.[108] It was against this backdrop that the most prolific champion of the Federalist cause, Alexander Hamilton, launched his bid for ratification of the new Constitution.

6

Statesmanship

AS A FIERCE DEBATE erupted in New York over the Constitution, Alexander Hamilton well understood that prejudice against Jews played a role in resistance to ratification in his home state. He pleaded with a prominent Anti-Federalist congressman from Albany, Abraham Yates Jr., to endorse the Constitution, warning that New York's failure to ratify would "divide the Southern from the Northern states and so divide the Union." Unmoved, Yates replied that he would sooner break up the country than "adopt the Constitution" and thereby "risk a government of Jew, Turk, or Infidel."[1] Anti-Federalists in Yates's mold may have been bigoted, but in a sense they were not wrong—the Constitution, if approved, really *would* benefit Jews by granting them equality in the eyes of the federal government. The Jewish community understood this as fully as the antisemites did. Hamilton and American Jewry thus found themselves aligned on the momentous question of ratification.[2]

Among Hamilton's many contributions to the ratification effort was his primary authorship of what became known as the Federalist Papers. He envisioned a series of essays designed to rally New Yorkers behind the Constitution. To assist in the enterprise, Hamilton first recruited John Jay, who was then the nation's secretary of foreign affairs and had collaborated with Hamilton earlier that year to revise the Columbia charter. They were aided by James Madison, the most influential delegate at the Constitutional Convention and an acquaintance of Hamilton's from the early 1780s when they had both served in Congress. Though Hamilton, Jay, and Madison divided the work and largely wrote independently, they published under a single pseudonym, "Publius," the name of a Roman statesman who helped depose a monarch and establish a republic. Pseudonyms were standard at the time for political debate in print; an essay was supposed to stand on the rigor of its argument rather than rest on the public stature of its author. In the end, the Federalist Papers comprised eighty-five installments, most of which appeared in newspapers between October 1787 and April 1788. Hamilton penned fifty-one of them, churning out his forceful defense of the Constitution at a rate of productivity that was impressive even by his standards.[3]

He also lobbied for the Constitution in less anonymous ways. Hamilton was a delegate at the New York ratifying convention during the summer of 1788 in Poughkeepsie, some seventy miles north of Manhattan. Hostility to ratification in New York was intense; even the chair of the convention was an Anti-Federalist. As the sole delegate in Poughkeepsie to have signed the Constitution in Philadelphia, Hamilton shouldered the primary burden of swaying the state convention toward approval. So impassioned were his pleas that spectators were moved to tears.[4]

Article VII of the Constitution specified that the document would take legal effect if nine of the thirteen states ratified it, and this breakthrough was reached with New Hampshire's approval on June 21, just as New York was beginning its convention.[5] Although the nine-state threshold had been crossed, the ongoing New York convention remained critical. After all, the Constitution would apply only to states that ratified, and given New York's sizable population and geographic centrality, the success of the Union likely hinged on an affirmative vote from the delegates in Poughkeepsie.[6]

As Hamilton labored for ratification in New York, Philadelphia played host to a "Grand Federal Procession," a parade conducted on the Fourth of July to celebrate the nine-state milestone.[7] The event exhibited the Jewish embrace of the Constitution at a time when enthusiasm for the new frame of government was far from universal among Americans. Benjamin Rush—who had been a delegate to the Continental Congress and signer of the Declaration of Independence—marveled at the parade's demonstration of unity across religious divides: "The Rabbi of the Jews, locked in the arms of two ministers of the Gospel, was a most delightful sight." (This "Rabbi" was, in fact, the *hazzan* of Philadelphia's synagogue.) To Rush, these intertwined religious leaders personified the constitutional prohibition on religious tests. "There could not have been a more happy emblem contrived of that section of the new Constitution, which opens all its powers and offices alike not only to every sect of Christians, but to worthy men of every religion," he reflected.[8] A minister interpreted the same sight as "a complete triumph over religious prejudices. The Jew joined the Christian . . . arm in arm, exhibiting a proof of brotherly affection and testifying [to] their approbation of the new Constitution."[9] The respect for Jews extended to culinary matters as well. At a feast that concluded the day's fete, the Committee of Provisions for the parade had arranged a kosher table with raisins, crackers, and—according to one Jewish participant—a "full supply of soused salmon."[10]

In a similar parade that Federalists organized in New York City later that month, the political stakes were higher. Philadelphia's Grand Federal Procession celebrated a feat already accomplished, but New York had yet to ratify the Constitution. The Federalists in New York City hoped that their parade would galvanize support for the Constitution in a state deeply divided over ratification.[11]

The parade's Committee of Arrangements had scheduled the procession for July 22, but this conflicted with the Fast of Tammuz, a mournful Jewish holiday marking the date that the Romans breached Jerusalem's walls in the year 70 CE. Remarkably, the parade organizers postponed the event for a day so that the city's Jews could partake. Perhaps the Jew most relieved by this turn of events was the artisan Asher Myers, who would now be available to claim the honor of leading the coppersmiths in the procession.[12] One Gentile explained in a letter to a business associate that the purpose of the delay was "to give the Jews an opportunity to join in the festivals, the 22nd being one of their holidays."[13] And another noted to his brother that the "procession is put off to the 23d," which he thought "a great compliment paid the Jews."[14] Indeed. With the state ratifying convention deadlocked, time was of the essence. What's more, Jews comprised little more than 1 percent of New York City's population.[15] The postponement of the parade underscores the strength of the Jewish alliance with the Federalists; such an extraordinary gesture would not have been made for a religious community whose allegiance to the Constitution was in doubt.

If the timing of the event was a courtesy to the Jews, then the substance of it was an effusive homage to New York's premier proponent of the Constitution: Alexander Hamilton. The central feature of the parade was a model warship called the "Hamilton" that rolled on wheels pulled by a team of ten horses. Though much smaller than an actual warship, the twenty-seven-foot "Hamilton" was still large enough to maintain thirty-two guns and about as many sailors. At various points along its journey through Manhattan, the ship would fire thirteen times to recognize the thirteen states of the Union. The "Hamilton" concluded its journey in Bowling Green near the southern tip of the island, where a crowd of thousands cheered its arrival.[16]

New York's tradesmen, who marched in the parade grouped by profession, considered Alexander Hamilton to be the human embodiment of the Constitution. The sailmakers unfurled a flag with a depiction of Hamilton at its center. Grain measurers, too, displayed a flag, featuring the likeness of Hamilton on one side and of George Washington on the other. As for the candlemakers, they opted to place Hamilton and Washington on the same side of their flag, with the image of thirteen candles between the two civic leaders. Each candle bore the name of a state, with those that had already approved the Constitution sharing a common flame and those yet to ratify featuring singular flames. Meanwhile, the flag of the cartmen offered a poetic tribute to "Hamilton" the warship:

Behold the Federal ship of fame
The "Hamilton" we call her name
To every craft she gives employ
Sure cartmen have their share of joy.[17]

The day culminated with an interdenominational meal that included representation from several of New York's religious communities:

Anglican, Lutheran, Calvinist, Presbyterian, Catholic, and Jewish.[18] Meanwhile, Hamilton—the person—was still procuring votes for ratification in Poughkeepsie. Three days after the parade, New York became the eleventh state to endorse the Constitution. The 30–27 vote was the slimmest majority yet of any state ratifying convention.[19]

———

With the Constitution duly enacted, the first representatives and senators soon convened in the new Congress, and George Washington ascended to the presidency. Congress formally recommended that Washington decree a countrywide day of thanksgiving, and he chose the fourth Thursday of November in what would eventually become a recurring national holiday. His Thanksgiving Proclamation of 1789 called on the American people to "unite" in expressing gratitude to "Almighty God" for "protection" during the war and "for the peaceable and rational manner, in which we have been enabled to establish constitutions of government . . . particularly the national one now lately instituted." Washington further gloried in "the civil and religious liberty with which we are blessed."[20]

Among those clergy heeding the president's call was the leader of Shearith Israel, Gershom Seixas, who delivered a Thanksgiving sermon to his congregants in New York. Keenly aware that most state constitutions denied a measure of religious freedom that the national Constitution upheld, Seixas did not share the Anti-Federalist fear that a strong central government posed a threat to individual liberty. Instead, his sermon celebrated the federal government for protecting freedom.[21] Seixas praised the Constitution as a legal charter inspired by God himself that ensured equality for Jews. "We are, through divine goodness, made equal partakers of the benefits of government by the Constitution," he affirmed in an allusion to the ban on religious tests for office. It now fell upon Jews, Seixas maintained, to prove themselves worthy of a government that afforded them first-class citizenship. He asked his congregants to "behave in such a manner as to give strength and stability to the laws entered into by our representatives" and "to support that government which is founded upon the strictest principles of equal liberty and justice."[22]

Hamilton—who served with Seixas on the Columbia board—had recently been tapped to run the Department of the Treasury, and Seixas's sermon called upon the members of Shearith Israel to "consider the burden imposed on those who are appointed to act in the executive department." Then came a benediction for government officials: "May the Supreme King of Kings, through his infinite mercies, preserve them, and grant them life, and deliver them from all manner of trouble and danger." The congregants also chanted the festival morning prayer service and concluded with the singing of *Adon Olam*, a hymn that had been a staple of Jewish liturgy for centuries.[23]

That the Jewish veneration of the Constitution was genuine and not just politically prudent was manifest in the constitution that Shearith Israel adopted for itself around 1790, which broke from the synagogue's colonial-era conventions. Before the Revolution, power was concentrated in the hands of a few elite congregants, consistent with the hierarchical structure of Sephardic synagogues back in Europe. Shearith Israel's presidents, together with a board of elders, controlled most congregational matters. To the extent that decisions were made beyond this small circle, only those Jews who paid dues were entitled to vote. Sitting presidents in consultation with the elders chose the succeeding presidents, and dues-paying members alone were eligible to serve as president.[24]

The synagogue's constitution of 1790 reflected the influence of the federal Constitution in both style and substance. Its opening lines echoed the famous "We the People . . ." preamble: "We the members of the K. K. Shearith Israel . . ." (K. K. was shorthand for *Kahal Kadosh*, meaning "Holy Congregation"). In contrast to the prewar era, now all men age 21 who adhered to the tenets of the Jewish faith (except indentured servants) "shall be entitled to every right and privilege belonging to this society and are hereby declared to be in every respect on an equality with those now convened." No longer would the board of trustees choose the congregation's presidents. Election of all officers was instead vested in the synagogue members. The new charter was explicit in drawing parallels between the broader political context and Shearith Israel's new mode of self-governance, championing "the principles of equal liberty, civil and religious."[25]

The synagogue's constitution even included a bill of rights animated by the same Enlightenment ideals about sovereignty and liberty that informed the federal Bill of Rights (which the states were still in the process of ratifying). Shearith Israel's version began, "In free states all power originates and is derived from the people, who always retain every right necessary for their well being individually." Among the rights "which ought to be preserved inviolate" for congregants were the prerogative to read from the Torah at services, to have the *hazzan* present at weddings and funerals, to discuss "any subject whatsoever with decency" in synagogue meetings, and to receive a copy of the Shearith Israel constitution.[26] Hamilton's former client Solomon Simson, then serving as the congregation's president, was the most likely architect of the synagogue's 1790 code.[27]

These developments at Shearith Israel were part of a democratic movement at Jewish congregations throughout the country. In Richmond at newly founded Beth Shalome ("House of Peace"), the synagogue's constitution also drew inspiration from the preamble of the federal Constitution: "We the subscribers of the Israelite religion . . ." Beth Shalome, too, extended equal standing to all of its adult males. Charleston's Beth Elohim congregation ("House of God") soon followed suit. Farther south, in Savannah, Mickve Israel ("Hope of Israel") formulated a code of laws with the democratic tenet that any three congregants could challenge a decision of the board by presenting the matter to the synagogue's membership at large for its collective consideration.[28] The fact that these synagogues used the word "constitution" to describe their new charters is itself revealing of the influence of democratic values on Jewish life. Congregations traditionally had called their governing codes *haskamot*, which roughly translates to "covenants," but in postrevolutionary America, synagogues preferred to use the civic term over the religious one.[29]

Unlike these synagogues' constitutions, the U.S. Constitution did not speak to the question of eligibility for suffrage; that matter was the prerogative of each state to determine for itself. Still, it is telling that Jewish congregations looked to the federal Constitution as a model worthy of emulation *and* simultaneously embraced a relatively democratic system of synagogue governance. This suggests that American Jewry perceived the national Constitution as reflecting the egalitarian ideals of the Revolution, versus the Anti-Federalists who often depicted the Constitution as an elitist scheme that would imperil freedom.[30] George Mason, for instance, was a Virginia delegate to the Constitutional Convention who refused to sign it, predicting that the new frame of government would "produce a monarchy or a corrupt oppressive aristocracy; it will most probably vibrate some years between the two, and then terminate in the one or the other."[31] An Anti-Federalist delegate to South Carolina's ratifying convention employed even more dire language about the Constitution: "It evidently tends to promote the ambitious views of a few able and designing men, and enslave the rest."[32] These kinds of critiques would have sounded erroneous to those Jews who bristled at religious limitations for office at the state level and celebrated the explicit ban on religious tests in the federal Constitution. It was a quintessentially Hamiltonian position for them to believe that an energetic central government could flourish alongside robust individual liberty.[33]

———

With the U.S. Constitution ratified and the new federal system in effect, Hamilton assumed the role of treasury secretary in September 1789. He took office with a bold economic vision in mind for the young country, one that would prove highly divisive. Hamilton's opponents had already weaponized antisemitism amid the ratification debates, and that tendency only intensified during his tenure at the Treasury. As we will see, tropes about conniving Jewish financiers, bankers, and merchants were sufficiently widespread that they provided ready fodder for those who hoped to derail Hamilton's plans. Motivated by genuine prejudice or a perception that popular antisemitism could be gainfully exploited—or both—a number of his adversaries would repeatedly accuse him of peddling policies to enrich greedy Jews. In all likelihood, no other self-professing Christian in the early republic saw antisemitism invoked against him with greater frequency than did Hamilton.

Reflecting on his appointment to the federal government, Hamilton would later write that he had felt "an obligation to lend my aid towards putting the machine in some regular motion."[34] His modest language belied the enormity of the task that confronted him in those early days of the Washington administration. It was not at all clear that the nation would survive much longer. The political and economic turbulence of the 1780s bred legitimate fears that the country might descend into anarchy. Shays' Rebellion demonstrated in bloody terms that citizens could see violence as a proper remedy for their frustration. Moreover, a sense of a national identity among the citizens was underdeveloped, and civil war between American states seemed a disturbingly real prospect. As the founders were well aware, history was replete with failed attempts to establish republics. The creation of the new central government now offered them a unique, and perhaps final, opportunity to cohere the thirteen states into an enduring union.[35]

Hamilton understood that the fate of the country hinged on the imminent performance of its civic leaders. Shortly after the Constitutional Convention, he predicted that the future depended upon "a wise choice of men to administer the government." While "a good administration will conciliate the confidence and affection of the people," conversely the absence of capable leadership would foment "in the course of a few years" the nation's "dissolution."[36]

Because the government had only recently come into existence and was thus unencumbered by precedent, Hamilton enjoyed enormous latitude to craft policy. This novel occasion to create federal programs from scratch meant that he could succeed on a grand scale—or fail just as spectacularly. A man of towering ambition, Hamilton had the right disposition for the moment. Recall that he had studied monetary and fiscal matters during the war. Now as the steward of the country's finances, Hamilton wasted little time in advancing an audacious agenda to revive the economy.[37]

His sweeping policy prescriptions polarized the American political scene, dividing the cabinet, the Congress, and the country. Resistance

Federal Hall, on Wall Street in lower Manhattan, housed all three branches of the newly instituted national government. *Source*: George Holland, *A View of the Federal Hall of the City of New York, as Appeared in the Year 1797; with the Adjacent Buildings Thereto*. New York: H. R. Robinson. Library of Congress, Prints and Photographs Division [1847].

to Hamilton was not well organized at first because political parties did not yet exist in the early years of the Washington administration. The Federalists simply thought they *were* the government; in reality, they were a political faction within the government (granted, the dominant one at that moment). Federalists considered their critics to be seditious traitors rather than members of a loyal opposition.[38]

The anti-Hamilton faction included many Anti-Federalists who had unsuccessfully tried to rally their countrymen against the Constitution during the ratification debates. In the wake of their defeat, Anti-Federalist leaders tended to reconcile themselves to the Constitution, run for office, and combat government overreach from within the system. Opposition to Hamilton was not limited to Anti-Federalists.

Joining them were erstwhile Federalists who had advocated ratification but grew increasingly alarmed that Hamilton's vision of federal power was far more expansive than their own.[39] Foremost among these figures in Congress was James Madison, Hamilton's onetime collaborator on the Federalist Papers. Hamilton was saddened by what he considered Madison's betrayal of both personal friendship and political principle.[40] Madison had a staunch ally in Washington's cabinet, Secretary of State Thomas Jefferson. Hamilton and Jefferson each suspected that the other, if left unchecked, would destroy the republic. Perhaps never again in American history would cabinet infighting reach such fevered intensity.[41] The anti-Hamiltonians would become known in time as Republicans.

Hamilton spent his first months as treasury secretary drafting a report for Congress on how the nation should remedy its budgetary woes. America's chief fiscal challenge was the colossal public debt. The national and state governments alike had funded the Revolutionary War with borrowed money that now amounted to $54 million for the federal government and a combined $25 million for the states. On January 14, 1790, Hamilton submitted his fifty-one-page *Report on Public Credit*, a historic blueprint for the country's financial future.[42]

The key insight in the report was that the national debt, when properly managed, could actually become a "national blessing." Hamilton posited that if the country were reliable in its debt payments, then the value of depreciated government bonds would fully recover. Those bonds, in turn, could stimulate the domestic economy by serving as currency. At that time, bartering was commonplace throughout much of the United States, an inefficient practice that hamstrung growth. The report set forth how liquid capital in the form of stable government bonds would allow a nation as rich in entrepreneurial spirit and material resources as America to realize its full potential in trade, manufacturing, and agriculture. Consistent debt payments would also serve to lower interest rates on loans for both the government and private individuals. In addition to suggesting import duties to reduce the debt, the report called for a luxury tax on spirits, wine, coffee, and tea to help ensure the regularity of debt payments.[43]

A centerpiece of Hamilton's scheme was "assumption"—that is, the federal government's assumption of the states' debts into a singular national debt. Hamilton hoped to "cement more closely the union of the states" at a time when the perpetuity of the Constitution was not yet assured and the future unity of the thirteen states remained very much in question.[44] If the nation but not the states were in debt, then creditors would have a significant stake in ensuring the survival of the federal government. It was a deft move on Hamilton's part to leverage an economic problem toward a political goal.[45] Although he was often condemned—in his lifetime and beyond—as a lackey of the moneyed elite, Hamilton's aim was not to exploit the government to advantage the already affluent. Rather, he sought to incentivize those with financial clout to lend their support to the preservation of the republic.

As Congress and the nation debated whether the *Report on Public Credit* should translate into legislation, many of Hamilton's opponents infused their animosity toward his agenda with antisemitism. They accused Hamilton of crafting policies to favor Jews. A "Farmer" writing for the *Pennsylvania Gazette* warned of "the dangerous consequences of the Secretary's funding report to the true interests of our country." Hamilton and his allies—the "Farmer" alleged—were overly concerned that "there is not a Jew nor a broker in London or Amsterdam that will ever trust" the United States for failure to pay the debt. In other words, the Hamiltonians would sooner sacrifice the prosperity of genuine patriots than lose credit with Jews. Not coincidentally, London and Amsterdam were two major centers of Jewish banking at the time.[46] Although this "Farmer" expressly mentioned foreign rather than domestic Jews, given the common view of Jewry as a network of border-crossing swindlers, negative depictions of European Jews could only redound to the detriment of their American coreligionists.

One aspect of Hamilton's plan engendered more antisemitism than any other: government bonds. The government had paid veterans of the war in bonds whose worth was severely eroded by the economic and political uncertainties of the 1780s. Some speculators had bought these bonds from veterans for as little as one-seventh of their face value. But now the prospect of invigorated public credit meant that these bonds could rebound. Even the mere anticipation of Hamilton's report spurred a rise in the value of government bonds. If Congress approved Hamilton's proposal, speculators stood to reap windfall profits.[47]

Hamilton understood the problematic optics of speculators prospering off bonds originally conferred to soldiers. In his report he acknowledged the commonplace argument that the original bondholders should be the ones to collect the rewards but insisted that such a scenario was untenable. The financial marketplace could not function in the future if the government voided contracts from the past, Hamilton explained, because markets rested on the foundational principle that when a buyer acquires an asset, that buyer enjoys all future earnings and suffers all future losses. He pointed out that the text of the Constitution itself expressly upheld the validity of transactions predating its ratification. His report further contended that soldiers who willingly sold their bonds in exchange for cash had showed little faith in the country's future, whereas the speculators who purchased these bonds had demonstrated their confidence in America.[48]

According to some of Hamilton's adversaries, the beneficiaries of these inflated government bonds were sure to be Jews and other voracious groups. A piece in the *Poughkeepsie Journal* listed "brokers, speculators, Jews, members of Congress, and foreigners" as exploiters of the "dupes" who "are likely to become the victim of the specious artifice."[49] In the same vein, the pages of the *Pennsylvania Gazette* featured a satirical verse that referred to Hamilton as "Belcour," a character in a play who, like Hamilton, was of Caribbean origin:

"Tax on Tax," young Belcour cries,
More imposts and a new excise.
"A public debt's a public blessing,
Which 'tis of course a crime to lessen."
Each day a fresh report he broaches,
That *Spies* and *Jews* may ride in coaches.
Soldiers and Farmers, don't despair,
Untax'd as yet, are Earth and Air.[50]

By alluding to Hamilton's West Indian roots, and by associating spies with Jews, the poet's unsubtle implication was that Hamilton and his Jewish allies were not true Americans but malevolent foreign agents conspiring to bilk ordinary veterans and soil tillers. This poem was of a piece with novels of the era that frequently depicted Jews as shady operatives in covert international networks. In an age when Americans were anxious about foreign interference in their fledgling republic, Jews were often maligned as rootless outsiders whose loyalty to the country was doubtful.[51]

A column in the *New York Journal* assumed a somewhat different form of antisemitism. It condemned those Christians who were poised to profit off the inflated bonds for *acting* like Jews. "In our Christians, who tampered with the distress of their fellow soldiers, avarice was the homogenous quality of their souls," the author fumed. Referring to the character of Shylock in *The Merchant of Venice*, he remarked, "Shakespeare's Jew, the character of a vigorous imagination, is surpassed in avarice by the real character of these Christians." The editorialist suggested that although these greedy Christian speculators still had their foreskins, they were no better in their behavior than circumcised Jews. He used asterisks to denote male genitalia in lamenting, "The ***** of these people may be unmutilated, and may be in the original Christian state, but their minds are far gone in Israelitish avarice."[52]

In the face of resistance, Hamilton and his acolytes vigorously lobbied Congress to pass his plan into law. One critic commented that Hamilton's relentless campaign included "nightly visits—promises—compromises—sacrifices—and threats."[53] The prospect of federal assumption of states' debts was proving especially contentious. Those states that had already paid off their war debts decried the notion that other states' outstanding debts would now become a shared national obligation. In response, Hamilton maintained that the war had been a mutual endeavor, the benefits of freedom were shared by all states, and the debts accrued in the course of winning independence hence comprised a collective responsibility. And at the same time that Congress was torn on the question of assumption, the future location of the country's capital emerged as another controversial issue. The capital was then in New York, and some prominent Virginians were eager to see the locus of federal power migrate considerably southward.[54]

On June 20, 1790, Hamilton sat down for a fateful meal with the two most influential Virginians other than the president: Jefferson, who hosted the meal, and Madison. (There may have been another guest or two.) While Hamilton *wanted* the capital in New York, he *needed* assumption, and was willing to trade away the former to ensure congressional approval of the latter. And so—over a decadent meal of stuffed rooster, French pot roast, and, for dessert, cookies and ice cream—these leaders brokered one of the most significant deals in American political history. Hamilton agreed to use his sway in Congress to transfer the capital to Philadelphia for ten years before a permanent move to a site on the banks of the Potomac River, where it would sit adjacent to Virginia. Negotiations along these lines were already afoot between the Virginia and Pennsylvania delegations. Now with Hamilton's backing, a southern capital would be sure to come to fruition. In turn, Jefferson and Madison (while not openly endorsing assumption) lined up sufficient votes for Hamilton's bill to pass. The debt plan that Hamilton dreamed up became codified as the Funding Act of 1790 in August.[55]

The legislation was an extraordinary feat for the thirty-six-year-old treasury secretary. Although he bargained away to the Virginians the seat of government, Hamilton had won the more important concession on the reach of government. He understood far better than Jefferson and Madison that his funding system would irreversibly consolidate power in the federal state.[56] Hamilton—haunted by the specter of anarchy—had forged a national government potent enough to ensure its own survival. And the Funding Act was merely the beginning of his grander vision.

———

In December 1790, just four months after the Funding Act garnered approval, Hamilton submitted a second major treatise to Congress, his *Report on a National Bank*. He set forth, in typical Hamiltonian fashion, a deluge of arguments for why America needed a central bank. The country still suffered from a shortage of sound currency; such a bank could increase the money supply by printing paper currency based on deposits of gold and silver. Another advantage of a bank was that it would retain a repository of funds from which the government could draw during emergencies. Tax collection would also become more effective because the bank could loan money to individuals who were otherwise unable to meet their tax obligations and because the proliferation of paper currency would obviate the onerous practice of paying taxes in coin. The bank would be a joint public-private enterprise. Individual investors would hold most of the bank's stock, while the government would become a minority shareholder—albeit one with sufficient weight to influence the bank's course of business. Hamilton noted that the Bank of North America, which he conceived a decade earlier and Robert Morris made a reality, was now operating under a new charter from Pennsylvania that rendered the bank more local than national in character. Hamilton's plan hence required an entirely new bank whose operations extended beyond the limited remit of the Bank of North America.[57]

Jefferson and Madison once again emerged as Hamilton's principal adversaries, fearing that his scheme privileged northern mercantile interests over southern agrarian ones. When Congress passed legislation for the Bank of the United States in early 1791, the Virginians had one recourse left—persuade the president to veto the bill.[58] Jefferson wrote to Washington that establishing the bank was unconstitutional. Article I, Section 8 of the Constitution enumerates several financial powers that belong to Congress: "borrow money," "regulate commerce," and "coin money." Section 8 additionally stipulates that Congress can "make all laws which shall be necessary and proper for carrying into execution the foregoing powers."[59] Whether a central bank was a necessary instrument for facilitating the enumerated powers hinged on the meaning of "necessary." To Jefferson, any justification for the bank would require a tortured reading of that word. "The constitution allows only the means which are 'necessary,' not those which are merely 'convenient' for effecting the enumerated powers," he opined. Jefferson warned that a loose construction of "necessary" would expand federal authority beyond constitutional limits.[60]

Hamilton issued a forceful rebuttal with characteristic verbosity—a handwritten draft extended fifty-eight pages—for Washington's consideration.[61] "So erroneous a conception of the meaning of the word *necessary* should be exploded," maintained Hamilton. "*Necessary* often means no more than *needful, requisite, incidental, useful,* or *conducive to.*" He further insisted that the delegates' intent at the Constitutional Convention was not to unduly debilitate the government with a restrictive reading of "necessary."[62]

Jefferson and Hamilton construed the Constitution differently because they were plagued by different anxieties. Whereas Jefferson dreaded a government of boundless power, Hamilton feared a government too feeble to function. Their battle over the bank set the terms of a larger debate over how to interpret the Constitution—narrowly or broadly—that would engage every successive generation. In 1791, it was the Hamiltonian approach that won over Washington.[63] When the Bank of the United States opened on the Fourth of July of that year, aspiring investors rushed the building, and stock subscriptions were sold out in under an hour.[64]

Yet again, some of Hamilton's antagonists saw in his design a plot to fill Jewish coffers. A contributor to the *Philadelphia General Advertiser* bemoaned, "The only infallible way to wealth in our country is to be neither honest nor industrious. . . . The late sudden subscriptions to the national bank are ample proofs." He suggested "Amsterdam Jews" were among those lacking in "honesty or industry" who profited from the bank.[65] The piece was signed with the symbolic pseudonym "Square Toes." This reference to thrifty wooden shoes intended to convey to readers that the author counted himself among the honorable poor whom rapacious Jews and other elites supposedly victimized.[66] His association of Jews with the Hamiltonian agenda resonated beyond Pennsylvania, as several newspapers in other states reprinted his commentary.[67]

Even before Congress approved Hamilton's bank in February 1791, he managed to produce yet another exhaustive treatise on economic matters: his *Report on the Mint,* tendered to Congress in late January.

Bank of the United States. *Source: The City of Philadelphia, in the State of Pennsylvania, North America; as It Appeared in the Year 1800 consisting of 28 Plates Drawn and Engraved by W. Birch and Son.* Published by W. Birch, Springland Cot, near Neshaminy Bridge on the Bristol Road, Pennsylvania, December 31, 1800.

Hamilton was distressed at the condition of coinage. Coins had no uniform value across states. Merchants were hesitant to accept gold and silver coins, which were often alloyed with cheaper metals that debased their value. Counterfeit coins circulated widely.[68]

As early as 1781, Robert Morris had discussed the prospect of a mint with Benjamin Franklin, and the following year Congress approved a plan for one. But the endeavor stalled and no mint came to fruition.[69] The Jewish merchant Solomon Simson, a legal client of Hamilton's, sought to revive congressional interest in a national mint in 1785. By that point in time, Hamilton's tenure in Congress had come to an end, and Simson turned to the like-minded John Jay, then serving as the country's secretary for foreign affairs, to forward his blueprint for a mint to lawmakers. While the text of Simson's plan no longer exists, Jay's covering letter to the head of Congress still does: "At the request of Mr. Simson, who sustains the character of a Whig citizen and an honest man, I take the liberty of transmitting to your Excellency, herewith enclosed, a paper containing proposals for establishing a mint."[70] It is difficult to say what, if any, credit is due Simson for spurring Congress to action, but the following year, Congress did pass another law providing for a mint. Yet once again, no mint actually materialized.[71]

Hamilton resuscitated the cause with his *Report on the Mint*, where he lamented the "immense disorder" of coinage in the United States and advised that the creation of a mint would benefit "trade and industry, the value of all property, [and] the whole income both of the State and of individuals."[72] The report was consummately Hamiltonian in its fine-grained detail; he had well-informed thoughts on such matters as the ideal thickness and breadth of coins. It also reflected the systematic thinking of a man who carefully designed his various programs to work in tandem. He explained how a national mint would help facilitate key goals outlined in his earlier reports, such as fortifying public credit.[73]

In 1792, Congress heeded Hamilton's call and passed the Coinage Act, which authorized a mint and instituted the silver dollar as the official unit of lawful currency.[74] Although coin manufacturing would have naturally fit within the purview of the Treasury, the mint was instead placed under the auspices of the Department of State to appease Thomas Jefferson, who had long nursed an interest in coinage.[75] Jefferson stepped down as secretary of state the following year, but the mint remained at the State Department, much to Hamilton's chagrin. Even on Hamilton's final day as treasury secretary in January 1795, he was trying, unsuccessfully, to persuade Washington that the mint ought to relocate to his own department.[76]

Hamilton had greater luck in vouching for a Jewish merchant, Jacob Mark, who sought to furnish copper for the mint. Mark, along with some business partners, had acquired the rights to a copper mine in New Jersey. In 1794, they reached out to Hamilton in the hopes of securing a government contract.[77] "If you have not already ordered the quantity which is required for the mint," Jacob Mark and Company wrote to Hamilton, "we beg to be favored with the preference of your commands."[78] Because coinage fell within the remit of the State Department, Hamilton took up the matter on Mark's behalf with then–Secretary of State Edmund Randolph, assuring Randolph, "the copper from that mine has always had the reputation of being particularly good."[79] Randolph, in turn, requested that Hamilton investigate "whether the contract can be punctually filled." If so, then Hamilton was free to "enter into an engagement [on] behalf of the United States, at a price not exceeding that of imported copper."[80] In a letter to Hamilton, Jacob Mark and Company confirmed that its mine could indeed expeditiously fill the order for eighty tons of copper and, at an affordable 36 cents per pound, Mark's copper would cost "very considerably less than it can be imported for."[81] Hamilton forwarded this message to Randolph and explained that his own involvement in the transaction could legally go no further, as Congress had reserved to the mint director the power to purchase copper for coinage.[82]

———

Hamilton's vast financial system succeeded brilliantly, even as antisemitic critics remained stubbornly blind to its merits.[83] In 1793, with the benefits of Hamilton's programs accruing, an obstinate "American Farmer" writing for the *National Gazette* claimed that the nation's debt enriched Jews and passed the burden to future generations. "Borrowing money from the bankers and Jews of Europe" served to "mortgage the labor of posterity to discharge debts thus contracted," he alleged.[84] But in reality, Hamilton had always considered it incumbent on the present generation to reduce the debt. The reliability of payment to the country's creditors was a centerpiece of his plan, and in practice it produced just the tonic effects he predicted. America had been bankrupt when Hamilton became treasury secretary; by the end of his tenure in that office, the United States would boast a credit rating on par with the world's greatest powers.[85]

That Hamilton's opponents often employed antisemitism against his agenda speaks to the persistence of Old World bigotries in the early republic. It also serves as a testament to the Hamiltonian-Jewish alliance. After all, the Jewish mercantile class *did* stand to gain from Hamilton's far-reaching economic vision—but not owing to some nefarious ruse, as his opponents sometimes alleged. Rather, Jews found themselves by virtue of their marginality in the very sectors of the economy that attracted Hamilton's attention. Jewish prominence in trade and banking was a reality rooted partly in the want of access to other professions. Jews could not easily pursue many other careers—attorney, legislator, professor— owing to legal prohibitions and cultural prejudices. In contrast, the financial and commercial spheres that Hamilton invigorated did provide opportunities to industrious outsiders, Jews and Gentiles alike. To deride Hamilton as elitist is to ignore that the marketplace of his day was more of a meritocracy than the courtroom, statehouse, or college.

Hamilton, to be sure, was not a populist crusader. He feared mob rule, as did most of the founders. But his concerns about populism hardly meant that he was endeared to the prospect of a self-contained oligarchy.[86] Hamilton saw danger in both populism and elitism, warning his fellow delegates at the Constitutional Convention, "Give all power to the many, they will oppress the few. Give all power to the few, they will oppress the many."[87] He championed meritocratic principles, unsurprisingly so given his own humble origins. As Hamilton wrote in the Federalist Papers, "There are strong minds in every walk of life that will rise superior to the disadvantages of situation, and will command the tribute due to their merit."[88] Any movement away from hereditary hierarchy and toward meritocracy would tend to improve the condition of talented immigrants—a reality that Hamilton and any number of his Jewish compatriots well understood.

While many Jews were favorably positioned to reap rewards from Hamilton's financial programs under Washington, economic opportunity for Jews was not singular to the United States. Jews had found a measure of material success in other tolerant nations. It was in the realm of civic equality more than commercial prosperity where the Washington administration would take an unprecedented step in the history of the Jewish people.

7

Church and State

WHEN GEORGE WASHINGTON first assumed the presidency, the question of Jews' political rights was still unsettled. The U.S. Constitution's ban on religious tests for office seemed to indicate that national citizenship would be independent of religious identity. Yet the Constitution as it was ratified in 1788 remained silent about the free exercise of faith. Nor did it mention government establishment of religion—that is, whether the federal state could sponsor an official church. Theoretically, the national government could mitigate Jewish gains by encroaching on free exercise or requiring Jews to contribute tax dollars to a state-sanctioned religion. The proposed Bill of Rights promised to preclude those prejudicial outcomes by protecting free exercise and prohibiting an established church. But the process of ratifying the Bill of Rights had ground to a halt in the early days of the Washington administration. It was unclear whether free exercise and disestablishment would ever achieve constitutional status.[1]

George Mason had been the first to advocate a bill of rights, recommending in the closing days of the Constitutional Convention that one be included in the Constitution's original text. Mason's fellow delegates, however, proved resistant for numerous reasons. Having toiled over constitutional language amid the heat of a long Philadelphia summer, they were understandably anxious to return home. Moreover, they feared that drafting a bill of rights would take longer than the few hours Mason anticipated, and that debate over the specifics of such a bill might jeopardize tenuous compromises forged earlier in the convention.

Opponents of a bill of rights also believed it was unnecessary, as the Constitution provided for a government of limited power with no authority to infringe on essential freedoms. Some delegates worried that enumerating fundamental rights might, counterintuitively, curb liberty because a finite list of rights could wrongly imply that other unlisted rights *were* subject to government encroachment.[2] Alexander Hamilton stood among those who were concerned that a bill of rights might unwittingly limit freedom.[3]

In rebuffing Mason, the framers failed to foresee that most people, upon reading the product of the convention, would want their most vital liberties enshrined in a bill of rights. The Constitution was ratified with the common understanding that a bill of rights would soon follow. In 1789, Congress approved the Bill of Rights, and the president sent the proposed amendments to the states for their consideration. Yet despite widespread enthusiasm, hopes for ratification soon began to dim. Amendments required approval of three-fourths of the states to take effect. Georgia, Connecticut, and Massachusetts had not ratified the Bill of Rights. The determining vote thus fell to the Virginia General Assembly, where the push for ratification became mired in protracted wrangling between the legislature's upper and lower houses.[4] Meanwhile, religious discrimination persisted at the state level. Most states denied Jews either the right to vote, hold office, or practice law—or some combination thereof.[5]

Jewish-Americans thus had just cause to be anxious about their civil status and eager for affirmation from the country's first president. Soon, leaders of America's various synagogues began discussing how to convey to George Washington their support for him and their aspirations for the Jewish people in the country he now led.[6] The effort began on June 20, 1790, with a circular that Shearith Israel in New York sent to sister congregations in Newport, Philadelphia, Richmond, and Charleston to collect their thoughts on a possible joint letter to Washington. Two of Hamilton's legal clients, Isaac Moses and Solomon Simson, authored the circular.[7] Shearith Israel explained, "We are desirous of addressing the President of the United States in one general address, comprehending all the congregations professing our holy religion in

America, as we are led to understand that mode will be less irksome to the president than troubling him to reply to every individual address." In truth, Shearith Israel meant all the congregations save one—the Jews of Savannah had already sent their own letter to the president, and Washington had written a gracious response. Shearith Israel's circular reflected its frustration with the Savannah congregation, bemoaning, "We do not, by any means, conceive ourselves well treated by the Georgians," whose failure to give Shearith Israel any "previous notice" of their solo missive was "hurtful to our feelings."[8]

Washington had already taken his oath of office nearly fourteen months earlier, and in its circular Shearith Israel insisted that it would have contacted the other synagogues sooner about a collective letter but mitigating circumstances intervened. Just what those circumstances were is unclear; the circular vaguely alluded to a "situation" which for "some time past prevented us" from taking timely action. Shearith Israel now requested that the other congregations suggest language for a letter that would then be combined into a single address.[9]

Moses Seixas was the warden of the Touro Synagogue (also known as Yeshuat Israel, meaning "Salvation of Israel") in Newport, and he issued his response to Shearith Israel on July 2. His home state of Rhode Island had ratified the Constitution only weeks earlier. Not even the Rhode Island General Assembly and other important bodies in the state had found opportunity to write to Washington yet. Seixas feared that it would entail "a great degree of indelicacy for us to address the President of the United States previous to any of them and therefore from motives of diffidence, and an ardent desire to avoid giving umbrage, [we] would wish to decline at present."[10]

While the Newport synagogue had ample reason for having delayed an address to Washington, Shearith Israel had none, in Seixas's view. After all, Shearith Israel was situated in New York, a state that had ratified the Constitution two years prior and thus been properly in the Union for the entirety of Washington's presidency. According to Seixas, Shearith Israel's delay was all the more egregious given its status as the first Jewish congregation in America and its location in a city that was, at the time, the national capital. "What plea you can now make to him for your apparent neglect, which almost amounts to disrespect, we cannot conceive," scolded Seixas.[11]

Not only did Seixas reprimand Shearith Israel, but he defended the Savannah Jews for having unilaterally sent a message to Washington. "We do not blame the conduct of the Georgians, they had an undoubted right to do as they did" after Shearith Israel had opted to "procrastinate," he protested.[12] That Moses Sexias's brother, Gershom, was the *hazzan* of Shearith Israel makes Moses's caustic attitude surprising at first glance. Then again, the authors of Shearith Israel's circular were on the board of trustees, a board that had routinely frustrated Gershom Seixas in negotiations over his salary. Moses Seixas's pique may have been a testament to, rather than betrayal of, brotherly loyalty.[13]

Toward the end of the letter, Seixas tempered his tone somewhat. He reserved the possibility that Shearith Israel had deliberately waited until Rhode Island's ratification of the Constitution because New York Jewry wanted to include their Newport coreligionists in a letter to Washington. If that were indeed the case, then the Touro Synagogue would sign on, Seixas offered. Still, he would not accede to Shearith Israel's request that his congregation draft a letter to the president for Shearith Israel's review. Sexias instead directed Shearith Israel to furnish *him* with a draft so that the Newport congregants could respond with "our opinion thereon in a few hours after we have perused it." In closing, he conceded that some of his diction was perhaps too heated: "You'll excuse my language."[14]

Meanwhile, the Beth Elohim congregation in Charleston was similarly irked by Shearith Israel. Beth Elohim had sent a draft letter on July 15 for Shearith Israel to incorporate into a joint address. When Shearith Israel failed to acknowledge receipt in due time, Beth Elohim complained, "We are left in the dark."[15]

As the first synagogue in America, Shearith Israel was the foundational congregation that had served as a model for—and provided money to—Jewish communities along the Atlantic seaboard. But the congregations in Savannah, Newport, and Charleston illustrate how Shearith Israel did not enjoy blind deference from other synagogues. An aversion to hierarchy was part of what made American Jews distinct from their coreligionists in Europe and the Middle East, where Jewish authority was not so decentralized.[16]

With Shearith Israel's attempt at a collective letter showing little momentum, the Touro Synagogue of Newport received news that prompted Moses Seixas to begin writing his own address to the president, independent of the other synagogues—George Washington was coming to Rhode Island. The president was slated to visit Newport, the state's capital city, where Seixas would be afforded an opportunity to read aloud a letter on behalf of his congregation in Washington's presence.

It is not without irony that this event, which would prove of great historical significance owing to the famous reply it elicited from Washington, came at an otherwise trying time for Newport and its Jews. The war had resulted in the evacuation of much of the city's population, especially of Jews faithful to the Patriot cause. British troops had destroyed many buildings, and postwar recovery was slow in coming to Newport. In 1790, the Jewish community, like the city at large, was still a poor imitation of its earlier self.[17]

Washington chose to make a celebratory trip because Rhode Island finally had ratified the Constitution. That Rhode Island became the last of the original thirteen states to do so was unsurprising. The state was something of a problem child in the early republic. Under the Articles of Confederation, which required unanimity among the states for amendments, Rhode Island sank more than one endeavor that otherwise enjoyed broad support. In so doing, the state unwittingly illustrated the shortcomings of the Articles and inadvertently helped hasten the call for the Constitutional Convention. Rhode Island was the only state that declined to send delegates to Philadelphia in the summer of 1787.[18] And even though in 1788 the Constitution garnered the approval of enough states to take effect, Rhode Island refused to ratify for another two years. Dubbed "Rogue's Island" by its critics,[19] the state had a unique political culture and economic system that made it fiercely protective of its autonomy.[20] But faced with the prospect of being treated as a foreign country, and thus subject to import duties, Rhode Island belatedly ratified the Constitution in May 1790.[21]

———

Washington left New York by boat on August 15 and headed east through Long Island Sound toward Newport.[22] A number of dignitaries joined the president on his excursion, including a U.S. Supreme Court justice, the governor of New York, two congressmen, and Hamilton's rival in the cabinet, Thomas Jefferson.[23] On the morning of August 17, expectant Newport residents spotted the ship approaching the harbor. The towns-folk quickly went into motion, raising the state flag, ringing bells, and firing thirteen cannons in honor of the states of the Union.[24]

Washington and his cohort were greeted at the wharf by a committee of leading citizens.[25] During his ensuing tour of Newport, the president was almost certainly shown the local synagogue, as it was the best pre-served building in a city otherwise ravaged by war.[26] A contemporary magazine noted of Newport, "The whole appearance of the place is shat-tered and out of repair" and its "churches have not much of the beauties of architecture to boast of." However, "the Jews' synagogue is the most ornamented of them all," with a "rich and elegant" interior featuring impressive brasswork.[27]

While in Newport, Washington met an elderly but entrepreneurial Jewish resident named Jacob Isaacks. The septuagenarian Isaacks had pioneered a technique for desalinating ocean water, thereby making it safe "for all common and culinary purposes," according to the *Newport Herald*. Isaacks gifted a fresh bottle of his water to the president, who was reportedly "pleased to express himself highly satisfied therewith."[28] Lest Washington entertain any doubts about the potability of the bottle's contents, Isaacks also handed him two certificates from local townsmen vouching for his purification process.[29]

A formal banquet with eighty attendees commenced at 5:00 p.m. in the State House.[30] As these were years of scarcity for this once bustling seaport, local families had to volunteer tableware from their homes so that every dish, goblet, and pitcher at the supper would be silver.[31] Thir-teen toasts followed the meal, as was the tradition in that era. Partici-pants raised their glasses to such admired subjects as the U.S. Constitu-tion, the fallen soldiers of the Revolution, and the women of America.

Touro Synagogue. *Source*: Samuel Adams Drake, *Nooks and Corners of the New England Coast*. New York: Harper, 1875.

"May the last be the first," rang one toast, expressing the hope that the last state to ratify the Constitution would be the first in its defense. A local federal judge, Henry Marchant, offered the evening's final toast to "the man we love," and those present stood up in Washington's honor.[32] The president and his contingent retired after dinner to an upscale boardinghouse, where they slept two or more men to a room, except for Washington, who enjoyed private quarters. He slumbered under a blue quilt made of silk (which no subsequent guest would be allowed to use until another president, Rutherford B. Hayes, visited Newport eighty-nine years later).[33]

The next morning, the community organized a series of orations to commemorate the occasion. Judge Marchant was scheduled to speak first, but he became overwhelmed by the moment and someone else stepped in to give his remarks. An address from the Christian clergy was then read aloud. Finally, Moses Seixas delivered not one but two speeches, the first in his capacity as master of the local Masonic fraternity known as King David's Lodge—Washington was himself a Mason—and the second as warden of the Touro Synagogue.[34]

Amid all their ritual and secrecy, Masonic lodges were foremost social gatherings where men found respite from their professional and familial obligations. That Seixas was Jewish and an officer at a lodge named after a legendary Israelite king was not coincidental; Jewish colonists had established King David's Lodge some twenty years earlier. There were Jewish masons on both sides of the Atlantic. Unlike religious institutions, Masonic lodges were open to Jews and Gentiles alike, thereby providing a unique space where a Jew could retain his religious identity while cultivating ties with those Christian neighbors who were amenable to interfaith friendship.[35] Seixas's address from King David's Lodge to Washington comprised a short series of pleasant platitudes, praising the president's "exemplary virtues and emanations of goodness."[36]

He then turned to his second oration of the day, this one on behalf of the Jewish community to Washington. "Permit the children of the Stock of Abraham to approach you with the most cordial affection," Seixas opened. After celebrating that the "God of Israel" had "shielded your head in the day of battle," he contrasted the denial of rights for Jews in the past with the commitment to political equality that the Constitution seemed to promise: "Deprived as we heretofore have been of the invaluable rights of free citizens, we now . . . behold a Government, erected by the majesty of the People—a Government, which to bigotry gives no sanction, to persecution no assistance—but generously affording to all liberty of conscience, and immunities of citizenship."[37] Seixas's remarks were, in some sense, aspirational. Although the Constitution's explicit repudiation of religious tests for office suggested that Jews (and other religious minorities) were in fact entitled to first-class citizenship, the political climate remained worrisome, with most state constitutions discriminating against Jews and ratification of the federal Bill of Rights still languishing. Seixas's speech embodied the Jewish hope that their national government did indeed see them as full-fledged citizens.

Following Seixas's address, the president and his coterie headed toward the wharf, as they were due to sail to Providence. Washington passed a store during this walk and sent an aide inside to purchase a pair of gloves. The shopkeeper stood at the window, mesmerized by the sight of the nation's first head of state on her street. She was unaware that the man requesting to see her stock of gloves did so on Washington's behalf and refused to serve him, fixated as she was on the president outside. The failure of the aide to speedily return prompted Washington to enter the store himself. Gloves were quickly furnished. No one else had such a hold on the American people; as Jews like Moses Seixas understood, no one else could lend greater prestige to the principle of religious liberty.[38]

After Washington and his travel companions boarded their boat, a final salute of thirteen cannons thundered as they passed Newport's fort.[39] Their ensuing visit to Providence was brief, for pressing business awaited the president—the relocation of the capital from New York to Philadelphia.[40] But despite the claims on Washington's attention in the aftermath of his trip, he found time to issue a response to the Touro Synagogue. The president had a critical opportunity to give voice to his belief in civic equality for Jews. Washington well understood that his words would reach far more people than just Moses Seixas and his fellow congregants. Presidential replies to constituents were often reprinted in newspapers and thus an essential means by which Washington communicated the policy of his administration to the country.[41] The message that he crafted to Newport's Jews would become among the most important in the annals of religious freedom.

Washington mixed his own wording with language borrowed from Seixas's oration, affirming, "All possess alike liberty of conscience and immunities of citizenship."[42] This marked the first time in world history that the head of a modern state recognized Jews as citizens.[43] He continued in the letter's most famous passage: "It is now no more that toleration is spoken of, as if it was by the indulgence of one class of people that another enjoyed the exercise of their inherent natural rights. For happily the Government of the United States, which gives to bigotry no sanction, to persecution no assistance, requires only that they who live under its protection should demean themselves as good citizens."[44] That the president lifted this phrasing nearly verbatim from Seixas's speech could leave the Jews of Newport with no doubt that their aspiration and the position of the Washington administration were one and the same.[45]

The letter's distinction between mere religious toleration and genuine religious liberty is significant. Toleration is probationary; liberty is permanent. The process of Jewish "emancipation"—that is, the granting of citizenship—in Europe illustrates the precarious nature of toleration. When European nations gradually emancipated their Jews (beginning with France in 1791 and culminating with Romania in 1923), the measures were often provisional. The specter of reversal loomed. Citizenship was indeed an indulgence.[46] In the Newport letter, by contrast, Washington exalted religious liberty as an inherent natural right, signaling to Jews that the free exercise of their faith was not simply tolerable for the moment—it was an inviolable element of life in the American republic. The Newport letter stands as close to a formal emancipation of Jews as can be found in the history of the presidency.[47]

Washington closed his message to the Touro Synagogue with language from his favorite verse in the Hebrew Bible. He assured Newport's Jews that in this new nation, "everyone shall sit in safety under his own vine and fig-tree, and there shall be none to make him afraid."[48] The "vine and fig-tree" reference, from Micah 4:4, appears no fewer than thirty-seven times in Washington's writings.[49] Invoking a line from the Hebrew Bible doubtlessly helped the Christian president identify common ground with his Jewish correspondents. The Newport letter reached a broad readership, appearing in newspapers in Massachusetts, Connecticut, New York, Maryland, Virginia, South Carolina, and, of course, Rhode Island.[50]

In some respects, Washington's authorship of what is arguably the most important document in American Jewish history may seem surprising. He had not been especially engaged with Judaism or Jewry. Unlike other founders, Washington drew no parallels between Americans and ancient Jews, offered little comment on Jewish suffering, and had sparse contact with Jewish people.[51] But if discussion of Jews or their faith is strikingly absent from Washington's writings, then so too is any hint of the religious prejudice that mars the records of so many other founders. At the close of the Revolution, he had voiced his aspiration that America would serve as "an asylum for the poor and oppressed of all nations and religions."[52] And Washington showed fidelity to that sentiment in his private life. In one of his only references to "Jews" in his correspondence, he asked an aide to seek out the services of a pair of tradesmen and was explicit that neither national origin nor religious identity should raise any bar to hiring someone with talent. "If they are good workmen, they may be of Asia, Africa, or Europe," Washington stipulated. "They may be Mahometans, Jews, or Christian[s] of any sect—or they may be Atheists."[53] The Newport letter embodied that same characteristic broad-mindedness.

Historians speculate about who in Washington's circle most likely influenced his views in the Newport letter.[54] While scholars have not previously considered Hamilton, he is a compelling candidate for several reasons. No one else in the president's orbit could claim closer ties to the people and faith of Judaism. Hamilton also had a preexisting relationship with the Seixas family, having served alongside Moses's brother, Gershom, on the Columbia board.[55]

What's more, the crucial point in the Newport letter that bare tolerance of minority faiths falls short of genuine religious freedom was a distinction to which Hamilton himself was sensitive. In a government report from 1791, he praised "a perfect equality of religious privileges" as "far more precious than mere religious toleration." Hamilton predicted that people would "flock from Europe to the United States" in part to enjoy the kind of true religious liberty unknown in the Old World.[56] Indeed, he personally knew a number of Jewish immigrants to America who fit that very description.

The Newport letter also spoke directly to the notion of Jewry no longer living in fear—"there shall be none to make him afraid"—which would have been particularly meaningful to Jews given their long history of persecution. It was a history familiar to Hamilton. He marveled at Jewry's improbable continuity through the millennia, observing in an essay that the "progress of the Jews . . . from their earliest history to the present time has been and is entirely out of the ordinary course of human affairs. Is it not then a fair conclusion that the cause also is an *extraordinary one*—in other words, that it is the effect of some great providential plan?"[57] To Hamilton, the Jews' unlikely survival was a sure sign of God's favor.

———

In the months following the Newport letter, the synagogues of New York, Richmond, Charleston, and Philadelphia persevered in their efforts to formulate a joint address to Washington. Finally, they produced one. With the president in the new capital of Philadelphia, a local Jew named Manuel Josephson found occasion to read aloud this collective letter to Washington on December 13, 1790. The missive reflected the esteem with which Jews held both the president and the Constitution he had helped shepherd into existence. As the "Leader of the American Armies," Washington had "opened the way to the reign of freedom, but never was it perfectly secure, till your hand gave birth to the federal Constitution, and you renounced the joys of retirement to seal by your administration in peace, what you had achieved in war."[58] The following day, Josephson sent word to Shearith Israel that Washington took no umbrage at New York Jewry on account of their delay in addressing him.

"I made it a point to inform the President verbally, the reasons of your Congregation's seeming remissness in not having paid their respects before," relayed Josephson, "and he appeared perfectly satisfied."[59]

In Washington's written reply—given to Mikveh Israel but addressed to all the congregations that signed the joint letter—he imputed to the American people his own embrace of pluralism: "The liberality of sentiment toward each other, which marks every political and religious denomination of men in this country, stands unparalleled in the history of nations." Given the enduring bigotry against Jews and other dissenters, the president's statement was perhaps more hopeful than literal. Washington closed his response by conveying his wish to the Jews that "eternal blessings" would "rest upon your congregations."[60] Newspapers in multiple states published the president's reply.[61] With this letter, in tandem with the earlier missives to Savannah and Newport, Washington had addressed every synagogue in the United States. His embrace of a religiously diverse America—one that he expressly extended to the country's Jews—created a model for inclusivity in the critical early years of the republic when the power of precedent was at its zenith.

Notwithstanding these synagogues' initial bickering over a joint letter and a culture of decentralized religious authority, it is revealing that several congregations spread out across the country chose to speak with a single voice. The Jews of New York, Philadelphia, Richmond, and Charleston consciously presented themselves as a national religious community to the national government. Massachusetts was founded by and for Puritans, Pennsylvania by and for Quakers, Maryland by and for Catholics—but the Jews had no colony of their own. With the Revolution, colonies turned into states, many of which continued the colonial tradition of protecting the rights of their majorities while excluding minorities like Jews from the full prerogatives of citizenship. It is only natural, then, that Jewish loyalties would principally lie with the federal government that bestowed the very equality so often denied by the states. At a time when many citizens felt an allegiance to their individual state first and the country second, the Jews generally maintained a nationalistic orientation consistent with that of Hamilton, who fervently believed that domestic needs had to supersede local ones for the American experiment to succeed.[62]

———

The Newport letter stands as Washington's most vivid expression of religious pluralism, and his accepting attitude toward Jews was certainly of a piece with Hamilton's own. In the abstract, it might seem that those who showed the most sympathy for minority faiths would have favored the separation of church and state.[63] Yet Washington and Hamilton upend that assumption. Fully committed to religious liberty for all, they *also* believed that faith could be a boon to the civic health of the republic. It was in Washington's canonical Farewell Address of 1796—which Hamilton ghostwrote—that we find their most explicit articulation of that view.[64]

Washington originally considered stepping down after one term as president, having grown weary of partisan squabbles and feeling the effects of ill health. In 1792, he tapped James Madison to write an address for him commemorating his departure from office. But several presidential aides, Hamilton included, persuaded Washington that only his continued service as head of state could stave off the rupture of a still fragile republic. And so Washington agreed to stay on for a second and final term; Madison's manuscript was shelved for the time being.[65]

Four years later, in February 1796, the president first indicated to Hamilton—by then a private citizen practicing law—that his help was needed in preparing what would become known as the Farewell Address.[66] Washington's decision to solicit Hamilton is unsurprising, not only because the president had recently fallen out with Madison but also because Washington had long leaned on Hamilton to draft written communications.[67] In the course of the Revolutionary War, Hamilton was an invaluable ghostwriter for Washington. Hamilton continued to pen documents for him during his administration, including diplomatic letters, speeches to Congress, and official proclamations.[68] Both as aide-de-camp in the 1770s and as presidential advisor in the 1790s, Hamilton enjoyed substantial leeway in shaping the content and tenor of

Washington's language. Washington had the humility to recognize Hamilton's intellectual talent and to see that talent as an asset rather than a threat.

After Washington made a few alterations to the Madison draft from 1792, he sent that updated version to Hamilton to use as a starting point. Hamilton, naturally, wanted to discard Madison's words and compose his own. But he was diplomatic enough to produce two versions of an address for Washington's consideration—the first, entirely his own creation; the second, a revised draft of the Madison text.[69] Eliza Hamilton would later pridefully recall of her husband, "The whole or nearly all the 'Address,' was read to me by him as he wrote it and a greater part if not all was written by him in my presence."[70]

Hamilton first submitted his wholly original address to Washington and waited several weeks before forwarding his Madison rewrite. This was probably an intentional tactic to ensure that Washington would have time to fully assimilate Hamilton's own draft into his thinking; the president would thus be more likely to dismiss the Madisonian alternative when it finally reached his desk. Indeed, Washington ultimately did conclude that the Hamilton draft was "more dignified." As was typical when Washington received a ghostwritten document from an aide, he removed some wording, added new thoughts, and refined the diction. Over the next several weeks, the president and his former treasury secretary continued to exchange drafts. The Farewell Address is a consummate example of the collaborative dynamic between the two men.[71]

Notably, Madison's draft from 1792 made no mention of religion. In 1796, by contrast, Hamilton crafted language exhibiting a clear conviction that faith was crucial to the civic vitality of the country: "To all those dispositions which promote political happiness, religion and morality are essential props." His draft asked rhetorically, "Can we in prudence suppose that national morality can be maintained in exclusion of religious principles? Does it not require the aid of a generally received and divinely authoritative religion?"[72]

The foregoing passage was one of many where Washington tweaked Hamilton's phrasing. In its final form, the Farewell Address—printed in newspapers rather than read aloud—differed slightly from its original

version: "Of all the dispositions and habits which lead to political prosperity, religion and morality are indispensable supports." The rhetorical
questions became declarative statements. "Let us with caution indulge
the supposition that morality can be maintained without religion," the
Farewell Address warned. "Reason and experience both forbid us to
expect that national morality can prevail in exclusion of religious
principle."[73]

Hamilton's introduction of this passage on religion was not an anomalous contribution from someone otherwise unconcerned with matters
of faith. Elsewhere, he decried the French Revolution as a "volcano of
atheism."[74] Hamilton also lauded Americans for their "just reverence
for religion."[75] To be sure, he was not especially invested in the practice
of Christianity—despite the piety of his wife, Hamilton never joined a
church[76]—but his lack of interest in the Christian faith should not be
mistaken for ambivalence toward religion generally.[77]

Hamilton's language in the Farewell Address touted the role of religion in advancing civic goals but did not go so far as to endorse the re-
verse: government support for faith. Washington, however, had already
taken that step. More than a decade earlier, he demonstrated how religious pluralism might coincide with state funding of religious institutions.[78] In 1785, the Virginia General Assembly debated a bill that would
have used public dollars to bankroll Christian education. Washington
proved amenable to this kind of legislation—but only if Jews, Muslims,
and other dissenters were exempt from taxation that would subsidize
Christian teachers. In his words, "I am not amongst the number of those
who are so much alarmed at the thoughts of making people pay towards
the support of that which they profess, if of the denominations of Christians, or declare themselves Jews, Mahomitans or otherwise, and
thereby obtain proper relief."[79] The bill, ultimately, did not pass into
law.[80] We should be wary of projecting Washington's views in their totality onto Hamilton. Both men were pluralists, and both saw religion as
key to civic well-being, but Washington alone expressed comfort with
public monies subsidizing Christian institutions.

The Hamiltonian and Washingtonian models of church-state relations were similar, then, if not quite identical. Neither approach was

necessarily at odds with the Establishment Clause in the federal Bill of Rights. The First Amendment begins, "Congress shall make no law respecting an establishment of religion . . ." Americans in the founding era agreed that this language plainly prohibits the federal government from recognizing any particular denomination as an official state faith. Consistent with that common understanding, neither Washington nor Hamilton ever endorsed the idea of a state-sanctioned religion. There was no uniform opinion in their day on any additional meaning that might be wrung from the Establishment Clause. While a number of commentators in the early republic maintained that the text wholly divorces church and state, that interpretation would not become dominant until the twentieth century.[81] Another reading of the Establishment Clause, one in conformity with the Farewell Address, holds that religion can indeed bolster civic life so long as the federal government does not establish a church.

———

Some Republicans sought to exploit antisemitic sentiment in their bid to oppose Hamilton and the Federalist Party on the issue of church-state relations. They argued, erroneously, that Federalists favored a total unity of church and state; these Republicans further claimed that such an approach was a nefarious revival of the ancient Israelite government, wherein the same officials had been invested with power over religious and civil matters alike. A Republican pamphleteer, Abraham Bishop, traced a supposed lineage beginning with ancient Jews, continuing with the Catholic Church, and culminating with leading Federalists of his own day. "Federalism passed by another name among the Jews and Catholics" but "has always been found in a union of church and state," he insisted. Bishop maintained that this Federalist agenda was used to justify one of Hamilton's signature policies—the national assumption of states' debts—by falsely lending it the imprimatur of religion: "Church and state has taught the blessedness of a national debt." According to Bishop, Federalists also conferred upon Hamilton himself an aura of religious credibility by gushing over the "resemblance between

General Hamilton and his army and Michael and his angels," an allusion to Hamilton's stint as a general during the Adams administration.[82]

The Baptist clergyman Nehemiah Dodge resorted to similarly anti-Jewish polemics. In an address about the alleged Israelite origins of Federalist policy, he referred to Federalists as "those Federal gentleman, who are fond of blending church and state in this nation because they were *one* in the Jewish nation." Dodge suggested that proponents of such church-state blending were "most likely to promote rulers, and laws, favorable to their Jewish plan."[83]

Both Bishop and Dodge were distorting the Federalist position. Whatever ideological diversity existed within Federalist circles, no faction of the party supported a theocratic government.[84] And Hamilton, for his part, never endorsed a "union" or "blending" of church and state. Rather, he took the much more moderate stance that religious rectitude was important to the nation's welfare. It is a testament to the lingering antisemitism of the early republic that Hamilton's opponents believed they could score political points by conflating him and his party with ancient Jews.[85]

Hamilton did once allude to the Hebrew Bible to make a constitutional argument, but it was in defense of the separation of powers, not church-state unity. In an 1802 piece in the *New-York Evening Post*, a paper that Hamilton founded, he affirmed as a "fundamental maxim of free government" that "the three departments of power, ought to be separate and distinct." Drawing on biblical imagery, he continued, "In a representative republic, the legislative department is the 'Aaron's Rod' most likely to swallow up the rest." His symbolism here was drawn from Exodus 7:10: "Aaron cast down his rod before Pharaoh and before his servants, and it became a serpent."[86] As the most widely disseminated text of the era, the Bible offered a singularly useful reference point for readers.[87]

————

The Hamiltonian and Washingtonian models were not the only approaches to church-state relations in the early republic, nor would they win out in the course of American constitutional history.[88] Jefferson and Madison adopted a different philosophy that sought to keep government and religion mutually exclusive. And just as Hamilton and Washington illustrate that sympathizers with minority faiths could see a role for religion in civic affairs, Jefferson and Madison reveal how advocates of the separation of church and state could be tainted by antisemitic bias.

For Jefferson, religious freedom could only flourish in the absence of government involvement in faith.[89] "Religion is a matter which lies solely between Man and his God," he insisted. "He owes account to none other for his faith or his worship." Fearing that state engagement with faith would inevitably lead to the coercion of religious belief, Jefferson declared, "The legitimate powers of government reach actions only, and not opinions."[90] The Hamiltonian notion of a harmony between the religious and the civic had no place in the Jeffersonian worldview.

As politicians are apt to do, Jefferson saw in the Constitution a vindication of his preferred ideology. He penned a letter to a Baptist association—more than a decade after the First Amendment was ratified—in which he maintained that the Establishment Clause had constructed "a wall of separation between Church and State." Jefferson thereby coined the phrase that only much later would become synonymous with the actual text appearing in the First Amendment. To be sure, Jefferson's interpretation of the Establishment Clause resonated with some people in his age, Madison among them, but it did not garner universal acceptance.[91]

Although Jefferson is celebrated today as a champion of religious liberty, his attitudes about Judaism and Jewry were more complicated than popular memory of him might suggest. Much of his private correspondence with non-Jews exhibits a measure of hostility toward the Jewish faith and its people. Jefferson told a Christian protégé of his that the Jewish priesthood in antiquity comprised a "bloodthirsty race" that was "cruel and remorseless." These priests peddled "superstition" under the false guise of divine revelation. "The whole religion of the Jews" was based on "the fumes of the most disordered imaginations" masquerading as "special communications of the Deity." These myths, as Jefferson saw them, not only corrupted biblical Judaism but had "preserved their credit with the Jews of all subsequent times."[92] Jefferson similarly remarked to the former secretary of the Continental Congress that ancient Jews had "vicious ethics."[93] And in a letter to Benjamin Rush, Jefferson derided the Jewish understanding of God in the Bible as "degrading and injurious."[94] His lack of respect for Judaism was of a piece with his concerns about organized religion generally.[95]

Jefferson also analogized his political nemeses to Jews. Writing to a fellow Republican about the Federalists, he commented, "They are marked, like the Jews, with such a peculiarity of character."[96] And in a letter to the French hero of the American Revolution, Marquis de Lafayette, Jefferson claimed that Quakers and Jews alike had failed to embrace an American identity; instead, the Quakers were "dispersed, as the Jews" and "they still form, as those [Jews] do, one nation, foreign to the land they live in."[97]

To be fair, during Jefferson's tenure as president, he appointed a Jew to serve as the U.S. marshal in Maryland, a significant federal law enforcement post.[98] And whatever skepticism Jefferson expressed about Judaism and Jewry in private correspondence with Christians did not resurface in his personal interactions with Jews. Indeed, Jefferson's letters to Jews indicated an awareness of the persecution that their people had long endured. After the Jewish leader Mordecai Noah sent Jefferson a speech he had given, Jefferson thanked him for sharing "valuable facts in Jewish history" and acknowledged of the Jewish people, "Your sect, by its sufferings, has furnished a remarkable proof of the universal spirit of religious intolerance, inherent in every sect, disclaimed by all while feeble, and practiced by all when in power."[99] And upon receiving a similar missive from a Jewish doctor in Georgia, Jefferson replied that he was "happy in the restoration of the Jews particularly to their social rights." He further expressed his "hopes they will be seen taking their seats on the benches of science, as preparatory to their doing the same at the board of government."[100] This latter sentiment, while intended as a compliment, implied that Jews were not yet sufficiently cultivated for political leadership.[101]

Despite some misgivings about the religion and people of Judaism, Jefferson believed that everyone—Jews included—deserved to practice their faith freely. In a bid to attract immigration to Virginia in 1776, he sponsored an unsuccessful bill that would have extended citizenship in the state to foreigners, including members of minority faiths.[102] Jefferson scribbled "Jews advantageous" on the back of a copy of the bill.[103] He considered among his greatest achievements his authorship of the Virginia Statute for Religious Freedom, which protected the free exercise of faith and made the state government blind to religion. In the words of the statute, "All men shall be free to profess, and by argument to maintain, their opinions in matters of religion, and that the same shall in no wise diminish, enlarge, or affect their civil capacities." While free exercise was commonplace across the United States, the language about protecting "civil capacities" differentiated Virginia from a number of other states where Jews could practice their faith but, for doing so, faced disqualification from the ballot box, state legislature, and legal profession. Jefferson later affirmed in his autobiography that the statute was "meant to comprehend, within the mantle of its protection, the Jew and the Gentile, the Christian and Mahometan, the Hindu, and infidel of every denomination."[104] If Jefferson was an important defender of Jews' right to religious freedom, it was a role he played despite his dim view of Judaism and mixed take on its practitioners.

———

James Madison, too, flatly rejected the Hamiltonian position that religion is an essential element of civic prosperity. Madison was aware of those who felt that without an integration of "religious and civil polity, neither could be supported," and he condemned such a conceit as an "error so long rooted in the unenlightened minds of well meaning Christians, as well as in the corrupt hearts of persecuting usurpers."[105] That Madison and Washington sharply diverged on the politics of faith may help explain why Madison, who looms so large in the history of church-state relations, offered no comment whatsoever on religion in the ultimately discarded 1792 Farewell Address.

As with Jefferson, Madison's commitment to the separation of church and state did not mean that he was free of antisemitism. A glaring episode from Madison's presidential history marks the limit of his religious tolerance. The central player in this saga was the aforementioned Mordecai Noah, a Jewish journalist and playwright in Charleston who aspired to a diplomatic post. During the Madison administration, he petitioned the Department of State for an appointment to an American consulate in any of the Barbary states, which consisted of Morocco, Algiers, Tunis, and Tripoli.

Noah well understood that his identity as a Jew could be a strategic advantage in North Africa. Jews were considered impartial intermediaries between Christian and Muslim states; both Britain and the Netherlands had made use of Jewish envoys to that region. And the Barbary was home to powerful Jewish communities whose local clout could be leveraged by a Jewish-American consul to the benefit of his home country. Noah explained to the State Department that "it would be a favorable circumstance in sending a member of the Hebrew nation to the Barbary Powers . . . supported as I would be with the wealth and influence of forty thousand [Jewish] residents." He anticipated still other advantages if Madison elevated him to such a position. Wealthy Jews in any number of nations would see the appointment as a reflection of America's devotion to religious freedom and thereby entice them to immigrate to the United States. It would also send a strong message to other countries about American values. "I wish to prove to foreign powers," Noah wrote, "that our government is not regulated in the appointment of their officers by religious distinction." Madison would prove just the opposite in the end.[106]

Noah was appointed the consul to Tunis in 1813. As he prepared to leave for the Barbary, the administration gave him a secret mission to execute on his voyage. Algiers had abducted the American crew of a merchant ship. Secretary of State James Monroe instructed Noah to pay a ransom of up to $3,000 ($50,000 today) for each of the twelve captives. Noah was to engage in these negotiations under the false premise that he acted on behalf of the crew's friends rather than the U.S. government.[107] Monroe surely feared that any indication the administration was paying for the captives would only incentivize further abductions.

An unexpectedly serpentine path across the Atlantic and through Europe found Noah in Cádiz, Spain, where he came across the American expatriate Richard Keene. The two discussed the clandestine negotiations that Noah intended to initiate in Algiers. Keene told Noah that he could, for a finder's fee, travel there on Noah's behalf and settle the matter. After the American consul to Cádiz fulsomely vouched for Keene, Noah enlisted him for the cause. Noah had little idea that Keene was a notorious figure, with a scandal-ridden past, whom Madison profoundly distrusted.[108]

Once in Algiers, Keene managed to secure the release of only two of the twelve seamen in question, and, in a twist, he paid ransom for another four hostages who were supposedly from Louisiana and whose captivity was unbeknown to the U.S. government. Noah billed the State Department for the ransom, Keene's fee, the cost of returning the captives stateside, and Noah's own expenses, plus interest—a total of $25,910 ($436,000 today). With this, Noah continued onward to Tunis to assume his duties as consul.[109]

News of the affair and Noah's sizable bill were both met with frustration back in Washington. The State Department was displeased with Noah for several reasons. Not only did he hire an agent to complete a covert assignment that he had been expected to undertake himself, but he tapped none other than the disreputable Keene for the job. Moreover, the rescue of the Louisianans was beyond Noah's remit. And he proved loose-lipped, divulging to Keene and others that he operated at the behest of the Madison administration. Although Noah had indeed been indiscreet, not all of these charges were fair. Monroe never expressly forbade Noah from using a proxy, and Noah acted on the advice of America's own consul in Spain in selecting Keene. Nevertheless, the mission was largely a failure, and Noah was to take the blame.[110]

That Madison would fire Noah from his diplomatic post was inevitable; the question remained what the stated rationale would be. It was at this point that Noah's status as a Jew became injected into a diplomatic imbroglio that otherwise bore no connection to his religious identity. In discussing Noah's imminent recall, Monroe relayed to Madison the opinion of an American naval captain who "says that the Turks and other people on the Barbary coast believe that every Jew who dies turns into a jackass, and that the Christians mount and ride them instantly, and directly, to the Devil. If this is the impression, the reason for removing him [i.e., Noah] is the stronger."[111] By Monroe's lights, purported antisemitism in the Barbary states made the case for discharging Noah all the more compelling.

Madison proceeded to predicate Noah's ouster squarely on his Jewish background, with no mention of the Algiers fiasco. "In recalling Noah," the president instructed Monroe, "it may be well to rest the measure pretty much on the ascertained prejudices of the Turks against his religion."[112] Monroe, in turn, penned a letter of dismissal and entrusted it to an American squadron bound for the Barbary to deliver to Noah. The letter notified Noah that his Jewish faith posed an insurmountable hurdle to his continued public service, explaining, "At the time of your appointment, as Consul at Tunis, it was not known that the religion which you profess would form any obstacle to the exercise of your consular functions. Recent information, however, on which entire reliance may be placed, proves that it would produce a very unfavorable effect."[113]

Perhaps Madison was genuine in ridding the consulate of Noah because he was a Jew. Or maybe the president exploited ostensible bigotry against Jews as a convenient pretext for the dismissal, thereby avoiding commentary on a furtive operation to which the U.S. government was supposed to be officially unconnected. Either way, antisemitism played a part. Madison had thus changed the terms of the affair from concern about Noah's mismanagement of the mission to a far weightier question about the role of religious discrimination in American statecraft. Noah was eager to defend himself and his faith. He produced a pamphlet about the Algiers affair that criticized the Madison administration and extolled the patriotism of Jews in the United States. Although Noah did not formally publish the pamphlet, it circulated widely enough that Jewish-American leaders, along with Gentiles at home and abroad, sent letters to the State Department in his support.[114]

He pressed the issue further with Madison shortly after the latter's tenure as president had come to an end. The ex-consul wanted to impress upon Madison that his Jewish faith had not at all undermined his capacity to fulfill his diplomatic duties. "No injury arose in Barbary to the public service from my religion as relating to myself," Noah assured Madison. "On the contrary, my influence and standing abroad was highly creditable." He went on to share his worry that Madison had established a dangerous norm at the State Department by making religious identity a valid cause for dismissal. Noah requested that the letter recalling him from the consulate—one that "refers solely to my religion" as the grounds for removal—either "be erased from the books of the Department of State" or at least have some "explanations" attached to his file so as to "prevent any evils arising from the precedent."[115]

Madison's response flatly denied that Judaism played any factor in Noah's expulsion from Tunis and, in so doing, simply ignored that the letter of dismissal had unequivocally stated otherwise. He told Noah, "Your religious profession was well known at the time you received your commission; and that in itself it could not be a motive for your recall." To address Noah's unease about the State Department records, Madison suggested that James Monroe, who had succeeded him in the White House, would surely permit an addendum. This concession, however, was somewhat backhanded. Whereas Noah had asked for "explanations" to be appended to the annals for the sake of safeguarding future Jewish diplomats, Madison intimated that Noah's real concern was his own reputation. As Madison put it, "An official preservation will be readily allowed to explanations necessary to protect your character."[116] Madison was likely irked at the accusation that his administration had set a precedent for prejudice. After all, at the twilight of his presidency, he had appointed a Jewish consul to Scotland, a move that was perhaps sufficient in Madison's eyes to rectify any earlier damage wrought to Jews.[117]

Noah was apparently underwhelmed by Madison's letter because the following year he published a travelogue about his experiences abroad that included a devastating critique of Madison's role in the Algiers affair. He chastised the ex-president for forgetting "that the religion of a citizen is not a legitimate object of official notice from the government." According to Noah, Madison's reference to antisemitism in the Barbary as the justification for his removal did not square with reality; North African Jews were respected figures who served in important diplomatic and domestic positions for their countries. Noah revealed that Madison had been confronted with allegations "that my religion would produce injurious effects, and the President, instead of closing the door on such interdicted subjects, had listened and concurred." And even if—Noah reasoned hypothetically—the Barbary did suffer from endemic animus toward Jews, the United States should never abandon its principles to accommodate the hatred of others. "Are we prepared to yield up the admirable and just institutions of our country at the shrine of foreign bigotry and superstition?" he asked. "Are we prepared to disenfranchise one of our citizens to gratify the intolerant views of the Bey of Tunis?" Noah deplored how Madison had effectively signaled to foreign powers that they were entitled to determine the faith of American diplomats. He also voiced anxiety about the fate of the Jewish people, for if Jews who "fought and bled for American Independence" could not have their rights secured by the U.S. government, then "what nation may not oppress them?"[118] Noah's travelogue was so popular that it sold out.[119]

To be sure, Madison had other experiences with Jews that cast him in a more favorable light. While he lacked sustained exposure to Jewish individuals, Madison did borrow money from Haym Salomon, the adroit bill broker who helped the superintendent of finance remedy America's financial woes in the 1780s. An entry in Madison's ledger shows a £100 loan from Salomon in 1782 when Madison was serving as a congressional delegate in Philadelphia.[120] Madison then solicited funds from a fellow Virginian, Edmund Randolph, to avoid staying in hock to Salomon: "I cannot in any way make you more sensible of the importance of your kind attention to pecuniary remittances for me than by informing you that I have for some time past been a pensioner on the favor of H. S. Haym Solomon, a Jew Broker."[121]

Madison's aversion to remaining in Salomon's debt had nothing to do with the broker's Jewish identity; rather, Madison was discomfited by the excessive generosity of Salomon, who refused to charge interest. In a subsequent letter to Randolph, Madison referred to Salomon as "our little friend in Front Street" who provided a "fund which will preserve me from extremities, but I never resort to it without great mortification, as he obstinately rejects all recompense." Madison added that Salomon's benevolence stemmed from the latter's distaste for all-too-common "usurious" creditors. Salomon undoubtedly saw his interest-free loans as opportunities to subvert stereotypes about Jewish money-lenders.[122] At the twilight of Madison's life, he received a letter from Salomon's son looking for details about his long-deceased father. Madison replied that a number of congressmen had borrowed money from Salomon, and assured the son that "we regarded him as upright, intelligent, and friendly in his transactions with us."[123] Tropes about predatory Jewish financiers, so common in the writings of Franklin and Adams, were conspicuously absent from Madison's pen.

While Madison was not focused on religious liberty for Jews specifically, he was instrumental in the passage of laws that protected minority faith groups generally. Notably, Madison shepherded the Virginia Statute for Religious Freedom through the state legislature. He also endorsed the U.S. Constitution's ban on religious tests. And the federal Bill of Rights, which included the Free Exercise Clause, was Madison's handiwork.

After a Jewish leader in Savannah sent Madison a copy of a speech he had delivered on Jewish-American history in 1820, Madison responded that the "good citizenship" of domestic Jews was a vindication of the nation's noble experiment in religious liberty that had begun in its early years. The Jewish community provided a "happy illustration of the safety and success of this experiment of a just and benignant policy." Although Jews were "distrusted and oppressed elsewhere" around the world, in the United States they enjoyed with all others "the perfect equality of rights." Madison's missive was not quite accurate—civil disabilities on Jews persisted in a number of states—but nevertheless it reflected his own fidelity to religious freedom. His letter also expressed gratitude for the speech on the Jewish past, observing that "the history of the Jews must forever be interesting" and "every ray of light on the subject has its value."[124] Madison's words were not just empty flattery. When Jefferson asked him which books he would suggest for the library at the University of Virginia, Madison included on his list the works of Flavius Josephus, a first-century Jewish scholar who recorded Jewish history.[125]

The Madisonian-Jewish relationship, then, presents a complex picture. Madison helped institute legal regimes in Virginia and nationally that extended religious protections to all people, Jews included. And his limited interactions with individual Jews were largely respectful. Still, Madison's dismissal of an American diplomat on the basis of his Jewish identity is a significant blemish.

———

Hamilton, Washington, Jefferson, and Madison taken together illustrate a counterintuitive reality. Among the foregoing founders, the two who did not advocate the separation of church and state were unmarred by antisemitism, while the two who did were tainted by incidents of bias against Jews and Judaism. It is with deliberate intent that the preceding pages have avoided recommending or rejecting the Hamiltonian approach to church-state relations. His model—which endorsed both religious pluralism and religious support for civic life—should not necessarily guide us today. Current proponents of the separation of church and state argue that their position is the most beneficial for religious minorities. They fear that in the absence of separation, the majority will exploit its power to favor its faith at the expense of other denominations. A consideration of such concerns is beyond the scope of this chapter. The aim here is, instead, to sound a cautionary note against projecting the logic of our modern politics backward onto the past.

8

Law and Politics

AS TREASURY SECRETARY, Alexander Hamilton helped create the economic foundations on which the American republic could endure. But his focus on the country's finances led him to neglect his own. A cabinet member's salary was simply too modest to provide for his five children and pay off personal debts that he had accrued. By reviving his legal practice, Hamilton could triple or even quadruple his earnings. And so, in February 1795, not even halfway through George Washington's second term, he resigned his government post, returning to Manhattan and the New York bar.[1] It was a professional move that immersed Hamilton in the Jewish merchant class to an even greater degree than his first stint in law had prior to his service in the Washington administration.

Hamilton was a polarizing figure to the country at large, but New Yorkers saw him as their champion. The Chamber of Commerce celebrated his homecoming by holding a dinner in his honor. Among the luminaries on the 200-person guest list were the president of Columbia, the speaker of the New York State Assembly, and many of the city's businessmen. At the meal, Hamilton paid homage to "the merchants of New York, may they never cease to have honor for their commander, skill for their pilot, and success for their port," a toast that elicited nine cheers from the crowd.[2]

The 1790s were years of expanding trade for America in general and New York in particular. Thanks to the Constitution that Hamilton helped write and ratify, the federal government was empowered to stimulate economic growth with unprecedented efficacy. The United States also benefited from an ongoing war between Britain and France, which increased the importance of neutral American shippers in the global marketplace. New York fared especially well, outpacing both Boston and Philadelphia in exports by 1797. The economic boom in New York went hand-in-hand with a population boom; the city nearly doubled its census count from about 33,000 to 60,000 over the last decade of the eighteenth century.[3]

Business in New York was often transacted in taverns or coffeehouses. The Tontine coffeehouse on Wall Street was famous for its lively mix of traders, brokers, and financiers. At the base of the Tontine steps, auctioneers would stand atop barrels of rum or bales of cotton, taking bids shouted down from a balcony. "Everything was in motion; all was life, bustle, and activity," one British visitor recorded.[4]

The kinds of disputes that inevitably resulted from commercial enterprise demanded the talents of lawyers such as Hamilton. His sweeping knowledge of law, relentless work ethic, and flair for courtroom oratory made him arguably the city's preeminent litigator. He threw himself into his cases with his typical fervor. As a French diplomat in New York remarked of Hamilton, "I have seen a man who made the fortune of a nation laboring all night to support his family."[5]

———

Jews were important players in Hamilton's legal career as both witnesses and clients. Indeed, the witness stand was a critical site in the Jewish battle for equality. The integrity of Jews under oath had long been questioned in Europe and America. During medieval times, Jews who dared to give testimony in court were regularly subjected to degrading rituals. Jewish witnesses in Byzantium, for instance, had to wear a loincloth made of thorns. Meanwhile, Jews testifying in southern France were lacerated with thorns while forced to invoke upon themselves curses from the Hebrew Bible. And a law in Silesia (in modern-day Poland) mandated that any Jewish litigant balance himself on a stool during his testimony; he was subjected to a fine the first three times he fell off and automatically lost his case in the fourth instance.[6]

Antisemites had long justified such perverse treatment of Jewish witnesses by erroneously alleging that Judaism actually encouraged its adherents to lie in court. This invidious stereotype about Jews was rooted in a severe misrepresentation of the *Kol Nidre* prayer, which opens religious services on *Yom Kippur*, the Day of Atonement. *Kol Nidre* means "all vows," and the prayer includes this language: "All vows, obligations, oaths . . . or whereby we may be bound, from this Day of Atonement until the next (whose happy coming we await), we do repent. May they be deemed absolved, forgiven, annulled, and void, and made of no effect; they shall not bind us nor have power over us." Rabbis consistently interpreted this prayer to apply only to vows that a Jew made to himself or to God, and not to oaths taken in court. Nevertheless, those seeking to discredit Jewish witnesses ignored these rabbinic explanations and invoked *Kol Nidre* as evidence of Jews' dishonesty.[7]

Doubts about Jewish integrity on the witness stand sometimes resurfaced in the New World. Even New York—the most religiously tolerant of Britain's thirteen American colonies—was not wholly immune to this particular prejudice. Amid legal proceedings that pertained to a contested election in 1737, the General Assembly in New York categorically excluded testimony from Jews, declaring that "it was the opinion of the House that none of the Jewish profession could be admitted in evidence, in the controversy now depending."[8] Unease about Jewish witnesses persisted long past the era of colonial rule. Not until 1846 would New York adopt a new state constitution that definitively settled the question of religious tests for giving sworn testimony: "No person shall be rendered incompetent to be a witness on account of his opinions on matters of religious belief." As late as 1871, a court in Georgia was still considering whether a Jew could testify.[9]

It was a case concerning the trustworthiness of Jewish testimony that provided Hamilton a platform for the most fervent rebuke of antisemitism to be found in the annals of the American founders. His client, Louis Le Guen, was a Gentile merchant accused of fraud. Le Guen also hailed from a French nation that was then embroiled in a quasi-war against the United States on the high seas.[10] This suit promised to be particularly challenging for Hamilton. Although the allegations against Le Guen were without merit, a foreign merchant purportedly engaged in swindling—and from a hostile power no less—was not the most sympathetic of litigants whom Hamilton could have represented. What's more, Hamilton's cocounsel was a man for whom he had little regard: Aaron Burr.[11] Compounding these difficulties, the opposing party comprised two of New York's most highly reputed businessmen, Isaac Gouverneur and Peter Kemble. And, perhaps most vexing of all for Hamilton, his principal witnesses were Jews.

The controversy began in 1794, when Le Guen arrived in New York as "a perfect stranger," in his words. He carried with him a cargo of indigo and cotton from a French island in the Indian Ocean, and entered into a financial arrangement with Gouverneur and Kemble to serve as agents for the sale of his inventory. Despite numerous advertisements in a local paper, buyers failed to appear. Le Guen, Gouverneur, and Kemble began to strategize about overseas markets.[12]

They resolved to partner with three traders who would arrange for the distribution of Le Guen's goods in Europe. Under the care of one of these traders, Isaac Gomez, the freight was loaded onto a vessel called the *White Fox* in May 1795 and headed east. Five weeks later, Gomez sent word from the northern coast of France that demand there was no better than it had been in New York. "The cotton and indigo has come to a most miserable market," he reported. From Hamburg, Gomez conveyed similarly disappointing news the following month: "Markets being in a most miserable situation in France, induced me to bring the cotton and indigo here, which proves as bad, as it will not yield the amount of invoice and expenses thereon attending, by a loss of sixty percent." Reaching England in the fall, Gomez relinquished the cargo to London-based agents for Gouverneur and Kemble, who then sold it for a considerable shortfall.[13]

Le Guen was miffed. He insisted that the clearance of his inventory in London violated the terms of his partnership with Gouverneur and Kemble; their contract had specified a higher sale price. When Le Guen looked to the courts to recover damages, Gouverneur and Kemble in

turn accused Le Guen of bamboozling them with inferior goods. Le
Guen had the facts on his side—after all, Gomez's letters plainly indicated that the failure to realize a profit stemmed from market conditions
rather than the quality of the cotton and indigo. But Gouverneur and
Kemble were intractable. Two of the key witnesses for Le Guen were
Sephardic Jews: a trader who helped facilitate the transport of the
freight, and a merchant who examined Le Guen's inventory and vouched
for its caliber.[14]

The litigation, which would stretch on for years, became noteworthy
less for the obscure legal questions it raised than for the eminent lawyers
involved in the case, their spirited performances in court, and the sheer
hostility that the suit fomented between the two sides. Hamilton's general tendency to polarize those around him was on full display in this
case; the intense devotion to Le Guen's cause that inspired admiration
from Hamilton's supporters also led his detractors to malign him as an
extremist who would too readily sacrifice civility for victory.

After winning only nominal damages in an initial trial for Le Guen in
the spring of 1797, Hamilton successfully moved for a new trial that was
scheduled for the following fall.[15] Gouverneur and Kemble were frustrated that the proceedings would drag out but exceedingly confident
in their case. As Gouverneur wrote in a letter that summer, "Nothing
have we yet been able to finish with that troublesome Mssr Le Guen
who has got himself involved in a ridiculous lawsuit, which will take of
a handsome slice of his property."[16] In another missive, Gouverneur
expressed the same combination of resentment and optimism. He complained of being mired "in the same unpleasant situation with Le Guen,
who prefers to be wandering in law than to settle his affairs" but predicted that "the lawyers will get more than he shall and may cost him
yet a few years in the pursuit."[17] Le Guen was no less sanguine than his
opponents, assuring Hamilton, "Your talents, your zeal, and the integrity of those who must be my judges . . . will make me get a favorable
judgment."[18]

Then in October, with the trial just days away, Le Guen took the
unusual step of printing a public letter in a New York newspaper deplor-
ing how the accusations of fraud had incited "prejudice against me" in

the community at large. "These cruel surmises tend no less to obstruct the impartial course of justice than to injure my reputation," he lamented, adding that they were utterly "unfounded." Le Guen further noted that Gomez's letters exonerated him from wrongdoing—they "manifest great distress at the expectation of a loss, to the extent of 60 percent, but ascribe it solely to the declension and badness of the market, without the least allusion to any defect or mistake of quality" of the cargo.[19]

In the same newspaper appeared an anonymous editorial that summarized the reaction of Gouverneur and Kemble to Le Guen's letter. The author informed readers that Gouverneur and Kemble were outraged by "the recent unwarrantable attempt of Mr. Le Guen to prejudice the public mind, and that of the jury" on "the eve of a trial." Although piqued at what they considered a bid to pervert the due process of law, Gouverneur and Kemble reportedly took solace that "there is too much good sense in this community, to be imposed upon by so shallow an artifice." Le Guen then issued a swift rebuttal, maintaining that the allegation of fraud was bogus and thus extraneous to the real matter: the contractual agreement stipulating an acceptable sale price for the goods. Thus, his initial letter in the newspaper had not indulged in the "impropriety" of "bringing into discussion, before the public, the merits of a controversy, which is depending before the tribunal of justice." If anything, Le Guen had sought "studiously to avoid" litigating the matter in the press, and merely wanted "to obviate suggestions collateral and foreign to the merits" of the case.[20]

The trial commenced on October 24, and three days later, the jury awarded Le Guen the staggering sum of $119,302.47 (more than $2.6 million today). Given the cocksure attitude on the part of Gouverneur and Kemble, the verdict came as an abrupt shock. Brockholst Livingston, a lawyer for Gouverneur (and future U.S. Supreme Court justice), confessed to his client his own bewilderment that Hamilton managed to rob them of certain victory. "No event in the course of my professional career," Livingston exclaimed, "has ever given me more concern or excited so much astonishment as the influence of Mr. Hamilton with the Court."[21]

This portrait of Alexander Hamilton was originally owned by his childhood friend from St. Croix, Edward Stevens. *Source*: William J. Weaver, *Alexander Hamilton*. Indianapolis Museum of Art [ca. 1806].

The court still had to decide whether to approve the jury's verdict, with the judgment from a five-man bench to come down in late January.[22] Meanwhile, Gouverneur turned to the press to air his grievances against Hamilton. In the *Commercial Advertiser,* Gouverneur addressed Hamilton directly, imploring him to "act with more caution in committing yourself with a mistaken opinion" and advising that "it would also be more becoming in the practice, to be less abusive." Gouverneur felt "extremely hurt" by Hamilton's courtroom performance that had challenged Gouverneur's integrity. Apparently, at trial Hamilton had tried to turn an antisemitic trope on its head by referring to the Jewish villain, Shylock, who inhumanely demands a pound of flesh for an unpaid debt in Shakespeare's *The Merchant of Venice.* It seems that Hamilton insisted it was not Le Guen—whose central witnesses were Jews—but rather Gouverneur whose behavior approximated Shakespeare's loathsome caricature of a Jewish moneylender. Hamilton's mention of Shylock is known through Gouverneur's retelling, and no extant trial transcript exists with the original wording, so it is difficult to discern with certainty the context or meaning of Hamilton's remark.[23] Although the invocation of "Shylock" usually would have indicated antipathy toward Jews by the speaker, in this instance it was the speaker whose case relied upon Jewish testimony.

On the very day that Gouverneur published his broadside against Hamilton, an anonymous letter—likely from Hamilton himself—appeared in the *New-York Gazette and General Advertiser.* Signed under the pen name "Fair Play," the author showed little inclination to rein in the heated rhetoric that had thus far prevailed: "If intrigue and artifice can ensure success in a suit at law, Mr. Gouverneur, in his controversy with Mr. Le Guen, will not fail to have it."[24]

Notwithstanding their lawyer's consternation, Gouverneur and Kemble were still convinced that the jury's verdict against them was an anomaly and that they would ultimately be vindicated by the court. In a letter to an associate, they wrote of Le Guen, "You may take our word for it, he is wasting both time and property."[25] Once again, their assumptions proved faulty. The judges upheld the jury's verdict in a three-to-two vote.[26]

Gouverneur and Kemble pressed on with further appeals for another two years until the Court of Errors—the highest tribunal in the state of New York—agreed to hear the case in Albany. The Court of Errors was a unique legal body that combined all three branches of state government, comprising the lieutenant governor, the members of the senate, the justices of the supreme court, and New York's highest ranking judicial officer, the chancellor.[27] With the trial set for February 1800, a lawyer for Gouverneur and Kemble named Robert Troup wrote to a friend on January 25 that he anticipated high drama. "The cause of Gouverneur and Kemble with Le Guen is beginning to excite attention," Troup observed. He predicted "that some of the counsel will have their passions much excited" and knew firsthand that Hamilton in particular was prone to fervor. Invoking Hamilton's military title, Troup offered by way of metaphor, "With my moderation of temper, I hope to escape the General's pistols as well as his sword." Troup did not detect any insecurities on Hamilton's part, inferring, "General Hamilton is very confident of success."[28]

Although Troup was intimately acquainted with Hamilton—they had been roommates at King's College[29]—his estimation of Hamilton's optimism was mistaken in this instance. "Today the hearing of Le Guen's cause began," Hamilton wrote to his wife, Eliza, from Albany. "I fear prepossessions are strongly against us. But we must try to overcome them."[30] He seemed to brace for the worst, adding, "If I should *lose* my cause I must console myself with finding my friends. With the utmost eagerness I will fly to them."[31]

Troup may have misjudged Hamilton's faith in his case, but the prediction of Hamilton's ardor in court was wholly on the mark. "Hamilton has pushed this cause to the utmost extremity, and in my opinion with the utmost animosity and cruelty against Gouverneur and Kemble," Troup wrote to a New York merchant after opening arguments. "He has attacked the whole body of witnesses on the part of Gouverneur and Kemble." Troup expected that "the manner of his treating the witnesses and persecuting poor Gouverneur" would not play well with the court. Despite Hamilton's earlier triumphs in the case, still, reported Troup, "Mr. Gouverneur himself is very confident of success and is in good spirits," a laudable feat for Gouverneur "considering the treatment Hamilton has given him." Troup concluded, "You can scarcely conceive the public attention which the cause of Gouverneur and Kemble has excited!"[32]

Already a spectacle, the trial's sensationalism was further heightened by the arrival of a political giant of the era, Gouverneur Morris, who joined Isaac Gouverneur and Peter Kemble's legal team. Morris had served in the Continental Congress during the war, drafted the Constitution's famous preamble in 1787, and been named the American ambassador to France under Washington. The Le Guen suit marked Morris's return to law after a hiatus of twelve years.[33] Hamilton and Morris were themselves friends, but whatever affinity they had for one another did not mitigate each man's vigorous commitment to his duty in court.[34]

That Hamilton's legal expertise and rigor surpassed Morris's was indisputable. But when it came to oratorical ability, Morris stood among the very few who could rival Hamilton. James Kent, a New York Supreme Court justice, observed, "If the one [Hamilton] was the superior in logic and law learning, the other [Morris] was presumed to be his equal in eloquence, imagination, and wit." Morris cut a "commanding" figure, Kent recalled. "His noble head, his majestic mien, the dignity of his deportment were all impressive."[35]

After Hamilton delivered a forceful closing argument spanning six hours, Morris knew he could not compete with Hamilton on legal grounds. Instead, Morris told the court that he had no intention of referencing law books and alternatively would "appeal to the principles written on the heart of man."[36] Morris's flowery address soon degenerated into a base attack on Hamilton's two witnesses of the Jewish faith.[37] Alluding to them as "these Jew witnesses," Morris sought to impugn their credibility on the basis of their religion.[38] "Jews are not to be believed upon oath," he insisted bluntly.[39]

Hamilton had already given his closing remarks, but he could not leave such slander unanswered. He rose to his feet and asked the court if it would allow him a rebuttal; the court acceded to his request and announced that time would be allotted the following day. Upon leaving to prepare his rejoinder, Hamilton spoke to a law clerk about Morris's address:

"This speech has made a great impression, has it not?"

"It had," the clerk conceded.

"How then do you think it should be met?"

"In the same manner."[40]

A large crowd gathered in court the next day to see how Hamilton, ever the relentless fighter, would respond. This case had become about something more than a mere legal dispute between merchants. At issue was the momentous question of whether American justice would be blind to religion. The Revolution had rested on a radical promise of equality. That a figure as esteemed as Morris believed antisemitism would be an effective tactic with the court suggested that the egalitarian rationale for the war had perhaps yielded to entrenched prejudice. Hamilton understood the stakes for both Jewry and the country, and he resolved to defend the former to realize his vision for the latter.

Referencing Morris's attack on the Jews, Hamilton asked the court, "Has he forgotten, what this race once were, when, under the immediate government of God himself, they were selected as the witnesses of his miracles, and charged with the spirit of prophecy?" Hamilton moved from a discussion of the Jews as the Chosen People to the sordid history of their suffering. He decried how, as "remnants of scattered tribes," adherents of Judaism were "the degraded, persecuted, reviled subjects of Rome," an empire that oppressed Jews "in all her resistless power, and pride, and pagan pomp." Roman rule had left Jewry "an isolated, tributary, friendless people." Hamilton's message was clear—Morris was perpetuating a dark history of antisemitism that had plagued Jews since antiquity.

For Hamilton, Le Guen's Jewish witnesses were righteous heirs to a divinely ordained religion. "Were not the witnesses of that pure and holy, happy and Heaven-approved faith?" he inquired rhetorically. Hamilton proclaimed that Lady Justice would judge no people because of the manner in which they worshipped: "Be the injured party . . . Jew, or Gentile, or Christian, or Pagan, Foreign or Native, she clothes him with her mantle, in whose presence all differences of faiths or births, of passions or of prejudices—all are called to acknowledge and revere her supremacy."[41] Jews had suffered oppression for nearly two millennia at the hands of European powers; now an icon of American civic life was declaring that Jew and Gentile must stand equal before the law. In a young republic caught between Old World hierarchies and New World hopes, Hamilton's defense of equality for Jews was a powerful vindication of revolutionary ideals.

Although rarely lacking in confidence, Hamilton had been circumspect about Le Guen's chances for success. Yet Le Guen emerged victorious in the Court of Errors by a 28-to-6 vote.[42] Burr, for his part, had skillfully argued portions of the case; even Morris conceded in his diary, "Burr is very able and has, I see, made [a] considerable impression."[43] It was, however, Hamilton's eloquent appeal for equal justice that moved the members of the court. Justice Kent was unequivocal in identifying the determining factor in Le Guen's unlikely win: "the overbearing weight and influence of General Hamilton's talents."[44] Le Guen, by his own account, was "deeply moved" and "full of gratitude" to Hamilton and Burr alike, offering both lawyers substantial sums for their efforts. To Le Guen's disappointment, Hamilton refused a penny above $1,500 ($32,000 today); Burr accepted nearly three times that amount.[45]

Hamilton was generally renowned for the verve of his legal performances, but he demonstrated an emotional investment in Le Guen's case that exceeded even his usual standards. Justice Kent later recollected that among the countless trials Hamilton litigated with "energy and fervor," there was at most one other—involving freedom of the press—in which his zeal was so "strikingly displayed."[46] Opposing counsel Troup drew similar conclusions. In a letter to the American ambassador to Great Britain, Troup relayed the details of the Le Guen trial and observed, "Our friend Hamilton never appeared to have his passions so warmly engaged in any cause."[47] It was readily apparent that the case touched Hamilton personally. No other American founder ever denounced antisemitism with such conviction.

———

Hamilton not only relied on Jewish witnesses for his Gentile clients, but he also served as a prominent advocate in court for the interests of Jewish parties.[48] One of the most notable cases featured Aaron Burr, though as a litigant rather than lawyer; Solomon Myers Cohen, a well-known Jew; and the meaning of the Fourth of July. In 1795, the retired general Roger Enos issued a promissory note to the politician Francis Lewis for $3,500 ($75,000 today), redeemable on July 1. Aaron Burr also endorsed the note, rendering Burr liable for that sum in the event that General Enos failed to make payment. Enos was out of town at the beginning of July, and so Lewis turned to his Jewish agent, Cohen, to retrieve the $3,500 from Burr.[49] Cohen wrote to Burr in the hopes of an uncontentious transaction: "As General Enos is not in town and his note with your endorsement for 3500 dollars is payable . . . the holder desired me to give you this notice, that he looks to you for payment of the same. . . . I hope my conduct in this business will meet with your approbation."[50]

Normally, the endorser of a promissory note had a three-day grace period to fulfill the obligation, but Cohen made his request on July 3, only two days into the grace period. Burr accordingly refused to produce the $3,500. Cohen had opted not to wait until the customary third day because that third day happened to fall on the Fourth of July, the anniversary of America's secession from the British Empire. In a nation too new to have many public holidays, the Fourth of July was a revered day indeed. The outcome of the case would hinge on whether the special status of July 4 meant that Burr was liable to Lewis for the promissory note on July 3.[51] That Francis Lewis had been a signer of the Declaration of Independence made the case almost poetic in its symbolism.

Hamilton, representing Lewis, began collecting evidence to prove that financial institutions regularly executed transactions due on July 4 one day prior to the holiday. He obtained letters from bank cashiers who confirmed that "our practice is to demand payment of notes which fall due on the 4th [of] July, the day before, as in [the] case of Sundays and Christmas days."[52] In court documents, Hamilton's language suggested that he saw in Burr's behavior not an honest error but a lack of character.

Burr "faithfully promised" to cover the $3,500, but "Aaron Burr in no way regard[ed] his said promises and undertakings." Instead, Burr sought "craftily and subtly to deceive and defraud the said Francis Lewis." Hamilton derided Burr as "contriving."[53] The jury favored Hamilton's side, finding that "the anniversary day of the Declaration of Independence of these United States of America" is "generally observed by the citizens of this state of New York as a public festival." Accordingly, the promissory note was payable on July 3.[54]

In the New York Supreme Court, Hamilton emerged victorious again as the justices upheld the jurors' verdict. The court noted that the custom of honoring the Fourth of July by requiring that debts be paid the preceding day was a "generally known" convention and "all contracts" were to "be interpreted and governed by it." Therefore, the bench concluded "that the note in question is to be adjudged as having fallen due on the 3d day of July, the *second* day of grace, and, consequently, that the plaintiff is entitled to recover."[55] This judgment against Burr surely stoked his growing resentment toward Hamilton. Four years earlier, Hamilton had been instrumental in quashing Burr's bid for the governorship of New York. Now he bested Burr in court. And Hamilton's most intolerable acts of sabotage, as Burr would perceive them, still lay ahead.

———

The same year as the foregoing case, Hamilton's services were solicited for a dispute involving Jews on all sides. His client in this suit was Isaac Gomez, a Sephardic Jew who sat on the board of Shearith Israel (the very same Isaac Gomez who struggled to find European buyers for Le Guen's cargo). In 1794, Gomez and another Sephardi named Moses Lopez established a commercial partnership whose terms specified that for seven years neither of them could unilaterally transact business outside the partnership to the detriment of their shared enterprise. In the words of their legal agreement, "Neither of the said parties should, during the said term . . . carry on any private trade for and on his account to the prejudice of the said joint business." Before the seven years expired, Gomez and Lopez created a three-man partnership with yet another Sephardic trader, Abraham Rods Rivera. This arrangement proceeded on terms whose exact meaning became a source of controversy: "No contract, dealing, purchase, or other business shall be entered into on account of the said copartnership by either of the said parties without the previous consent and approbation of them." This wording left two matters ambiguous. For one, the tripartite contract did not clarify whether it existed in tandem with or superseded the earlier bilateral agreement between Gomez and Lopez. Moreover, it failed to stipulate whether any two or all three partners had to agree to a given business deal.[56]

With Hamilton as his legal counsel, Gomez sued Lopez for £3,000 on the basis that Lopez had engaged in private business outside the terms of their first agreement. Lopez, in turn, maintained that this business had been transacted with Rivera's consent and thus was consistent with the language of their second agreement. Hamilton persuaded the court that there was a legitimate cause of action against Lopez, and the defendant accordingly was sent to jail while awaiting trial. The parties were able to settle out of court before the trial date.[57]

———

Little is known about the merchant Isaac Roget other than that he was Jewish and a Hamilton client.[58] In a complex case involving 220 barrels of flour, Roget tapped Hamilton to represent him before the New York Supreme Court. Roget had agreed in early 1800 to purchase the flour in exchange for a note endorsed by one Joseph Lyon for $2,250 ($48,000 today). When the suppliers of the flour discovered that Lyon was insolvent and the note thereby worthless, they refused to turn over the flour. Roget then filed suit against the suppliers.[59]

The case hinged on two legal intricacies. First, the agreement had been signed by only one of the parties, not both. Whereas counsel for the suppliers insisted that the contract was accordingly void, Hamilton contended, "If one sign and deliver [the contract] over, it is enough" to make that contract enforceable. The second point of controversy centered on who shouldered responsibility for the note. Hamilton here proffered some clever logic: once the parties had agreed in writing to exchange the note for flour, the suppliers assumed the risk that the note might be unredeemable, just as Roget took the risk that the flour he had bought could be mediocre. In Hamilton's reasoning, "a note was to be given for the flour, not money to be paid; therefore, the loss from the note's proving bad [was] to be borne by the defendants." The suppliers' legal team vigorously challenged Hamilton's arguments as unsupported by the law and the facts of the case.[60]

When the state supreme court issued its decision, the justices found that Hamilton had been persuasive on the first matter—a contract signed by merely one party was not necessarily void. "If there are acts to be done by both parties," wrote the court, "and the one who is to perform a principal part (as here the delivery of the flour) sign, and it is accepted by the other party, there can exist no doubt . . . that such contract would be mutually obligatory." However, on the question of whether the suppliers bore the risk for the note, Hamilton's logic was too clever by half. The court concluded, "The offer by the plaintiff to pay in the note of a bankrupt was not an offer of payment," and ruled in favor of the suppliers.[61]

Among the most notable Jewish additions to Hamilton's client roster was Alexander Zuntz. A native of Germany, Zuntz arrived in New York during the Revolution as a sutler selling goods to Hessian mercenaries who worked for the British. Zuntz joined the handful of Loyalist Jews in New York who kept Shearith Israel functioning through wartime. He became the de facto head of the synagogue in those years and helped convince the British not to repurpose their house of worship as a hospital.[62] Gershom Seixas, though allied with the Patriots, stole into the city in 1779 to officiate Zuntz's wedding.[63]

After the war, Zuntz decided to stay in New York and opened a factory for starch and hair powder. He advertised that his "starch is equal to any from Europe but can be prepared of inferior quality if required." Although that enterprise foundered, Zuntz later met with success by opening a broker's office on Little Dock Street near the synagogue. His leadership in Jewish life continued into the 1790s. He served three terms as president of Shearith Israel, donated funds to the synagogue, and held the special honor of leading the morning service on *Yom Kippur* every year.[64] Hamilton's ledger suggests that he did not litigate on Zuntz's behalf but rather offered him legal advice.[65]

––––––

The income from Hamilton's law practice allowed him to fulfill a long-standing dream—he could finally afford a plot of land on which to build a country residence for his family.[66] The site that Hamilton chose was in upper Manhattan, then comprised of unspoiled woods and river views. It was common for New Yorkers with sufficient means to seek relief from the congestion and disease of lower Manhattan by retreating to uptown country estates. Although Hamilton enlisted New York's most celebrated architect to design the house, he was not content to defer entirely to the discretion of the expert. Hamilton poured himself into the architectural plans with characteristic intensity.[67]

The result was a graceful and dignified home of yellow paneling with white trim. Visitors stepping through the front doors would encounter, tellingly before anything else, Hamilton's study. Even at this stage of his life, in which he was more dedicated to family than ever before, Hamilton's legal work remained a priority. There were bedrooms aplenty for his children, who now numbered seven. Various touches in the home betokened Hamilton's cosmopolitan tastes: the parlor featured French furniture, and the fireplaces were crafted from Italian marble. But there could be no question that this worldly immigrant was foremost an American—a giant portrait of George Washington hung in the foyer. In a quiet allusion to his Caribbean past, Hamilton called the property, "The Grange," the name of the plantation on St. Croix where his mother was buried.[68] Here, then, is another reminder that although Hamilton did not speak of his childhood, neither did he forget.

––––––

The Grange, where Hamilton resided with his family in his later years. *Source: The Grange, Kingsbridge Road, the Residence of Alexander Hamilton.* Miriam and Ira D. Wallach Division of Art, Prints and Photographs: Picture Collection, New York Public Library.

As Hamilton defended the credibility of Jewish testimony, represented Jewish citizens in the courts, and continued his tenure alongside Gershom Seixas on the Columbia board, some of his fellow Federalists forsook the party's earlier commitment to Jewish rights. Recall that it had been Anti-Federalists who sought to exploit religious bigotry during the ratification debates; similar tactics were then employed by some in the anti-Hamilton contingent that opposed the sweeping legislative reforms passed by the first Congress under the new Constitution. But as the French Revolution echoed across the Atlantic, it altered the role of antisemitism in the American political landscape.

Initially, the revolution in France, which began in 1789, elicited widespread enthusiasm in the United States. French revolutionaries were seen as heirs to the same values that had animated America's War of Independence. Jewish-Americans had additional cause to champion the French Revolution once France granted political equality to its Jews in 1791. By the following year, however, the French Revolution was less

uniformly embraced throughout the United States. Reports of massa-
cres and anarchy in France disturbed many Federalists, who began re-
nouncing the French Revolution. Political factions in the United States
were then becoming organized political parties, and a significant portion of American Jewry shifted to the Republican camp because of Republicans' continued endorsement of the French revolutionaries.[69]

Several Federalists, in turn, started peddling the kind of antisemitism
that formerly had been the preserve of their opponents. In 1795, for instance, a Federalist printer took aim at a Republican group in New York
that had named a Jew as its vice president (none other than Hamilton's
former legal client, Solomon Simson). The printer sought to taint the
entire organization as a cabal of Jews with stereotypically Jewish features, physical and otherwise: "This itinerant gang will easily be known
by their physiognomy; they all seem to be, like their Vice-President, of
the tribe of Shylock: they have that leering underlook, and malicious
grin, that seem to say to the honest man—*approach me not*."[70] This sneer
managed to compress multiple antisemitic clichés into a single sen-
tence: Jews were rootless in geography, unsettling in appearance, and
immoral in character.

Similar prejudice surfaced in Pennsylvania two years later when a
state senate race resulted in a narrow win for a Republican politician
who, though born and raised Christian, had a Jewish father. A Federalist
newspaper in Philadelphia considered the politician a Jew all the same,
warning, "Since the *Jews* obtained such a complete triumph over the
Gentiles, it is said they have conceived the idea of imposing on us a *general circumcision*."[71] The myth that Jews secretly plotted to circumcise
Gentiles was an anti-Jewish trope dating back centuries.[72]

Still, it would go too far to suggest that Federalists and Republicans
entirely reversed in their respective attitudes toward Jewry. There were
Republicans who continued to malign Jews into the early nineteenth
century. A Republican piece from 1803 appearing in a Hartford newspaper unfavorably associated Federalists with ancient Judaism, which the
writer considered a debased religion. He argued that the Federalists in
Connecticut spuriously professed to govern the state in the name of
freedom, just as Jews in antiquity had falsely claimed to serve the

Almighty. In his words, "The system of policy here was as distant from the principles of liberty as the Jewish washings and oblations were from the law of God."[73] Evidently, casual antisemitism still had traction in Republican circles.

Some Federalists were quick to condemn Republican animus against Jews. An 1802 column in the *New-England Palladium*, a Federalist organ, derided Thomas Jefferson and his "adherents" for their "bitter, vindictive spirit" toward those who had bought government securities under Hamilton's economic scheme. The author deplored how such purchasers "have been denounced as speculators, usurers, and Jews, and held up as objects so odious, that to cheat them would almost be deemed a virtue."[74] Yet again, Republicans were contemptuously linking the Hamiltonian agenda to Jewry.

A number of Federalists disavowed anti-Jewish bigotry within their own ranks as well. In 1802, for instance, a Federalist paper in rural Pennsylvania leveled an antisemitic attack on a Republican editor who had one Jewish grandparent; Federalists in nearby Pittsburgh organized a gathering to disaffiliate themselves from that kind of religious intolerance.[75] They further announced in the *Pittsburgh Gazette* their "abhorrence of the vile calumnies, falsehood, and slander which have so frequently appeared in certain newspapers disgracing the name of liberty."[76] Hamilton, too, was willing to criticize a fellow Federalist for antisemitism—his adversary in the Le Guen case, Gouverneur Morris, was a prominent member of the Federalist Party.

———

Hamilton was hardly a devout Christian, but there were isolated instances when he sought to instrumentalize Christianity for political ends. As French-American relations deteriorated in 1797 and anxieties about a possible war increased, he wrote a message to a congressman that touted the prospect of a "national appeal to Heaven for protection." Hamilton made plain that his rationale was rooted in utility, not theology: "The politician will consider this as an important means of influencing opinion."[77] A year later, Hamilton attempted to use religion to sway public sentiment, publishing an essay in a New York paper that vilified "the disgusting spectacle of the French revolution" for exhibiting "animosity to the Christian system."[78] He was not wrong on the facts—revolutionaries in France had confiscated church property and even executed nuns.[79]

The election of 1800 then saw the Federalists lose control of both the presidency and Congress, prompting Hamilton to propose as a political tonic a Christian Constitutional Society. This was a passing thought that he mentioned once in a letter to an ally in Congress. Hamilton never broached the topic again, much less brought it to fruition. Moreover, the tenor of the letter makes clear that he was motivated by partisan strategy rather than religious conviction. In Hamilton's view, the Republicans understood the advantage of appealing to the heart over the head. The Federalists, on the other hand, were overly reliant on the "reason of men" and insufficiently attuned to the "impulse of passion." To win back "popular favor," the Federalist Party ought to appeal to Christian voters in religious terms, he explained.[80]

Hamilton did not discuss Christianity in his personal correspondence, with one exception—letters to his pious wife, Eliza. Yet even those allusions to Christianity were sporadic, occasioned only by the illness or death of someone in Eliza's family. At those trying times, Hamilton would urge his wife to find resolve in either "Christian fortitude" or "Christian resignation."[81] He also rented a pew for her in Trinity Church in Manhattan, where their children were baptized,[82] and he expected his eldest son, Philip, to attend church.[83] Hamilton and his law partner, Richard Harison, even provided Trinity Church with pro bono legal counsel, although that likely owed much to the fact that Harison was a vestryman at Trinity.[84] Hamilton was not himself a member of the church.[85] Trinity's surviving communion book from that time period shows Eliza's name, while her husband's is conspicuously absent.[86] Indeed, Hamilton did not belong to any church, meaning that in the eyes of some denominations, he simply was not a Christian at all.[87]

In the few instances when Hamilton discussed God, he described God as an engaged participant in world events. Hamilton credited "the blessing of providence" with having staved off "national bankruptcy" under the feeble Articles of Confederation.[88] During John Adams's presidency, Hamilton grew frustrated with the administration's foreign policy and told Washington, "My trust in Providence, which has so often interposed in our favor, is my only consolation."[89] And in an 1803 essay in the *New-York Evening Post*, Hamilton attributed "the kind interpositions of an over-ruling Providence" for both America's victory in the Revolution and its purchase of the Louisiana Territory from France.[90] Because of Hamilton's distance from Christian practice, historians have at times described him as a deist,[91] but his belief in an activist God was directly at odds with deism's conception of divinity as noninterventionist.

———

The developments leading up to the coda of Hamilton's life—his notorious duel—offer some additional insight into his complicated relationship with religion. Although he was a private citizen in the early 1800s, Hamilton still managed to exploit his residual clout to foil Aaron Burr's political ambitions. Hamilton believed that Burr answered to nothing beyond his own ego. "His public principles have no other spring or aim than his own aggrandizement," Hamilton once scoffed.[92] He helped derail Burr's designs on both the presidency in 1800 and the New York governorship four years later.[93]

Tensions between them reached dangerous proportions after Hamilton openly maligned Burr at a dinner in Albany around the time of the 1804 gubernatorial election. One of the supper companions recounted Hamilton's disparaging remarks in a letter that was reprinted in a newspaper.[94] Diminished by Hamilton in the courtroom, the political arena, and now the press, Burr would suffer his antagonist no longer. He asked Hamilton to either disavow the alleged insults or own them outright.[95] Hamilton well understood that taking the former path meant a truce and the latter a duel. But he could not bring himself to offer concessions to a man for whom he had so little respect.[96]

As he prepared for his encounter with Burr, Hamilton penned a statement to be made public afterward in which he explained the balance of factors that informed his tortured decision to step onto the dueling grounds. Hamilton acknowledged a number of reasons not to partake in a potentially fatal duel. For one, there was Eliza and their brood to think of: "My wife and children are extremely dear to me." Hamilton also recognized that dueling was an illicit practice that undermined the very rule of law to which he dedicated his career. He worried, too, about his creditors. The man who had consolidated the nation's debt was steeped in his own; his death would leave his creditors partially repaid at best. And, notably, Hamilton entertained religious objections. "My religious and moral principles are strongly opposed to the practice of dueling," he stressed.[97] Hamilton was not alone in having reservations about duels. Numerous ministers, newspapers, and scholars across the country deprecated dueling as a barbaric relic.[98]

Yet dueling still enjoyed a certain prestige in American culture, especially among soldiers and politicians—and Hamilton fell into both categories.[99] He typified many contemporary duelists who, despite misgivings, were nonetheless in thrall to the honor code.[100] They fashioned themselves gentlemen whose stature and self-worth were predicated on their willingness to hazard their lives in defense of their honor.[101] As Hamilton's statement put it, "All the considerations which constitute what men of the world denominate honor, impressed on me (as I thought) a peculiar necessity not to decline the call."[102]

Hamilton went on to explain that only if he stood his ground against Burr could he maintain, in the eyes of his fellow citizens, the credibility needed to help the nation navigate future "crises of our public affairs." Plainly, Hamilton had not abandoned hope that he might one day reclaim the reins of state power. Yet he was also mindful that dueling was not uniformly embraced by Americans. And so Hamilton added that he was determined, if "it pleases God to give me the opportunity, to reserve and throw away my first fire"—that is, he would aim his pistol away from Burr.[103] While Hamilton's participation in the duel was a gesture to those who commended the practice, his pledge to "throw away" his bullet was a nod to those who condemned it. This was a deft exercise in political optics that promised to preserve his standing with the greatest number of people whether he lived or died.

By his own admission, Hamilton was driven to duel by outward concerns about his public reputation, but his motives were likely rooted as well in a lifelong inward struggle to grapple with his harrowing past. The honor code would have appealed to Hamilton not just as a former soldier and statesman but as a Caribbean orphan forever plagued by anxiety about his status in the world.[104] Despite Hamilton's heroics in battle and achievements in government, he remained overly sensitive to slights. One of his allies observed of Hamilton, "No man, not the Roman Cato himself, was more inflexible on every point that touched . . . integrity and honor."[105] Perhaps only glory in death would provide him what the feats of a lifetime could not.

Hamilton's insistence that he owed a duty to God to direct his gun away from Burr appears to be not solely opportunistic but also heartfelt. The night before the duel, a confidant urged Hamilton to fire at Burr and thereby increase his chances for survival. Hamilton, however, was immovable. "My friend, it is the effect of a religious scruple, and does not admit of reasoning," he explained. "It is useless to say more on the subject, as my purpose is definitely fixed."[106]

Both in the statement that he prepared for public consumption and in his foregoing remark to his friend, Hamilton spoke of faith in broad terms with no specific references to Christianity. But he also authored a secret letter to Eliza, to be delivered to her only in the event of his death, which framed the occasion in Christian terms that would have been meaningful to her. Hamilton assured her that he would not discharge his weapon at Burr owing to the "scruples of a Christian" and offered these final instructions: "I charge you to remember that you are a Christian."[107] Eliza was unaware of the imminent duel as her husband steeled himself for this final mission, one whose tragic aftermath raises questions anew about the authenticity of his Christian bona fides.

Epilogue

AT DAWN ON JULY 11, 1804, on a stony ledge above the Hudson River, Aaron Burr and Alexander Hamilton broke the morning calm with the sounds of gunfire. A bullet tore into Hamilton's spine, and he sprang up on his toes for a moment before collapsing to the ground.[1] He knew straight away that the wound would be fatal. "I am a dead man," Hamilton declared.[2] The surgeon on the scene was equally certain of his mortal fate, later recalling, "His countenance of death I shall never forget."[3] Burr stood unharmed. Hamilton's bullet had hit a tree branch more than twelve feet from Burr; either Hamilton shot first and did so, as promised, without an intent to kill, or he pulled his trigger merely as a reflexive muscle spasm when his body absorbed Burr's bullet.[4]

Hamilton was quickly rowed from the dueling grounds in Weehawken, New Jersey, to lower Manhattan for urgent medical care and conveyed to a bedroom in the house of the director of the Bank of New York. As word spread through the streets that Hamilton was on his deathbed, the usual bustle of the city gave way to a stunned stillness.[5] Crowds gathered outside the home where Hamilton rested.[6] Though paralyzed, he was still lucid in mind and intelligible in speech. Hamilton asked first that his wife be sent for, and then that a bishop give him communion.[7]

Maybe a man who had exhibited relative indifference toward Christianity for decades suddenly accepted Jesus. But there is another explanation more consistent with the rest of Hamilton's life. Eliza took Christian rites seriously, and she would soon be at her husband's deathbed.

Hamilton no doubt understood that if he were to finally take communion, it could provide Eliza with a measure of solace amid the grief about to envelop her life.

Bishop Benjamin Moore came to Hamilton's side but refused to administer communion. For one, Moore condemned dueling as a "barbarous custom." And it seems that the bishop also entertained doubts about the sincerity of someone who neither belonged to a church nor previously had taken communion, for Hamilton felt compelled to plead that his request for an eleventh-hour communion did not spring from a sudden impulse but was actually a long-standing desire. He tried to reassure Moore: "It has for some time past been the wish of my heart, and it was my intention to take an early opportunity of uniting myself to the church by the reception of that holy ordinance." The bishop eventually acceded to his wishes.[8] When Eliza arrived, Hamilton invoked her faith: "Remember, my Eliza, you are a Christian."[9]

With steady doses of opiate, Hamilton persisted through the night under the watchful gaze of his wife and friends. Bearing witness to the slow and painful death of the man they all loved was almost insufferable. The next day, as Hamilton grew weaker, his seven children were brought to his bed so that he could gaze upon them a final time. His rivals— Jefferson, Madison, Adams—would live into their golden years. But on the afternoon of July 12, 1804, Alexander Hamilton, no older than fifty, took his last breath.[10]

———

Contemporary commentary on Hamilton's deathbed communion is revealing of his apathy toward Christianity prior to the duel. The *Daily Advertiser* newspaper wrote of Hamilton that by "receiving in attestation of his faith the sacrament of the Lord's Supper" in "his last hours," he "has not left the world to doubt of his faith." The article thus intimated that without such a display of religiosity at the end, his Christianity would otherwise have been in doubt. Similarly, a pastor in Albany insisted of Hamilton's communion, "This last act, more than any other, sheds glory on his character. Everything else death effaces. Religion alone abides with him on his deathbed. He dies a Christian."[11] To stress how Hamilton died a Christian was to concede that he did not live as one. Had Hamilton practiced Christianity before the duel, there would be little impetus for the pastor to proclaim that death effaced all else in his life.

Hamilton's enemies also took note of his last-minute Christian awakening but were unmoved. A remorseless Burr (who would spend years in exile avoiding criminal charges for the duel) complained to a friend that Hamilton's "last hours . . . appear to have been devoted to malevolence and hypocrisy."[12] John Adams, who had been publicly besmirched by Hamilton,[13] wrote in his autobiography that he would not "suffer my character to lie under infamous calumnies, because the author of them, with a pistol bullet through his spinal marrow, died a penitent."[14] And so Hamilton's admirers and adversaries alike considered his communion an anomalous departure from his usual lack of Christian piety. These accounts from the time of Hamilton's passing—as well as Hamilton's own deathbed acknowledgment that he wished to, but had not yet, united himself to the church—serve to cast doubt on a claim made by his son fully sixty years later that Alexander had espoused Eliza's faith well before the duel.[15]

———

As tolling bells announced Hamilton's death, a dark cloud of bereavement engulfed New York.[16] One of the best surviving descriptions of the scene comes from Rebecca Gratz, a twenty-three-year-old Jew from Pennsylvania renowned for her philanthropic work and striking beauty.[17] "The whole city of New York is in a state of consternation. You can have no idea of the general mourning here," she shared with her sister.[18] For Gratz, the grief was personal. Her family members had long been political devotees of Hamilton, and she herself had grown up as a friend to Hamilton's children when he lived in Philadelphia as treasury secretary.[19] That Hamilton allowed the sons and daughters of Jews to play with his own stands as further testament to his personal comfort with Jewish people.

A founding father, still in his prime, gunned down on the field of honor was a tragedy of devastating proportions, and the grandeur of Hamilton's funeral befitted the gravity of the loss. Shopkeepers closed their businesses, flags were lowered to half-staff, and throngs packed the route of his funeral procession. Only the death of George Washington had occasioned public grief of this magnitude. Hamilton's corpse wound through the streets of lower Manhattan to the sounds of chiming bells and firing cannons. Spectators mounted rooftops and scaled trees to see above the heads of the tear-drenched crowds below. The slow-moving cortege took two hours to reach Eliza's church, where Hamilton was eulogized before his burial there.[20] The following day Rebecca Gratz recorded, "Yesterday was a day of sorrow and lamentation. I never witnessed so distressing a scene. The procession was conducted with the utmost solemnity and [in] every countenance might be traced the heart's affliction."[21] Alexander Hamilton had come to New York an anonymous immigrant. He died there its greatest citizen.

———

Among the founders, Hamilton has always cut a unique figure—his Caribbean origins, financial ingenuity, and dramatic death all distinguish him from the other icons of his era. Hamilton's ties to the people and faith of Judaism make him that much more singular. In all probability he had a Jewish identity in childhood, and in all certainty he attended a Jewish school. Though not a Jew in his American years, the adult Hamilton expressed deep reverence for Judaism and demonstrated sensitivity to the age-old oppression of its adherents. He also cultivated numerous connections to the Jewish community in the United States. As a famed lawyer, Hamilton advocated for Jewish citizens in the courts. As an influential alumnus, he proved critical in making Jews eligible for the Columbia presidency and placing the first Jew on the college's board. As a far-sighted treasury secretary, he willed into existence a financial system that created opportunities for Jews who were excluded from other professions. Hamilton's efforts to build a society where Jew and Gentile would partake as equals underscore the democratic possibilities of the young nation, even as the persistence of antisemitism meant that the radical promise of the Declaration of Independence would remain only partially realized for the Jews of the early republic.

Indeed, Hamilton was distinct from other founders in part because his relationship to Jewry was unsullied by antisemitic bias. If Jefferson and Hamilton both defended civic equality for Jews, Jefferson alone described them as heirs to a corrupt religion. If Jay and Hamilton both claimed credit for Jewish-friendly reforms at Columbia, Jay alone advocated the mass conversion of Jews to Christianity. If Madison and Hamilton both acknowledged the long history of Jewish persecution, Madison alone relied on antisemitism as a rationale for firing a government official. If Adams and Hamilton both conveyed great respect for Judaism, Adams alone invoked the word "Jew" as a slur. To be sure, Washington matched Hamilton in the absence of prejudice toward Jews, and the Newport letter marked a seminal moment in Jewish history; still, Washington's exposure to Jews was minimal compared to Hamilton's.

What's more, no founder aside from Hamilton saw antisemitic sentiment mobilized against his goals with such regularity. He tirelessly promoted the Constitution, whose ratification was resisted by a number of Anti-Federalists because it opened federal office to Jews. At trial, opposing counsel slandered Hamilton's witnesses as liars whose testimony ought to be discounted purely on the basis of their Jewish faith. Hamilton's economic policy in particular unleashed a torrent of anti-Jewish vitriol. According to his detractors, the treasury secretary was forming an unholy alliance with rapacious Jews. It was alleged that he would sell out his countrymen to Jewish creditors. Hamilton and his Jewish accomplices, critics claimed, did not produce wealth through honest work on farms; they reaped their profits from the dark arts of finance. Common soldiers and soil tillers were supposedly the innocent victims of Hamilton's collusion with Jews. Unlike the other founding fathers, he had not been born in the original thirteen colonies, and so Hamilton was conveniently smeared as an outsider whose loyalty was as suspect as the border-crossing Jews with whom he purportedly conspired.

Hamilton's antagonists were peddling a pernicious breed of bigotry. And yet, in many respects, the embattled Hamilton and his Jewish compatriots *were* outsiders. In a world that was largely rural, they flocked to city life. At a time when agriculture predominated, they engaged in trade and banking. Amid a society where many feared centralized power, Hamilton and his Jewish supporters embraced the new federal Constitution with its strong national government. Their very status as outsiders turned them into consummate modernizers.[22]

It is little coincidence, then, that the forces arrayed against Hamilton were often the very same that sought to relegate Jews to the margins of American life. Fear of Hamilton's agenda and fear of Jews were commonly conflated because they were both, ultimately, fears about modernization. The cosmopolitan marketplace that provided fresh opportunity to talented strivers was to many others a symbol of an ominous fate that threatened their way of life. Hamilton envisioned a future that belonged not to the sons of plantation aristocrats but to the itinerant, the enterprising, the urban—in other words, to people like him and his Jewish allies. While Jews were not fully accepted in the America of Hamilton's day, they surely could be in the America of Hamilton's dream.

ABBREVIATIONS

Archives

AHP Alexander Hamilton Papers, Library of Congress, Washington, DC.

AJA Jacob Rader Marcus Center of the American Jewish Archives, Cincinnati.

AJHS American Jewish Historical Society, New York and Boston.

GKP Gouverneur and Kemble Papers, New York Public Library.

GWP George Washington Papers, Library of Congress, Washington, DC.

NHCS Nevis Historical and Conservation Society, Charlestown, Nevis.

NYSA New York State Archives, Albany, NY.

RBML Rare Book and Manuscript Library, Columbia University in the City of New York.

RIGS Rigsarkivet (Danish National Archives, Copenhagen), Vestindisk-guineiske kompagni, Bogholderen på St. Croix, Mandtalslister og matrikler (scanned version).

YIVO YIVO Institute for Jewish Research Archives, New York.

Collected and Published Works

DHRC *The Documentary History of the Ratification of the Constitution Digital Edition.* Edited by John P. Kaminski, Gaspare J. Saladino, Richard Leffler, Charles H. Schoenleber, and Margaret A. Hogan. Charlottesville: University of Virginia Press, 2009.

LPAH *The Law Practice of Alexander Hamilton: Documents and Commentary.* Edited by Julius Goebel et al. 5 vols. New York: Columbia University Press, 1969–1981.

PAH *The Papers of Alexander Hamilton Digital Edition.* Edited by Harold C. Syrett. Charlottesville: University of Virginia Press, Rotunda, 2011.

PAJHS *Publications of the American Jewish Historical Society.*

PBF *The Papers of Benjamin Franklin.* Edited by Leonard W. Labaree et al. New Haven, CT: Yale University Press, 1959–.

PGWC *The Papers of George Washington Digital Edition—Confederation Series.* Charlottesville: University of Virginia Press, Rotunda, 2008.

PGWD *The Papers of George Washington Digital Edition—Diaries.* Charlottesville: University of Virginia Press, Rotunda, 2008.

PGWP *The Papers of George Washington Digital Edition—Presidential Series.* Charlottesville: University of Virginia Press, Rotunda, 2008.

PGWR *The Papers of George Washington Digital Edition—Revolutionary War Series.* Charlottesville: University of Virginia Press, Rotunda, 2008.

PJA *The Adams Papers Digital Edition—Papers of John Adams.* Edited by Sara Martin. Charlottesville: University of Virginia Press, Rotunda, 2008–2021.

PJAD *The Adams Papers Digital Edition—Diary and Autobiography of John Adams.* Edited by Sara Martin. Charlottesville: University of Virginia Press, Rotunda, 2008–2021.

PJMC *The Papers of James Madison Digital Edition—Congressional Series.* Edited by J. C. A. Stagg. Charlottesville: University of Virginia Press, Rotunda, 2010.

PJMP *The Papers of James Madison Digital Edition—Presidential Series.* Edited by J. C. A. Stagg. Charlottesville: University of Virginia Press, Rotunda, 2010.

PJMR *The Papers of James Madison Digital Edition—Retirement Series.* Edited by J. C. A. Stagg. Charlottesville: University of Virginia Press, Rotunda, 2010.

PTJ *The Papers of Thomas Jefferson Digital Edition—Main Series.* Edited by James P. McClure and J. Jefferson Looney. Charlottesville: University of Virginia Press, Rotunda, 2008–2021.

PTJR *The Papers of Thomas Jefferson Digital Edition—Retirement Series.* Edited by James P. McClure and J. Jefferson Looney. Charlottesville: University of Virginia Press, Rotunda, 2008–2021.

NOTES

Introduction

1. For the purposes of this claim, this book follows historian Richard B. Morris, who identifies the "founding fathers" as the seven foremost leaders—Alexander Hamilton, George Washington, Benjamin Franklin, John Adams, Thomas Jefferson, John Jay, and James Madison—in his book *Seven Who Shaped Our Destiny: The Founding Fathers as Revolutionaries* (New York: Harper & Row, 1973).

2. Allan McLane Hamilton, *The Intimate Life of Alexander Hamilton* (New York: Charles Scribner's Sons, 1910), 8.

3. He drafted a letter to a friend that acknowledged, "my birth is the subject of the most humiliating criticism"—see Alexander Hamilton to William Jackson, August 26, 1800, *PAH*, 25:88. Hamilton showed this letter to James McHenry, who urged Hamilton not to send it to Jackson—see Ron Chernow, *Alexander Hamilton* (New York: Penguin, 2004), 615–616.

4. Gertrude Atherton, "The Hunt for Hamilton's Mother," *North American Review* 175 (August 1902): 237–238.

5. Comments on Jews, [n.d.], *PAH*, 26:774.

6. Quotations appear in John C. Hamilton, *History of the Republic of the United States of America, as Traced in the Writings of Alexander Hamilton and of His Contemporaries*, 2nd ed. (Philadelphia: J. B. Lippincott, 1864), 7:710–711. Alexander Hamilton described the witnesses in court as "converts" to Judaism—many Sephardic Jews were converts to Judaism in that their Jewish ancestors relinquished their faith amid the Inquisition centuries earlier and then subsequent generations reclaimed their Jewish heritage after fleeing Spanish or Portuguese territory.

7. Stephen F. Knott, *Alexander Hamilton and the Persistence of Myth* (Lawrence: University Press of Kansas, 2002), 4–5, 25–26.

8. Thomas Jefferson to John Adams, January 24, 1814, *PTJR*, 7:146; Thomas Jefferson to Benjamin Rush [enclosure], April 21, 1803, *PTJ*, 40:254, 253.

9. Hamilton helped found the New York Manumission Society and engaged in various abolitionist activities. His opposition to slavery is complicated by the fact that he married into a prosperous slave-owning family. Whether Hamilton himself owned slaves is uncertain, but slave ownership was not mutually exclusive to abolitionism in the early republic; a number of abolitionists owned slaves. For Hamilton's relationship with slavery and antislavery, see Leslie M. Harris, "The Greatest City in the World? Slavery in New York in the Age of Hamilton," in

Historians on Hamilton: How a Blockbuster Musical Is Restaging America's Past, ed. Renee C. Romano and Claire Bond Potter (New Brunswick, NJ: Rutgers University Press, 2018), 81–85.

10. Thomas K. McCraw, *The Founders and Finance: How Hamilton, Gallatin, and Other Immigrants Forged a New Economy* (Cambridge, MA: Harvard University Press, 2012), 15–17.

Chapter 1

1. Ron Chernow, *Alexander Hamilton* (New York: Penguin Press, 2004), 8–10.

2. Philip Freneau, "Account of the Island of Santa Cruz," *United States Magazine* 1 (February 1779): 82.

3. Richard B. Sheridan, *Sugar and Slavery: An Economic History of the British West Indies, 1623–1775* (1974; repr., Kingston, Jamaica: Canoe Press, 2000), 14; J. H. Galloway, *The Sugar Cane Industry: An Historical Geography from Its Origins to 1914* (New York: Cambridge University Press, 1989), 83.

4. Michelle M. Terrell, *The Jewish Community of Early Colonial Nevis: A Historical Archaeological Study* (Gainesville: University Press of Florida, 2005), 7.

5. Helen Dewar, "Canada or Guadeloupe? French and British Perceptions of Empire, 1760–1763," *Canadian Historical Review* 91 (December 2010): 637; Chernow, *Alexander Hamilton,* 7.

6. Florence Lewisohn, *St. Croix under Seven Flags* (Hollywood, FL: Dukane Press, 1970), 80–81; Waldemar Westergaard, *The Danish West Indies under Company Rule (1671–1754)* (New York: Macmillan, 1917), 206n17.

7. Lewisohn, *St. Croix,* 90.

8. James Thomas Flexner, *The Young Hamilton: A Biography* (Boston: Little, Brown, 1978), 11.

9. Lewisohn, *St. Croix,* 90–92.

10. Terrell, *Jewish Community,* 12; Lois Dubin, "Introduction: Port Jews in the Atlantic World," *Jewish History* 20 (June 2006): 117–120; and generally, Yuri Slezkine, *The Jewish Century* (Princeton, NJ: Princeton University Press, 2004).

11. Laura Arnold Leibman, *Messianism, Secrecy, and Mysticism: A New Interpretation of Early American Jewish Life* (London: Vallentine Mitchell, 2012), 5–6.

12. Terrell, *Jewish Community,* 12.

13. Isaac S. Emmanuel and Suzanne A. Emmanuel, *History of the Jews of the Netherlands Antilles* (Cincinnati: American Jewish Archives, 1970), 1:277.

14. Lewisohn, *St. Croix,* 91. Not counting Levine, there were at least three adult male Jews (Jacob de Cordua, Emanuel Aboab, and Moses Mendes) in St. Croix in 1745. This number was derived from cross-referencing a list of Jews on St. Croix from the era found in William F. Cissel, "Alexander Hamilton: The West Indian 'Founding Father,'" Christiansted National Historic Site, National Park Service, U.S. Department of the Interior (July 2004), 23n10, with the island's *Mandtalslister* (census list) from 1745—see RIGS, 1741–1747: frame 192. It is impossible to state with precision the size of the Jewish population because it is unknown which, if any, of these men were married with children at that point in time.

15. Neville A. T. Hall, *Slave Society in the Danish West Indies: St. Thomas, St. John, and St. Croix* (Baltimore: Johns Hopkins University Press, 1992), 5.

16. Chernow, *Alexander Hamilton*, 19; Terrell, *Jewish Community*, 7.

17. Quoted in George F. Tyson and Arnold R. Highfield, *The Kamina Folk: Slavery and Slave Life in the Danish West Indies* (1994; repr., Virgin Islands: Virgin Islands Humanities Council, 1997), 41.

18. Richard Brookhiser, *Alexander Hamilton, American* (New York: Free Press, 1999), 15.

19. Lewisohn, *St. Croix*, 94.

20. Tyson and Highfield, *Kamina Folk*, 45.

21. Lewisohn, *St. Croix*, 97–100.

22. H. U. Ramsing, *Alexander Hamilton's Birth and Parentage*, trans. into English by Mrs. S. Vahl (1951), 2. Ramsing's original article appeared in 1939.

23. Lewisohn, *St. Croix*, 98, 115.

24. Lewisohn, *St. Croix*, 115, 118–120.

25. Chernow, *Alexander Hamilton*, 10; Flexner, *Young Hamilton*, 12.

26. Alexander Hamilton to William Jackson, August 26, 1800, *PAH*, 25:89.

27. Flexner, *Young Hamilton*, 10–12; Westergaard, *Danish West Indies*, 7.

28. Historians have debated whether Levine grew poor over time. Ramsing suggests that "before his death, he had had to pawn his gold buttons for a very small sum"—see *Alexander Hamilton's Birth*, 14. Conversely, Cissel argues that "assumptions of Lavien's unstable or diminishing finances" are "not corroborated by the relatively constant number of slaves owned by him"—see "Alexander Hamilton," 23n14. After Levine's death in 1771, the local paper announced that "2 houses, some lots of land, and other effects" from Levine's estate would be sold at auction, which would suggest that Levine did not die poor—see *Royal Danish American Gazette* (Christiansted, St. Croix), March 6, 1771, 1.

29. Arthur Hendrick Vandenberg, *The Greatest American: Alexander Hamilton* (New York: G. P. Putnam's Sons, 1921); William Graham Sumner, *Alexander Hamilton* (New York: Dodd, Mead, 1890); Lewis Henry Boutell, *Alexander Hamilton, the Constructive Statesman* (Chicago: Slason, Thompson, 1890); Henry Renwick and James Renwick, *Lives of John Jay and Alexander Hamilton* (New York: Harper & Brothers, 1841).

30. Brookhiser, *Alexander Hamilton, American*, 15; Noemie Emery, *Alexander Hamilton: An Intimate Portrait* (New York: G. P. Putnam's Sons, 1982), 15; Jacob Ernest Cooke, *Alexander Hamilton* (New York: Charles Scribner's Sons, 1982), 1; Forrest McDonald, *Alexander Hamilton: A Biography* (New York: W. W. Norton, 1979), 6; John C. Miller, *Alexander Hamilton: Portrait in Paradox* (New York: Harper & Brothers, 1959), 3; Ramsing, *Alexander Hamilton's Birth*, 14–15; David Loth, *Alexander Hamilton: Portrait of a Prodigy* (New York: Carrick & Evans, 1939), 17; Helen Nicolay, *The Boys' Life of Alexander Hamilton* (New York: Century Co., 1927), 14; Henry Jones Ford, *Alexander Hamilton* (1920; repr., New York: Charles Scribner's Sons, 1925), 5–6; Charles Conant, *Alexander Hamilton* (Boston: Houghton, Mifflin, 1901), 5; Henry Cabot Lodge, *Alexander Hamilton* (Boston: Houghton, Mifflin, 1883), 294; George Shea, *The Life and Epoch of Alexander Hamilton: A Historical Study*, 3rd ed. (Boston: Houghton, Mifflin, 1881), 147; John T. Morse Jr., *The Life of Alexander Hamilton* (Boston: Little, Brown, 1876), 1:1; John C. Hamilton, *History of the Republic, as Traced in the Writings of Alexander Hamilton and His Contemporaries* (New York: D. Appleton, 1857), 1:41; Samuel M. Schmucker, *The Life and Times of Alexander Hamilton* (Philadelphia: John E. Potter, 1856), 26.

31. Jews of Levitic descent transliterated the Hebrew letters for Levi (לוי) to a Latin-script alphabet in a variety of ways—see Alexander Beider, *A Dictionary of Jewish Surnames from the Russian Empire*, rev. ed. (Bergenfield, NJ: Avotaynu, 2008), 18. (Beider here discusses Levitic names in Europe generally, not just those endemic to the Russian Empire.) I use "Levine" throughout the book because Alexander Hamilton himself opted for that formulation when referencing Johan's son—see Alexander Hamilton to Elizabeth Hamilton, [1782], *PAH*, 3:235. (Elsewhere, Hamilton used "Lavine"—see, for instance, Alexander Hamilton to William Jackson, August 26, 1800, *PAH*, 25:89.) Johan's surname appears in different formulations in primary sources, including "Levine," "Levin," "Lewin," "Lavien," "Lavine," "Lavin," "Lawien," "Lawin," and "Lovien"—see Broadus Mitchell, *Alexander Hamilton: Youth to Maturity, 1758–1788* (New York: Macmillan, 1957), 1:472n34; and Cissel, "Alexander Hamilton," 23n10. The diversity of spellings is unsurprising given that the clerks who recorded names in the Danish records were not known for their consistency. It is worth noting, too, that Caribbean Jews often wrote their own names in multiple spellings—see Franklin B. Krohn, "The Search for the Elusive Caribbean Jews," *American Jewish Archives Journal* 45 (1993): 151. Two spellings of Johan's surname ("Levin" and "Lewin") match letter-for-letter Levitic surnames found among eighteenth-century Jews. See, for instance, the German-Danish Jew Joseph Meyer Levin, referenced in Martin Schwarz Lausten, *Jews and Christians in Denmark: From the Middle Ages to Recent Times, ca. 1100–1948*, trans. Margaret Ryan Hellman (Boston: Brill, 2015), 53–54; and the German Jew Hirschel Lewin, mentioned in Michael A. Meyer, ed., *German-Jewish History in Modern Times* (New York: Columbia University Press, 1996), 1:236. As I discuss later, Johan might himself have been German originally. The precise formulation "Levine" was not yet a standard spelling for Levitic Jews in the eighteenth century—see Joseph R. Rosenbloom, *A Biographical Dictionary of Early American Jews: Colonial Times through 1800* (1960; repr., Lexington: University of Kentucky Press, 2015), 87. "Lavien" also appears frequently in the St. Croix records as Johan's surname, which is a difference of only one vowel from "Levien," a name borne by known Jews in the Caribbean. See, for instance, Abraham Levien, a Jamaican Jew mentioned in Mordechai Arbell, *The Jewish Nation of the Caribbean: The Spanish-Portuguese Jewish Settlements in the Caribbean and the Guianas* (Jerusalem: Gefen, 2002), 256; and in Joshua Hezekiah DeCordova, *Reason and Faith, or, Philosophical Absurdities, and the Necessity of Revelation, intended to Promote Faith among Infidels, and the Unbounded Exercise of Humanity, among all Religious Men* (Jamaica: Strupar and Preston, 1778), viii. For a nineteenth-century example of a Jewish Levien in the Danish West Indies, see the discussion of Joseph Levien on St. Thomas in Judah Cohen, *Through the Sands of Time: A History of the Jewish Community of St. Thomas, U.S. Virgin Islands* (Hanover, NH: Brandeis University Press, 2004), 154–156. While "Levien" and "Lavien" differ by a vowel, transliterated variants of the same Hebrew name commonly had vowel differences—see Heinrich W. Guggenheimer and Eva H. Guggenheimer, *Jewish Family Names and Their Origins: An Etymological Dictionary* (Jersey City, NJ: KTAV Publishing House, 2007), 1:xxiv. Using Johan's surname to determine his religious identity is complicated by the fact that Gentiles occasionally had Levitic-sounding names—see, for instance, "Benjamin Levi" and "John Levy" in Rosenbloom, *Biographical Dictionary*, 86, 92. Johan's surname thus raises the possibility of his having a Jewish identity but cannot, on its own, settle the question.

32. Flexner mentions Levine's prior work on Nevis as a merchant in *Young Hamilton*, 12.

33. William Pencak, *Jews and Gentiles in Early America, 1654–1800* (Ann Arbor: University of Michigan Press, 2005), x.

34. Ramsing, *Alexander Hamilton's Birth*, 12; RIGS, 1752–1755: frame 69 #19. The property came into the possession of Aron Mothas de Gottero.

35. RIGS, 1752–1755: frames 106–108. Of the more than 300 names for 1753, Jews appearing on the list were Aron Mothas de Gottero, Joseph Robles, Jacob de Cordua, and Emmanuel Aboab. Isack Melhado appears elsewhere in the 1753 records—see RIGS, 1752–1755: frame 103. Johan Levine could be the sixth Jew on the island (but, of course, he could not sell his own plantation to himself and thus he does not factor into the calculation). For a list of Jews in St. Croix at this time, see Cissel, "Alexander Hamilton," 23n10. Although Cissel lists Cordua and La Pena as two individuals, Cordua is sometimes referred to as Jacob de Cordua La Pena in the historical record.

36. Allan McLane Hamilton, *The Intimate Life of Alexander Hamilton* (New York: Charles Scribner's Sons, 1910), 8. Levine may have been Danish in the sense that he spent most of his adult life as a resident of the Danish kingdom, but he perhaps had other origins. Levine wrote to a Danish-speaking lawyer in German, which has led some scholars to speculate, not unreasonably, that Levine initially hailed from Germany—see Flexner, *Young Hamilton*, 12. Lewisohn's history of St. Croix describes Levine as a "naturalized Dane"—see *St. Croix*, 108.

37. Willard Sterne Randall, *Alexander Hamilton: A Life* (New York: HarperCollins, 2003), 8; Holmes Alexander, *To Covet Honor: A Biography of Alexander Hamilton* (Belmont, MA: Western Islands, 1977), xiv; Nathan Schachner, *Alexander Hamilton* (1946; repr., New York: Thomas Yoseloff, 1957), 5; Mitchell, *Alexander Hamilton*, 1:6; Ralph Edward Bailey, *An American Colossus: The Singular Career of Alexander Hamilton* (Boston: Lothrop, Lee & Shepard, 1933), 18.

38. Gertrude Atherton, *A Few of Hamilton's Letters, Including His Description of the Great West Indian Hurricane of 1772* (New York: Macmillan, 1903), 273.

39. Flexner, *Young Hamilton*, 12, 468n11.

40. Robert A. Hendrickson, *The Rise and Fall of Alexander Hamilton* (New York: Van Nostrand Reinhold, 1981), 8.

41. Cissel, "Alexander Hamilton," 23n10. Chernow, for his part, suggests of Levine, "If he was Jewish he managed to conceal his origins" because otherwise Rachel's "snobbish" mother "would have certainly squelched the match," but Chernow furnishes no evidence to substantiate this claim—see Chernow, *Alexander Hamilton*, 10.

42. RIGS, *Jacob de Cordua*: 1741–1747: frames 192, 216 #44, 250 #44, 281 #44, 282 #45; 1748–1751: frames 18 #44 and #45, 30, 55 #44 and #45, 122, 156 #44 and #45, 183, 200, 243 #44 and #45, 274, 275, 285; 1752–1755: frames 19 #44 and #45, 31 #7, 37, 45, 78 #45, 93 #7, 107, 158 #7, 176, 197 #7, 239; *Aron Mothas de Gotero*: 1748–1751: frames 50 #32, 121, 198, 236 #32, 282, 284; 1752–1755: frames 14 #32, 69 #19, 71 #32, 106; *Emanuel Aboab*: 1741–1747: frames 54, 58, 95, 101, 156, 159, 192, 245 #1, 274 #1, 297 #9 and #13; 1748–1751: frames 12 #1, 30, 78, 156 #45, 185 #6, 199, 243 #45, 277, 278; 1752–1755: frames 12 #9, 19 #45, 23 #7, 39, 44, 82 #6 and #9, 103, 106, 147 #6 and #10, 174, 238; *Isack Melhado*: 1752–1755: frames 8 #53, 45, 60 #53, 103; *Moses Mendes*: 1741–1747: frames 139, 192, 297 #27; 1748–1751: frames 78, 190, 279; *Joseph Robles*: 1748–1751: frames 50 #32, 121, 198, 236 #32, 282, 284; 1752–1755: frames 14 #32, 71 #32, 106, 136 #32, 175, 231 #32.

43. RIGS, *Jacob de Cordua*: 1741–1747: frame 230.

44. For Levine's entries, see RIGS, 1741–1747: frames 210 #12, 245 #12, 275 #12; 1748–1751: frames 47 #12, 121, 144 #12, 146 #19, 284; 1752–1755: frames 13 #19, 69 #19, 107, 144, 175, 189.

45. Cissel, "Alexander Hamilton," 23n10.

46. A July 12, 1765, statement from the Privy Council noted that among the "Jewish families," two were "Danish families, the rest (being) Portuguese"—see Zvi Loker, *Jews in the Caribbean: Evidence on the History of the Jews in the Caribbean Zone in Colonial Times* (Jerusalem: Misgav Yerushalayim, 1991), 308.

47. While no marriage certificate exists with a fixed date, records show that Rachel did not reside with her mother in 1745 and thus was ostensibly living with Johan as his wife. Rachel bore him a son in 1746, which would also be consistent with a 1745 wedding—see Mitchell, *Alexander Hamilton*, 1:6. On the likelihood of the Grange hosting the ceremony, see Cissel, "Alexander Hamilton," 23n10. In the divorce proceedings for Johan and Rachel, a witness testified that he "had heard that she was married to John Michael Lavien, although he had not seen the priest marry them"—quotation appears in Michael E. Newton, *Discovering Hamilton* (Phoenix: Eleftheria, 2019), 79. This witness's reference to a priest on its own cannot determine the religious character of the marriage ceremony because Gentiles sometimes used the word "priest" to refer to Jewish faith leaders—see, for instance, Isaac Bangs's reference to Gershom Seixas as a "priest" in D. de Sola Pool, "Descriptions of the Synagogues in New York in 1776 and 1828," *PAJHS* 40 (December 1950): 188. In the same vein, the Jewish faith was sometimes referred to as a "church"—see, for example, *New Jersey Journal* (Elizabethtown), January 18, 1797, 1. It may also have been the case that no witness saw a "priest" officiate the nuptials of Johan and Rachel because they were not married by any priest.

48. Ramsing, *Alexander Hamilton's Birth*, 2; Cissel, "Alexander Hamilton," 31n89. The failure of Rachel and Johan to baptize Peter as an infant is a necessary deduction from the premise that Peter undertook an adult baptism because Anglican doctrine prohibits two baptisms. As *The Book of Common Prayer* (1662) specified, "Hath this child been already baptized, or no? If they answer, no: then shall the Priest proceed." Cissel acknowledges that two baptisms would have "contravened the theology and doctrine of the Church of England" ("Alexander Hamilton," 31n89).

49. While Baptists and Mennonites, who did not practice infant baptism, organized churches on the island, they did not do so until after Peter Levine's upbringing—see Lewisohn, *St. Croix*, 156, 193.

50. *The Book of Common Prayer* (1662) required the following Trinitarian formulation: "I baptize thee in the Name of the Father, and of the Son, and of the Holy Ghost."

51. For a list of denominations on St. Croix, see Lewisohn, *St. Croix*, xxvii.

52. Ramsing, *Alexander Hamilton's Birth*, 27.

53. Chernow, *Alexander Hamilton*, 26. Chernow is left to speculate: "One explanation is that Johann Michael Lavien had painfully concealed his Jewish roots but still did not want his son baptized." But if Levine intended to conceal his Jewish roots, then forgoing the practice of infant baptism for his son would have undermined rather than furthered such an end.

54. Cissel, "Alexander Hamilton," 31n89.

55. While conversion to Judaism was disallowed in Denmark proper, the authorities on St. Croix had wide latitude to disregard Danish law in part because Danish law was too

religiously restrictive for the diversity of the Caribbean. As Poul Erik Olsen explains, "In 1734, the island of St. Croix had just been bought from France and colonists for the new acquisition were in great demand. So as not to scare potential settlers away by a legal system that would be strange to most of them, and which criminalized all non-Protestant confessions, a royal charter to the West Indian & Guinean Company granted that the 'Danske Lov' should only be in force insofar as it could be applied under the local circumstances, and only when they did not conflict with local regulations"—see Olsen, "Slavery and the Law in the Danish West Indies," in *Negotiating Enslavement: Perspectives on Slavery in the Danish West Indies*, ed. Arnold R. Highfield and George F. Tyson (St. Croix, USVI: Antilles Press, 2009), 1. Even in Denmark proper, there was some flexibility in the state's approach to the question of conversion to Judaism. When a Gentile died in 1727 and evidence surfaced that the deceased had discreetly converted to Judaism, the police chief sought harsh punishments for the local Jewish community, but the king overruled the police chief and limited punitive sanction to a fine—see Lausten, *Jews and Christians*, 62–63.

56. Given that Jewish identity is matrilineal, this scenario would have required Peter to convert to Judaism.

57. The only scholar to take seriously the prospect of Rachel's Jewish identity is William E. Woodward, whose biography of George Washington mentions in passing that Rachel might have been Jewish. Woodward writes that "[Alexander's] mother was the wife of a Jewish merchant named Levine. It is said she was not a Jewess, though this is mere conjecture. Her name was Rachel, a Jewish name, and her husband was a Jew"—see *George Washington: The Image and the Man* (New York: Boni and Liveright, 1926), 371. Given that Woodward takes Rachel's first name as evidence of a possible Jewish identity, and considering the reality that she was born Christian, Woodward's evidence for his claim is faulty even if the claim itself has merit. In a similarly misguided vein, Johan J. Smertenko implies that Hamilton may have had Jewish ethnicity because Johan was Jewish and perhaps Hamilton's biological father—see Smertenko, *Alexander Hamilton* (New York: Greenberg, 1932), 4–5. There is no evidence to support the conceit that Levine might have been Hamilton's father. Some twentieth-century antisemites suggested that Hamilton was Jewish, but they did so for reasons rooted in prejudice rather than in historical evidence—see Michael E. Newton, *Alexander Hamilton: The Formative Years* (Phoenix: Eleftheria, 2015), 34–35.

58. Rosenbloom, *Biographical Dictionary*, 165, 136, 56. For an example of a Jewish Peter, see "Peter Hays" on p. 59.

59. Michael Hoberman, Laura Leibman, and Hilit Surowitz-Israel, eds., *Jews in the Americas, 1776–1826* (London: Routledge, 2018), 172nn4–5.

60. See, for instance, Jacob Rader Marcus, *Early American Jewry*, vol. 2: *The Jews of Pennsylvania and the South, 1655–1790* (Philadelphia: Jewish Publication Society of America, 1953), 185, for the case of Elizabeth Whitlock; and Rosenbloom, *Biographical Dictionary*, for the cases of Sarah Abrahams (formerly Betty Hart) married to Moses Nathan (pp. 5, 132); Ann Sarah Hugenin Irby married to Abraham Alexander Sr. (p. 6); and Jane (Jean) Nathan married to Joseph Nathan (p. 132).

61. Chernow, *Alexander Hamilton*, 11.

62. Ramsing, *Alexander Hamilton's Birth*, 8.

63. Alexander Hamilton to William Jackson, August 26, 1800, *PAH*, 25:89; Chernow, *Alexander Hamilton*, 12.

64. Chernow, *Alexander Hamilton*, 12–17.

65. William A. Smith, *A Natural History of Nevis and the rest of the English Leeward Charibee Islands in America* (Cambridge: J. Bentham, 1745), 308.

66. Regarding the monkeys, see Chernow, *Alexander Hamilton*, 20. The brown pelican is the national bird of St. Kitts and Nevis.

67. John Oldmixon, *The British Empire in America, Containing the History of the Discovery, Settlement, Progress and present State of all the British Colonies, on the Continent and Islands of America* (London: Printed for John Nicholson at the King's Arms in Little Britain, Benjamin Tooke at the Middle-Temple-Gate, Fleet Street, and Richard Parker and Ralph Smith under the Piazza of the Royal Exchange, 1708), 2:201–202, 197–198.

68. Marco G. Meniketti, *Sugar Cane Capitalism and Environmental Transformation: An Archaeology of Colonial Nevis, West Indies* (Tuscaloosa: University of Alabama Press, 2015), 99.

69. Oldmixon, *British Empire*, 2:196.

70. Oldmixon, *British Empire*, 2:196–197.

71. Quotation appears in Meniketti, *Sugar Cane Capitalism*, 100.

72. Vincent K. Hubbard, *Swords, Ships, and Sugar: History of Nevis* (Corvallis, OR: Premiere Editions International, 2002), 128.

73. Joan Robinson, *Nevis in the Time of Hamilton, His Contribution to His Adopted Country and Nevisian Legacy* (Ithaca, NY: Arnold Printing, 2005), 13; Brian Dyde, *Out of the Crowded Vagueness: A History of the Islands of St Kitts, Nevis, and Anguilla* (Oxford: Macmillan Caribbean, 2005), 97.

74. Smith, *Natural History of Nevis*, 309.

75. The year of Hamilton's birth has long been a matter of debate among scholars, with some opting for 1757 and others 1755. However, Michael Newton recently unearthed new sources from St. Croix that align with a 1754 birth—see *Discovering Hamilton*, 7–9.

76. Chernow, *Alexander Hamilton*, 17.

77. Chernow, *Alexander Hamilton*, 19.

78. Meniketti, *Sugar Cane Capitalism*, 86.

79. Smith, *Natural History of Nevis*, 57.

80. Terrell, *Jewish Community*, 12.

81. Arbell, *Jewish Nation*, 221; Terrell, *Jewish Community*, 45, 48, 69, 135.

82. Eli Faber, *Jews, Slaves, and the Slave Trade: Setting the Record Straight* (New York: New York University Press, 1998), 104.

83. Robert Robertson, *A Letter to the Right Reverend the Lord Bishop of London: From An Inhabitant of His Majesty's Leeward-Caribbee-Islands. Containing some Considerations on His Lordship's Two Letters of May 19, 1727. The First To the Masters and Mistresses of Families in the English Plantations abroad; The second To the Missionaries there. In which is Inserted, A Short Essay concerning the Conversion of the Negro-Slaves in our Sugar-Colonies: Written in the Month of June, 1727, by the same Inhabitant* (London: J. Wilford, 1730), 102, 12.

84. Terrell, *Jewish Community*, 61–62.

85. Ronald L. Eisenberg, *The JPS Guide to Jewish Traditions* (Philadelphia: Jewish Publication Society, 2004), 623.

86. See, for instance, Mordechai Arbell, "Return to Judaism: The Circumcisers of Curaçao," *Shofar* (Fall 1999): 5; Miriam Bodian, "'Men of the Nation': The Shaping of *Converso* Identity in Early Modern Europe," *Past and Present* (May 1994): 48–49.

87. Jonathan Israel, "Jews and Crypto-Jews, 1500–1800," in *Atlantic Diasporas: Jews, Conversos, and Crypto-Jews in the Age of Mercantilism, 1500–1800*, ed. Richard L. Kagan and Philip D. Morgan (Baltimore: Johns Hopkins University Press, 2009), 17; Bruno Feitler, "Four Chapters in the History of Crypto-Judaism in Brazil: The Case of the Northeastern New Christians (17th–21st Centuries)," *Jewish History* 25 (2011): 216.

88. Aviva Ben-Ur and Rachel Frankel, *Remnant Stones: The Jewish Cemeteries and Synagogues of Suriname/Essays* (Cincinnati: Hebrew Union College Press, 2012), 42–44; Leibman, *Messianism, Secrecy, and Mysticism*, 93.

89. Kiddushin 68b, Sanhedrin 44a, Yevamot 47b.

90. Terrell, *Jewish Community*, 13.

91. The St. John's records from the 1750s show no baptismal entry for either Hamilton brother—see Vere Langford Oliver, ed., *Caribbeana: Being Miscellaneous Papers Relating to the History, Genealogy, Topography, and Antiquities of the British West Indies* (London: Mitchell Hughes and Clarke, 1910–1919), 1:324–328. For copies of the original records from St. John's, see RG 16.10 St. Johns Register of Birth, Baptisms, Marriages and Burials, 1729–1825, NHCS. No baptismal records from the 1750s survive for either St. Paul's, which was near Alexander Hamilton's childhood home, or St. George's, where his mother's parents had been members.

92. John C. Hamilton, *History of the Republic*, 1:42.

93. Brookhiser, *Alexander Hamilton, American*; Cooke, *Alexander Hamilton*; Alexander, *To Covet Honor*; Miller, *Portrait in Paradox*; Loth, *Alexander Hamilton*; Ford, *Alexander Hamilton*; Vandenberg, *Greatest American*; Conant, *Alexander Hamilton*; Lodge, *Alexander Hamilton*; Sumner, *Alexander Hamilton*; Boutell, *Alexander Hamilton*; Schmucker, *Life and Times*; Renwick and Renwick, *Lives of John Jay and Alexander Hamilton*.

94. Cissel, "Alexander Hamilton," 25n29; McDonald, *Alexander Hamilton*, 8; Flexner, *Young Hamilton*, 24; Robert A. Hendrickson, *Hamilton* (New York: Mason/Charter, 1976), 1:26; Mitchell, *Alexander Hamilton*, 1:19; Schachner, *Alexander Hamilton*, 17; Bailey, *American Colossus*, 20; Shea, *Life and Epoch*, 149; Morse, *Life of Alexander Hamilton*, 1:4.

95. Lewisohn, *St. Croix*, 150.

96. Chernow, *Alexander Hamilton*, 17. See also Randall, *Alexander Hamilton*, 18; Marie B. Hecht, *Odd Destiny: The Life of Alexander Hamilton* (New York: Macmillan, 1982), 8.

97. Oliver, *Caribbeana*, 1:43–44; 1:88–91; 1:256; 1:303; 1:356; 3:221; 3:352. The latter two instances appear in the Faucette's family church. Sometimes such an infant is described as a "bastard," other times as "illegitimate." See also Newton, *Alexander Hamilton*, 521–522.

98. The theory that Hamilton was denied schooling on account of his illegitimacy is closely tied to another dubious claim in the secondary literature that Alexander's illegitimacy barred him from baptism. Hendrickson suggests, "To the vestry of white slave owners and prosperous artisans of St. George's Gingerland parish on Nevis she [Rachel Levine] would not have been particularly welcome to celebrate the sacrament of baptism for her illegitimate children"—see

Hamilton, 1:6. The church records cited above demonstrate that illegitimacy did not necessarily disqualify an infant from baptism.

99. Conventional Jewish education centered around a Talmud Torah, a communal school for the children in a given Jewish community. The school often had a close association with and financial support from the synagogue. Teachers and students at a typical Talmud Torah were male. Jewish girls, to the extent they received education at all, were usually taught informally by their mothers at home.

There were, however, numerous exceptions to these norms in the early modern Atlantic world. Not all Jewish schools were Talmud Torahs. We know that in mid-eighteenth century Curaçao, for instance, there were also *private* Jewish schools because, according to a pair of historians, the colonial governor "ordered the Jews to stop holding classes, private or communal, on Sunday, under penalty of a 25 pesos fine," and the governor "defended his action before his superiors on the ground that the Jewish schools 'disturbed the neighbors'"—see Emmanuel and Emmanuel, *History of the Jews,* 1:152. Moreover, not all teachers were male. As early as the 1500s, there were female educators called *melammedet* in Jewish schools—see Elijah Bortniker, "Jewish Education—16th–18th Centuries," in *Encyclopaedia Judaica,* 2nd ed., ed. Michael Berenbaum and Fred Skolnik (Detroit: Macmillan Reference USA, 2007), 6:179. The Villarreal School in London, founded circa 1730, was a private Jewish school for girls and had a female teacher. (No scholarship yet exists on the Villarreal School, but Julia Lieberman is currently undertaking research on the subject.) When Jewish girls did attend school, it was not necessarily the case that their teachers were exclusively female. For instance, the Hague in the eighteenth century had a Jewish school for girls where a brother and sister taught—see Tirtsah Levie Bernfeld, *Poverty and Welfare among the Portuguese Jews in Early Modern Amsterdam* (Oxford: Littman Library of Jewish Civilization, 2012), 350n203. Nor were student bodies at a given Jewish school necessarily all-male or all-female. There is evidence that as early as the mid-seventeenth century, Amsterdam had Jewish schools where boys and girls may have been present in the same classes—see Benjamin E. Fisher, *People of the Book: Jewish Society and the Turn to Scripture in the Seventeenth Century* (Cincinnati: Hebrew Union College Press, 2020), 50. In sum, Jewish schools were often communal but sometimes private, teachers were generally male but occasionally female, and student bodies were usually segregated by gender but not necessarily.

With this diverse educational landscape in mind, let us turn to two important details about Alexander Hamilton's school that emerge from his son's brief remark—the Judaic nature of the school and the gender of his teacher. A Jewish educator teaching portions of the Torah in the original Hebrew makes clear that the school was Judaic in character rather than a secular private school that had a teacher who happened to be Jewish. By way of contrast, there are examples of private schools in the nineteenth century that were nonsectarian with non-Jewish students and an educator who was, incidentally, a Jew. See for instance, Isaac Harby of Charleston, South Carolina, in Jacob Rader Marcus, *United States Jewry, 1776–1985* (Detroit: Wayne State University Press, 1989), 1:381; Jacob Mordecai of Warrenton, North Carolina, in Emily Bingham, *Mordecai: An Early American Family* (New York: Hill and Wang, 2003), 36; and Rebecca Cohen Belinfante in Curaçao in Emmanuel and Emmanuel, *History of the Jews,* 1:441. It is telling that when Suriname's David Cohen Nassy suggested in the late eighteenth century an evening school for children of any faith, his proposed curriculum was decidedly not Judaic. In the words of one

NOTES TO PAGES 28–30   207

historian commenting on the proposal, "The absence of religion is striking. . . . Clearly, the non-denominational character of the college made religion a subject to avoid"—see Robert Cohen, *Jews in Another Environment: Surinam in the Second Half of the Eighteenth Century* (New York: E. J. Brill, 1991), 101. Whereas Nassy's nonsectarian proposal underscores how Jews avoided any appearance of trying to Judaize Christian children, by the same logic the Judaic content of Alexander Hamilton's school points to its sectarian character as a Jewish school.

That Alexander's teacher was female suggests that the school in Nevis was probably a private Jewish school rather than a full-fledged Talmud Torah. While men traditionally taught boys, be it in communal or private Jewish schools, it is unsurprising that in Nevis a female teacher would educate boys. Gender roles were most likely to be renegotiated in fledgling Jewish communities on the fringes of the diaspora, communities whose members were too few in number to have the luxury of strictly enforcing traditional male-female divides. Indeed, Natalie A. Zacek identifies Nevis as the smallest of the major Jewish Caribbean communities in "Great Tangled Cousinries? Jewish Intermarriage in the British West Indies," in *A Sefardic Pepper-Pot in the Caribbean*, ed. Michael Studemund-Halévy (Barcelona: Tirocinio, 2016), 141n11. By way of analogy, Jonathan Sarna observes how in early America, women sometimes assumed male roles—such as reader during *Yom Kippur* services or even synagogue sexton—but "as frontier communities became larger and more organized, women found these kinds of opportunities foreclosed to them"—see *American Judaism: A History* (New Haven, CT: Yale University Press, 2004), 50.

So although a "Jewess" teaching boys was not a conventional practice, it would fall among the numerous exceptions to general patterns in Jewish education that can be found throughout the early modern Atlantic world, and what's more, Nevis was home to just the kind of frontier Jewish community where we are most likely to see a reworking of traditional gender roles.

100. For a discussion of the purpose of Jewish education, see Jacob Rader Marcus, *The Colonial American Jew, 1492–1776* (Detroit: Wayne State University Press, 1970), 2:1057–1059.

101. Sanhedrin 59a explains that although Gentiles could study the Noahide laws—that is, seven laws that Gentiles should follow, according to Jewish law—the Torah as a whole is the special preserve of the Jewish people and "a gentile who studies Torah robs the Jewish people of it." This interpretation is derived from a biblical verse: "Moses commanded us a law, an inheritance of the congregation of Jacob" (Deuteronomy 33:4), which the Talmud interprets to mean that the Torah "is an inheritance for us, not for them." To be sure, some Christian Hebraists engaged Jews for individualized tutoring, but these instances were limited. For a discussion of Ezra Stiles, a Christian Hebraist who was exceptional in colonial America in the extent of his ties to Jewry, see Marcus, *Colonial American Jew*, 2:1104–1107. There is a significant difference between isolated instances of a Jew offering one-on-one instruction to a Christian adult versus a Jewish schoolteacher instructing a Christian student in the Torah in a Jewish school. No known evidence suggests that the latter was a practice in the eighteenth-century Caribbean.

102. Terrell, *Jewish Community*, 40–41; C. S. S. Higham, "The General Assembly of the Leeward Islands," *English Historical Review* 41 (April 1926): 195.

103. Natalie Zacek, "'A People So Subtle': Sephardic Jewish Pioneers of the English West Indies," in *Bridging the Early Modern Atlantic World: People, Products, and Practices on the Move*, ed. Caroline A. Williams (Burlington, VT: Ashgate, 2009), 109; Terrell, *Jewish Community*, 50.

104. Terrell, *Jewish Community*, 50–51.

105. Quotation appears in J. W. Fortescue, ed., *Calendar of State Papers, Colonial Series, America and West Indies, 1689–1692* (London: Mackie and Co., 1901), 594.

106. Natalie A. Zacek, "The Freest Country: Jews of the British Atlantic World, ca. 1600–1800," in *The Atlantic World* (London: Routledge, 2014), 367.

107. Quotations appear in Zacek, "People So Subtle," 101.

108. Robinson, *Nevis in the Time of Hamilton*, 11.

109. Terrell, *Jewish Community*, 52–53.

110. Quotation appears in Dyde, *Crowded Vagueness*, 85.

111. Hubbard, *Swords, Ships, and Sugar*, 121, 126–127, 129.

112. Quotation appears in Terrell, *Jewish Community*, 54.

113. Terrell, *Jewish Community*, 53–54.

114. Terrell, *Jewish Community*, 135, 138.

115. Terrell, *Jewish Community*, 30.

116. Terrell, *Jewish Community*, 135. In Europe, Jews clustered as well, sometimes by choice so that they could have close proximity to Jewish institutions. In other instances, European Jews were coerced by state authority into Jewish ghettos—see Jacob Katz, *Out of the Ghetto: The Social Background of Jewish Emancipation, 1770–1870* (Cambridge, MA: Harvard University Press, 1973), 20. In sixteenth-century Venice, Jews were locked behind ghetto walls at night—see Dana E. Katz, *The Jewish Ghetto and the Visual Imagination of Early Modern Venice* (New York: Cambridge University Press, 2017), 33.

117. Terrell, *Jewish Community*, 141.

118. Smith, *Natural History of Nevis*, 10.

119. Terrell, *Jewish Community*, 140.

120. As Zacek writes, "Jewish populations within the individual West Indian colonies in the eighteenth century may have been as small as seventy individuals (in 1720s Nevis) or as large as a thousand (in 1780s Curaçao)"—see "Great Tangled Cousinries?," 141n11.

121. A possible clue that Rachel crossed back and forth between Christianity and Judaism depending on her location comes from the baptismal register of St. Eustatius, a Dutch island in the Caribbean. An entry for October 1, 1758, marks a "James Hamelton and Rachel Hamelton, his wife," who were present at the baptism of Alexander Fraser—see Baptismal Register of St. Eustatius 1743–1765 (microfiche), October 1, 1758, CBG/Centre for Family History, The Hague, Netherlands. Rachel here engaged in several falsehoods. First, Rachel was never married to James Hamilton Sr. Second, her surname was never Hamilton (or Hamelton). Third, she told someone on St. Croix that while she had been on St. Eustatius, she had kept the name "Lavien" even though the Fraser baptismal record indicates she (at least temporarily) discarded that surname. According to the divorce proceedings on St. Croix for Rachel and Johan Levine, a witness testified that he "had heard both from herself [Rachel] and others that she was married to John Michael Lavien and that she went on both Sainte Christopher [i.e., St. Kitts] and Sainte Eustatius under the name of Rachel Lavien"—quotation appears in Newton, *Discovering Hamilton*, 79–80. Flexner suggests, "On West Indian islands where they were not otherwise known, James and Rachel put themselves forward as a conventional couple"—see *Young Hamilton*, 23. Given her multiple lies concerning her status on St. Eustatius, it requires no great leap to imagine that she could have indulged in yet another measure of deception at the Fraser baptism and

hidden any Jewish identity. A fluid religious identity would make her somewhat akin to those Jews who were, in the words of Lois Dubin, neither strictly "Jews" nor "Crypto-Jews" but "something in-between, shuttling back and forth between religious professions"—see Dubin, "Introduction," 119.

Chapter 2

1. James Thomas Flexner, *The Young Hamilton: A Biography* (Boston: Little, Brown, 1978), 25; Ron Chernow, *Alexander Hamilton* (New York: Penguin Press, 2004), 21.

2. Chernow, *Alexander Hamilton*, 20–21.

3. Florence Lewisohn, *St. Croix under Seven Flags* (Hollywood, FL: Dukane Press, 1970), 113.

4. Neville A. T. Hall, *Slave Society in the Danish West Indies: St. Thomas, St. John, and St. Croix* (Baltimore: Johns Hopkins University Press, 1992), 88. Christiansted's population was 2,175 in 1758 and 2,203 in 1766.

5. *Royal Danish American Gazette* (Christiansted, St. Croix), March 9, 1771, 1; May 4, 1771, 1; March 2, 1771, 1; July 8, 1772, 1; August 12, 1772, 1. Quotations appear in the August 12 issue.

6. *Royal Danish American Gazette* (Christiansted, St. Croix), August 22, 1772, 1; August 12, 1772, 1; March 20, 1771, 1; November 14, 1770, 1; September 15, 1770, 1. Quotation appears in the March 20 issue. For the British primacy among the gentry and attendant British influence on the culture of St. Croix, see Hall, *Slave Society*, 15–16.

7. Chernow, *Alexander Hamilton*, 22.

8. H. U. Ramsing, *Alexander Hamilton's Birth and Parentage*, trans. into English by Mrs. S. Vahl (1951), 25.

9. Chernow, *Alexander Hamilton*, 23.

10. Flexner, *Young Hamilton*, 30.

11. The fragmentary nature of church records from this time (some of these records no longer exist and bugs have eaten large portions of the surviving documents) defy conclusive analysis of whether St. Croix's churches recorded Jewish deaths. The case of the Serina family demonstrates the challenge in ascertaining whether the St. John's Episcopal Anglican Church on St. Croix—which marked Rachel Levine's death—recorded Jews in its registers. Under "Baptisms, marriages, burials 1765–1787," the church register has an entry in its baptism file reading, "Rebecca Serina born of Jewish parents May 28th" (1769). If this entry recorded Serina's birth, then plainly it is an instance of a Jew appearing in the register. If, however, this entry is recording the baptism of a Jewish adult converting to Christianity, then Serina's name does not indicate that Jews as such were recorded. One piece of evidence in favor of the former possibility is the fact that those who were baptized usually had two dates listed next to their names—the first of the baptism, the second of the birth. Yet Serina has only one date next to her name, which would support the inference that the entry is recording her birth alone and thus she was Jewish. Then again, in the marriage file, there is an entry for the nuptials of "John Jones and Rebecca Serina" at the home of the Reverend Goodchild listed for August 14, 1769. If we assume that the Rebecca Serina "born of Jewish parents" was the same Rebecca Serina who married John Jones at a clergyman's house, then surely the May 28 entry mentioned does indicate an adult converting to Christianity. Perhaps, however, we ought not be so certain there was only one Rebecca Serina

on St. Croix—there were, for instance, two different people named "Mary" in the Serina family who appear in the church registers. Nor did the name "Mary" necessarily indicate a Christian identity in the Caribbean—see, for example, the Jewish Mary Asser Lyons in "Jacque Judah Lyons," *PAJHS* 21 (1913): xxiii. In the final analysis, the Serina family appears to have had both Jewish and Christian members, but whether St. John's recorded the names of all members or only the latter group remains indeterminate.

To complicate matters further, even a burial in a churchyard did not always indicate a Christian identity in the eighteenth century. David Salisbury Franks, despite always having a Jewish identity, was buried at Christ Church in Philadelphia—see Hersch L. Zitt, "David Salisbury Franks, Revolutionary Patriot (c. 1740–1793)," *Pennsylvania History* 16 (April 1949): 92.

12. Epitaphs in the Jewish cemetery at Christiansted, St. Croix, Virgin Isl., 1957–1958, [SC-13471], AJA.

13. Lewisohn, *St. Croix*, 119.

14. See appendix in Gertrude Atherton, *A Few of Hamilton's Letters, including His Description of the Great West Indian Hurricane of 1772* (New York: Macmillan, 1903). In land registers from the twilight of Rachel's life, she appears under "Lewin," which matches letter for letter how some Levitic Jews spelled their last name in that era—see, for instance, Rigsarkivet (Danish National Archives, Copenhagen), Matrikel for St. Croix (1758–1915) (scanned version); folder 1763–1768, frame 213 #49.

15. Ramsing, *Alexander Hamilton's Birth*, 26.

16. Broadus Mitchell, *Alexander Hamilton: Youth to Maturity, 1758–1788* (New York: Macmillan, 1957), 1:16, 1:478n6.

17. Probate court transaction on estate of Rachel Lavien, [February 19, 1768], *PAH*, 1:1–3.

18. Robert A. Hendrickson, *Hamilton* (New York: Mason/Charter, 1976), 1:17.

19. Willard Sterne Randall, *Alexander Hamilton: A Life* (New York: HarperCollins, 2003), 9.

20. Marie B. Hecht, *Odd Destiny: The Life of Alexander Hamilton* (New York: Macmillan, 1982), 7.

21. The Anglican register reads, "Rachael Levine Feb. 26 at Mr. Tuite's Plant. by D.O. aged 32"—see appendix in Atherton, *Few of Hamilton's Letters*. Cissel likewise doubts that the Reverend Goodchild was present, noting that the register's entry for Rachel's death makes no reference to Goodchild. Cissel surmises that the initials D. O. refer to one Daniel Oxley, who appears in the St. Croix *Matrikler*, and suggests that Oxley was the parish clerk—see "Alexander Hamilton: The West Indian 'Founding Father,'" Christiansted National Historic Site, National Park Service, U.S. Department of the Interior (July 2004), 11, 30n80.

22. Ramsing, *Alexander Hamilton's Birth*, 26.

23. Quotation appears in Ramsing, *Alexander Hamilton's Birth*, 28.

24. Chernow, *Alexander Hamilton*, 26–27.

25. Chernow, *Alexander Hamilton*, 27–28.

26. Erik J. Lawaetz, *St. Croix: 500 Years Pre-Columbus to 1990* (Herning, Denmark: Poul Kristensen, 1991), 307.

27. Chernow, *Alexander Hamilton*, 29, 32.

28. Thomas K. McCraw, *The Founders and Finance: How Hamilton, Gallatin, and Other Immigrants Forged a New Economy* (Cambridge, MA: Harvard University Press, 2012), 15–17.

29. Chernow, *Alexander Hamilton*, 31.

30. Alexander Hamilton to Tileman Cruger, February 1, 177[2], *PAH*, 1:23.

31. Alexander Hamilton to William Newton, February 1, 177[2], *PAH*, 1:24.

32. Alexander Hamilton to Nicholas Cruger, November 12, 1771, *PAH*, 1:11.

33. Michael E. Newton, *Discovering Hamilton* (Phoenix: Eleftheria, 2019), 189–190. Newton, who discovered this document, accepts the conventional wisdom that Hamilton was a lifelong Christian and does not discuss why Hamilton failed to receive communion.

34. *The Book of Common Prayer* (1662). While eighteenth-century Anglican theologians differed on the precise "age of discretion," plainly the practice of communion was common enough for youths on St. Croix that the court made it a prerequisite for a seventeen-year-old to provide sworn testimony. For discussion of the proper age for confirmation (and thereby communion), see Holly Brewer, *By Birth or Consent: Children, Law, and the Anglo-American Revolution in Authority* (Chapel Hill: University of North Carolina Press, 2005), 70; Robert Cornwall, "The Rite of Confirmation in Anglican Thought during the Eighteenth Century," *Church History* 68 (June 1999): 370.

35. Alexander Hamilton to Edward Stevens, November 11, 1769, *PAH*, 1:4.

36. See, for instance, Mordechai Arbell, *The Jewish Nation of the Caribbean: The Spanish-Portuguese Jewish Settlements in the Caribbean and the Guianas* (Jerusalem: Gefen, 2002), 223.

37. Chernow, *Alexander Hamilton*, 35.

38. Hugh Knox, *Discourses on the Truth of Revealed Religion and Other Important Subjects* (London: Thomas Cadell, 1768), 1:152, 197–198.

39. Jacob Rader Marcus, *The Colonial American Jew, 1492–1776* (Detroit: Wayne State University Press, 1970), 2:1090–1091.

40. *The Oxford Magazine* 8 (November 1772): 199.

41. Alexander Hamilton to the *Royal Danish American Gazette*, September 6, 1772, *PAH*, 1:35–36.

42. John C. Hamilton, *The Life of Alexander Hamilton* (New York: D. Appleton, 1840), 1:7.

43. Flexner, *Young Hamilton*, 49–50.

44. Nathan Schachner, "Alexander Hamilton Viewed by His Friends: The Narratives of Robert Troup and Hercules Mulligan," *William and Mary Quarterly* 4 (April 1947): 209.

45. Chernow, *Alexander Hamilton*, 42.

46. Miscellany, 1711–1820; Hamilton, Alexander; School exercises; Notes on Genesis and Revelations, 1773, box 38, reel 31, frame 13664, AHP.

47. Schachner, "Alexander Hamilton," 209–210.

48. Newton, *Discovering Hamilton*, 5.

49. Richard Brookhiser, *Alexander Hamilton, American* (New York: Free Press, 1999), 16; Flexner, *Young Hamilton*, 18; Hecht, *Odd Destiny*, 4; Forrest McDonald, *Alexander Hamilton: A Biography* (New York: W. W. Norton, 1979), 7. Other biographers subscribe to a 1755 birth year—see, for instance, Noemie Emery, *Alexander Hamilton: An Intimate Portrait* (New York: G. P. Putnam's Sons, 1982), 16; Jacob Ernest Cooke, *Alexander Hamilton* (New York: Charles Scribner's Sons, 1982), 2; Mitchell, *Alexander Hamilton*, 1:11–13; Chernow, *Alexander Hamilton*, 16–17; John C. Miller, *Alexander Hamilton: Portrait in Paradox* (New York: Harper & Brothers, 1959), 3.

50. Newton, *Discovering Hamilton*, 8.

51. To the Royal Danish American Gazette, [April 6, 1771], *PAH*, 1:6, 7n1.

52. Probate court transaction on estate of Rachel Lavien, [February 19, 1768], *PAH*, 1:3.

53. Newton, *Discovering Hamilton*, 8.

54. Robert McCaughey, *Stand, Columbia: A History of Columbia University in the City of New York, 1754–2004* (New York: Columbia University Press, 2003), 36.

55. Even after Hamilton's undergraduate tenure at King's College, he retained a boyish appearance. One contemporary recalled that in late 1776, "Hamilton's company marched into Princeton. It was a model of discipline; at their head was a boy, and I wondered at his youth; but what was my surprise, when struck with his diminutive figure, he was pointed out to me as that Hamilton of whom we had already heard so much"—quotation appears in John C. Hamilton, *Life of Alexander Hamilton*, 1:57.

56. David C. Humphrey, *From King's College to Columbia, 1746–1800* (New York: Columbia University Press, 1976), 112.

57. Bayrd Still, *Mirror for Gotham: New York as Seen by Contemporaries from Dutch Days to the Present* (1956; repr., New York: Fordham University Press, 1994), 34.

58. Humphrey, *From King's College*, 114–115, 185, 205–206.

59. McCaughey, *Stand, Columbia*, 34.

60. Humphrey, *From King's College*, 205, 190, 194; Leon Hühner, "Jews in Connection with the Colleges of the Thirteen Original States Prior to 1800," *PAJHS* 19 (1910): 118.

61. Humphrey, *From King's College*, 128, 135, 166, 176, 182.

62. Schachner, "Alexander Hamilton," 212–213; Humphrey, *From King's College*, 200. The first college president of King's offered tutoring in Hebrew before Hamilton arrived, and a professorship of "Oriental" languages, including Hebrew, was created in 1792, but it remains unclear if undergraduates could seek Hebrew instruction during Hamilton's tenure on campus—see Humphrey, *From King's College*, 163, 295.

63. Humphrey, *From King's College*, 187, 202–203, 160.

64. Alexander Hamilton to James A. Bayard, August 6, 1800, *PAH*, 25:56.

65. Humphrey, *From King's College*, 162, 226.

66. Schachner, "Alexander Hamilton," 213.

67. Douglass Adair and Marvin Harvey, "Was Alexander Hamilton a Christian Statesman?," *William and Mary Quarterly* 12 (April 1995): 314.

68. Schachner, "Alexander Hamilton," 206.

69. Thomas Jefferson to William Short, September 8, 1823, in *The Writings of Thomas Jefferson*, ed. H. A. Washington (1854; repr., New York: Cambridge University Press, 2011), 7:310.

70. Diary entry, August 23, 1774, *PJAD*, 2:109.

71. Howard B. Rock, *Haven of Liberty: New York Jews in the New World, 1654–1865* (New York: New York University Press, 2012), 72. Note that this book is part of a three-volume set by Rock, Deborah Dash Moore, Jeffrey S. Gurock, Annie Polland, and Daniel Soyer, *City of Promises: A History of the Jews of New York* (New York: New York University Press, 2012).

72. Still, *Mirror for Gotham*, 34–35.

73. Thomas Pownall and Samuel Holland, *The provinces of New York and New Jersey; with part of Pensilvania, and the province of Quebec* (London: Robt. Sayer & John Bennett, 1776),

Library of Congress, Geography and Map Division. Refer to this map for locations of sites in New York City described in this chapter.

74. Alexander J. Wall, *The Equestrian Statue of George III and the Pedestrian Statue of William Pitt* (New York: New York Historical Society, 1920), 37, 50, 54.

75. Still, *Mirror for Gotham*, 34–35.

76. John Adams to Benjamin Rush, November 11, 1806, in John Adams, Benjamin Rush, Julia Stockton Rush, and Alexander Biddle, *Old Family Letters* (Philadelphia: J. B. Lippincott, 1892), 118.

77. Carl Bridenbaugh, *Cities in Revolt: Urban Life in America, 1743–1776* (New York: Alfred A. Knopf, 1955), 384.

78. Still, *Mirror for Gotham*, 36.

79. Edwin G. Burrows and Mike Wallace, *Gotham: A History of New York City to 1898* (New York: Oxford University Press, 1999), 213–214.

80. Still, *Mirror for Gotham*, 35.

Chapter 3

1. William Pencak, *Jews and Gentiles in Early America, 1654–1800* (Ann Arbor: University of Michigan Press, 2005), 19, 37; Jonathan D. Sarna, "The Mystical World of Colonial American Jews," in *Mediating Modernity: Challenges and Trends in the Jewish Encounter with the Modern World*, ed. Lauren B. Strauss and Michael Brenner (Detroit: Wayne State University Press, 2008), 186–188.

2. Jacob Rader Marcus, *Early American Jewry*, vol. 1: *The Jews of New York, New England, and Canada, 1649–1794* (Philadelphia: Jewish Publication Society of America, 1951), 25.

3. Leonard Dinnerstein, *Antisemitism in America* (New York: Oxford University Press, 1994), 5.

4. Howard B. Rock, *Haven of Liberty: New York Jews in the New World, 1654–1865* (New York: New York University Press, 2012), 26.

5. Dinnerstein, *Antisemitism in America*, 6.

6. Rock, *Haven of Liberty*, 55.

7. Jacob R. Marcus, "The American Colonial Jew: A Study in Acculturation," in *The American Jewish Experience*, ed. Jonathan D. Sarna (New York: Holmes & Meier, 1986), 10; Rock, *Haven of Liberty*, 44–46; Jacob Rader Marcus, *The Colonial American Jew, 1492–1776* (Detroit: Wayne State University Press, 1970), 2:905.

8. Quotations appear in Carl Bridenbaugh, ed., *Gentleman's Progress: The Itinerarium of Dr. Alexander Hamilton, 1744* (Chapel Hill: University of North Carolina Press, 1948), 178.

9. Rock, *Haven of Liberty*, 46.

10. Rock, *Haven of Liberty*, 45, 46, 49. For a discussion of the role of kosher meat in relationships between Jewish communities, see Laura Arnold Leibman, *Messianism, Secrecy, and Mysticism: A New Interpretation of Early American Jewish Life* (London: Vallentine Mitchell, 2012), 189–192.

11. Leo Hershkowitz, ed., *Wills of Early New York Jews (1704–1799)* (New York: American Jewish Historical Society, 1967), 70.

12. Rock, *Haven of Liberty*, 48.

13. Abraham I. Abrahams to Moses Seixas, June 1, 1772, in Frank Zimmerman, "A Letter and Memorandum on Ritual Circumcision, 1772," *PAJHS* 44 (September 1954): 60.

14. Rock, *Haven of Liberty*, 48, 65; Marcus, *Colonial American Jew*, 2:988–991.

15. Rock, *Haven of Liberty*, 28–41.

16. Rock, *Haven of Liberty*, 38–40; Eli Faber, *Jews, Slaves, and the Slave Trade: Setting the Record Straight* (New York: New York University Press, 1998), 132; Leslie M. Harris, "The Greatest City in the World? Slavery in New York in the Age of Hamilton," in *Historians on Hamilton: How a Blockbuster Musical Is Restaging America's Past*, ed. Renee C. Romano and Claire Bond Potter (New Brunswick, NJ: Rutgers University Press, 2018), 79–81.

17. Rock, *Haven of Liberty*, 46.

18. Pencak, *Jews and Gentiles*, 14–15.

19. Pencak, *Jews and Gentiles*, 56–57, 60–62.

20. Jonathan D. Sarna, *American Judaism: A History* (New Haven, CT: Yale University Press, 2004), 29, 20–22.

21. Dinnerstein, *Antisemitism in America*, 3.

22. Dinnerstein, *Antisemitism in America*, 7; Marcus, "American Colonial Jew," 8–9, 16.

23. Rock, *Haven of Liberty*, 66, 40–41.

24. Dinnerstein, *Antisemitism in America*, 4. Fritz Hirschfeld places the Jewish population at 1,500–2,500 in *George Washington and the Jews* (Newark: University of Delaware Press, 2005), 13.

25. David A. Gerber, "Anti-Semitism and Jewish-Gentile Relations in American Historiography and the American Past," in *Anti-Semitism in American History*, ed. David A. Gerber (Champaign: University of Illinois Press, 1986), 14.

26. Marcus, *Colonial American Jew*, 3:1127.

27. Samuel Oppenheim, "Disgraceful Acts of a Mob at a Jewish Funeral in New York, 1743," *PAJHS* 31 (1928): 240.

28. Pencak, *Jews and Gentiles*, 2; Marcus, *Colonial American Jew*, 3:1127–1128.

29. Robert Rogers, *A Concise Account of North America* (London: J. Millar, 1765), 65–66.

30. Marcus, *Colonial American Jew*, 3:1123, 3:1121.

31. Gerard G. Beekman to Metcalf Bowler, February 14, 1760, in *The Beekman Mercantile Papers, 1746–1799*, ed. Philip L. White (New York: New York Historical Society, 1956), 1:352.

32. Pencak, *Jews and Gentiles*, x.

33. Rock, *Haven of Liberty*, 66, 71–72.

34. Robert Middlekauff, *The Glorious Cause: The American Revolution, 1763–1789*, rev. and expanded ed. (New York: Oxford University Press, 2005), 276–278, 316–317, 347; Pauline Maier, *American Scripture: Making the Declaration of Independence* (New York: Knopf, 1997), 156.

35. Rock, *Haven of Liberty*, 75–76.

36. Rock estimates that before the war New York had 250 Jews and that during the war thirty Jewish Loyalists lived in the city—see *Haven of Liberty*, 71, 80. Meanwhile, Pencak tallies sixteen confirmed Jewish Loyalists compared to "twenty-some patriots"—see *Jews and Gentiles*, 62. It is difficult to state with certainty the proportion of New York Jewry that sided with the Patriots versus the Loyalists. For one, not all Jewish Loyalists who were in New York during the war had

lived in New York prior to the Revolution. Moreover, Jews, like other Americans, sometimes switched their fealties in the course of the war. Pencak rightly insists, "It is best not to interpret the various numbers too precisely but to regard them as exemplifying not only a community, but many individuals, whose allegiances were divided and in flux"—see *Jews and Gentiles*, 65. Despite uncertainty over exact numbers, there is consensus among scholars that most New York Jews were Patriots.

37. Rock, *Haven of Liberty*, 78–79.

38. Richard Morris, "The Jews, Minorities, and Dissent in the American Revolution," in *Migration and Settlement: Proceedings of the Anglo-American Jewish Historical Conference Held in London Jointly by the Jewish Historical Society of England and the American Jewish Historical Society, July 1970* (London: Jewish Historical Society of England, 1971), 152.

39. Rock, *Haven of Liberty*, 75–78; Sarna, *American Judaism*, 31, 33.

40. Ron Chernow, *Alexander Hamilton* (New York: Penguin Press, 2004), 62–63, 72–73, 80, 84.

41. George Washington to Lieutenant Colonel Joseph Reed, January 23, 1776, *PGWR*, 3:173.

42. Karl-Friedrich Walling, *Republican Empire: Alexander Hamilton on War and Free Government* (Lawrence: University Press of Kansas, 1999), 1.

43. Quotation appears in Myron Magnet, *The Founders at Home: The Building of America, 1735–1817* (New York: W. W. Norton, 2014), 273.

44. Quotation appears in John C. Hamilton, *The Life of Alexander Hamilton* (New York: D. Appleton, 1840), 1:69.

45. Harry MacNeill Bland and Virginia W. Northcott, "The Life Portraits of Alexander Hamilton," *William and Mary Quarterly* 12 (April 1955): 187–188; Chernow, *Alexander Hamilton*, 51, 128–129.

46. Eulogy on Nathanael Greene, [July 4, 1789], *PAH*, 5:348.

47. Quotation appears in Tench Tilghman to William Tilghman, May 12, 1780, in *Memoir of Lieut. Col. Tench Tilghman* (Albany, NY: J. Munsell, 1876), 173; see also Chernow, *Alexander Hamilton*, 129–131, 136, 147.

48. As David L. Holmes notes of George Washington, Thomas Jefferson, James Madison, and James Monroe, "All of these men . . . continued to worship at least occasionally in the church of their ancestors"—see *The Faiths of the Founding Fathers* (New York: Oxford University Press, 2006), 36–37. Douglass Adair and Marvin Harvey, meanwhile, characterize this time in Hamilton's life as a "period of complete religious indifference" in "Was Alexander Hamilton a Christian Statesman?," *William and Mary Quarterly* 12 (April 1955): 314. See also Chernow, *Alexander Hamilton*, 132.

49. Benjamin Franklin, *Autobiography of Benjamin Franklin*, ed. John Bigelow (Philadelphia: J. B. Lippincott, 1868), 211–212.

50. Marcus, *Early American Jewry*, 1:252; Gerald E. Hart, *The Quebec Act, 1774* (Montreal: Gazette Printing Company, 1891), 12; Hersch L. Zitt, "David Salisbury Franks, Revolutionary Patriot (c. 1740–1793)," *Pennsylvania History* 16 (April 1949): 77; David Salisbury Franks to George Washington, May 12, 1789, *PGWP*, 2:278.

51. Marcus, *Early American Jewry*, 1:253–254.

52. Samuel Rezneck, *Unrecognized Patriots: The Jews in the American Revolution* (Westport, CT: Greenwood Press, 1975), 28–29.

53. Chernow, *Alexander Hamilton*, 140.

54. Chernow, *Alexander Hamilton*, 140.

55. D. A. B. Ronald, *The Life of John André: The Redcoat Who Turned Benedict Arnold* (Philadelphia: Casemate, 2019), 241.

56. Jared Sparks, *The Life and Treason of Benedict Arnold* (Boston: Hilliard, Gray, 1835), 230; Chernow, *Alexander Hamilton*, 140; Ronald, *Life of John André*, 241. Hamilton's correspondence makes clear that he was already acquainted with Franks before this episode—see Alexander Hamilton to Baron von Steuben, [July 23, 1780], *PAH*, 2:366–367.

57. Willard Sterne Randall, *Benedict Arnold: Patriot and Traitor* (New York: William Morrow, 1990), 558.

58. Benedict Arnold to George Washington, September 25, 1780, *PAH*, 2:440.

59. David Salisbury Franks to George Washington, October 16, 1780, GWP, series 4, General Correspondence, reel 71. See also Abraham S. Wolf Rosenbach, "Documents Relative to Major David S. Franks while Aid-de-Camp to General Arnold," *PAJHS* 5 (1897): 174, 159, 165; Zitt, "David Salisbury Franks," 81–82.

60. George Washington to David Salisbury Franks, October 21, 1780, GWP, series 4, General Correspondence, reel 71. Regarding Hamilton's authorship of the letter, see *PAH*, 2:485.

61. Quotation appears in Rezneck, *Unrecognized Patriots*, 30.

62. David Salisbury Franks to George Washington, November 24, 1780, GWP, series 4, General Correspondence, reel 72.

63. Pencak, *Jews and Gentiles*, 210.

64. Leibman, *Messianism, Secrecy, and Mysticism*, 243.

65. Pencak, *Jews and Gentiles*, 209–211. Pencak suggests that "anti-semitism" was "probably at work" (p. 209) in the Franks affair and concludes, "Franks's repeated defense of his honor, and insistence that a court clear his name when Washington and other generals were willing to drop the matter, typifies the behavior of colonial Jews in general. Realizing the existence of anti-semitism, they struck back verbally whenever criticized to make sure popular rumors and insinuations were at least formally refuted" (p. 211).

66. Joseph R. Rosenbloom, *A Biographical Dictionary of Early American Jews: Colonial Times through 1800* (1960; repr., Lexington: University of Kentucky Press, 2015), 39; Arthur Hertzberg, *The Jews in America: Four Centuries of an Uneasy Encounter: A History* (1989; repr., New York: Columbia University Press, 1997), 70.

67. Hirschfeld, *George Washington and the Jews*, 111.

68. [Diary entry: November 16, 1789], *PGWD*, 5:498.

69. During the Constitutional Convention, Washington dined at the home of a Mr. Prager, according to his diary. The editors of the *Papers of George Washington* write that the Prager mentioned in the diary was "probably" Mark Prager, whom they describe as a "nonprofessing Jew from England"—see [Diary entry: June 21, 1787], *PGWD*, 5:170; and *PGWC*, 1:532n1.

70. Zitt, "David Salisbury Franks," 92.

71. George Washington to Oliver Wolcott Jr., October 14, 1793, *PGWP*, 14:215.

72. Franks was not the only Jewish veteran to seek employment from Washington during the latter's presidency. Solomon Bush, who had earned the rank of lieutenant colonel during the war, suggested himself for a diplomatic post in London in 1789. Washington, while writing

back genially, did not grace Bush with a job—see Hirschfeld, *George Washington and the Jews,* 115, 119.

73. Max M. Edling, *A Hercules in the Cradle: War, Money, and the American State, 1783–1867* (Chicago: University of Chicago Press, 2014), 24–25; Janet A. Riesman, "Money, Credit, and the Federalist Political Economy," in *Beyond Confederation: Origins of the Constitution and American National Identity,* ed. Richard Beeman, Stephen Botein, and Edward C. Carter (Chapel Hill: University of North Carolina Press, 1987), 128.

74. Pay Book of the State Company of Artillery, [1777], *PAH,* 1:382. For the source of Hamilton's knowledge about Jewish commerce in Prague, see the entry for "Bohemia" in Jacques Savary des Brûlons, *The universal dictionary of trade and commerce, translated from the French of the celebrated Monsieur Savary, Inspector-General of the Manufactures for the King, at the Custom-House of Paris: With Large Additions and Improvements, Incorporated throughout the Whole Work; Which more particularly accommodate the same to the Trade and Navigation Of these Kingdoms, And the Laws, Customs, and Usages, To which all Traders are subject. By Malachy Postlethwayt, Esq,* 2nd ed. (London: J. Knapton, 1757), 1:302–303.

75. Jane Frances Amler, *Haym Salomon: Patriot Banker of the American Revolution* (New York: Rosen Publishing Group, 2004), 64.

76. Quoted in Marcus, *Colonial American Jew,* 3:1122. Morris saw his wealth evaporate after engaging in land speculation that failed to yield the spectacular profits he imagined. In 1798, Morris was confined to debtors' prison—see Ryan K. Smith, *Robert Morris' Folly: The Architectural and Financial Failures of an American Founder* (New Haven, CT: Yale University Press, 2014), 6–7.

77. Chernow, *Alexander Hamilton,* 155.

78. Alexander Hamilton to Robert Morris, April 30, 1781, AHP, box 1, reel 1, frames 410–433.

79. Alexander Hamilton to Robert Morris, [April 30, 1781], *PAH,* 2:606, 617.

80. Robert Morris to Alexander Hamilton, May 26, 1781, *PAH,* 2:645–646.

81. *Journals of the Continental Congress, 1774–1789* (Washington, DC: Government Printing Office, 1912), 20:546; Richard Sylla and David J. Cowen, eds., *Alexander Hamilton on Finance, Credit, and Debt* (New York: Columbia University Press, 2018), 36.

82. Alexander Hamilton to Robert Morris, [April 30, 1781], *PAH,* 2:632.

83. Amler, *Haym Salomon,* 6, 10, 16, 22–23, 26–27; quotation appears on 26. The limited literature on Salomon is riddled with errors, the residue of concerted efforts by later generations of Jews to aggrandize his role in the Revolution and trade on his embellished legacy to legitimize their presence in the United States—see generally Max J. Kohler, *Haym Salomon, Patriot Broker of the Revolution: His Real Achievements and Their Exaggeration: An Open Letter to Congressman Celler* (1931), Milton Gottesman Rare Book Collection, AJHS. In an indication of how little scholarship exists on Salomon, Pencak describes Charles Edward Russell's 1930 book *Haym Salomon and the Revolution* as "the modern biography of Salomon" (*Jews and Gentiles,* 294n90). Morris U. Schappes warns, "Legends and falsifications, however, die hard. . . . To be used with special precautions is the one biography of Salomon, Charles Edward Russell, *Haym Salomon and the Revolution*"—see *A Documentary History of the Jews in the United States, 1654–1875* (New York: Citadel Press, 1950), 579n2. Amler's book, while written for a lay readership and without citations, is the most recent and most accurate monograph on Salomon's life.

84. Amler, *Haym Salomon*, 33, 36, 38, 40, 43, 52–53; quotation appears on 56.

85. Amler, *Haym Salomon*, 64, 67, 73.

86. Amler, *Haym Salomon*, 67, 75.

87. Amler, *Haym Salomon*, 90, 80; Cash Book, [March 1, 1782–1791], *PAH*, 3:12.

88. Amler, *Haym Salomon*, 92–95.

89. Chernow, *Alexander Hamilton*, 149–165. Quotation appears in Alexander Hamilton to George Washington, [November 22, 1780], *PAH*, 2:509.

90. Chernow, *Alexander Hamilton*, 165.

91. Alexander Hamilton to Elizabeth Hamilton, [1782], *PAH*, 3:235.

Chapter 4

1. Ron Chernow, *Alexander Hamilton* (New York: Penguin Press, 2004), 168–169.

2. Chernow, *Alexander Hamilton*, 184–185.

3. Howard B. Rock, *Haven of Liberty: New York Jews in the New World, 1654–1865* (New York: New York University Press, 2012), 79–80, 86.

4. *LPAH*, 2:viii. Although no longer part of the British Empire, American courts continued to selectively use English law at their discretion. American lawyers sometimes argued for the continued validity of any given English doctrine but could just as readily dismiss its value and propose alternatives.

5. Jacob Rader Marcus, *Early American Jewry*, vol. 1: *The Jews of New York, New England, and Canada, 1649–1794* (Philadelphia: Jewish Publication Society of America, 1951), 163.

6. Jacob Rader Marcus, *American Jewry: Documents, Eighteenth Century* (Cincinnati: Hebrew Union College Press, 1959), 393.

7. Marcus, *Early American Jewry*, 1:164.

8. David de la Sola Pool, *Portraits Etched in Stone: Early Jewish Settlers, 1682–1831* (1952; repr., New York: Columbia University Press, 1953), 283–284.

9. Solomon Simpson v. Ebenezer Jones (1784), series JN519-17, New York State Supreme Court of Judicature judgment rolls and other documents on parchment, 1684–1848 (bulk 1765–1810), bundle 87, #K-5, NYSA.

10. Chernow, *Alexander Hamilton*, 191, 74, 85, 126, 169, 185–186, 287, 389, 660–661.

11. Chernow, *Alexander Hamilton*, 16, 24–25, 191, 74, 192.

12. Quotation appears in Eugene L. Didier, "Aaron Burr as a Lawyer," *Green Bag* 14 (October 1902): 453.

13. Didier, "Aaron Burr as a Lawyer," 454.

14. Tully No. III, [August 28, 1794], *PAH*, 17:159.

15. Chernow, *Alexander Hamilton*, 190.

16. Didier, "Aaron Burr as a Lawyer," 457–458.

17. Jacob Rader Marcus, *Early American Jewry*, vol. 2: *The Jews of Pennsylvania and the South, 1655–1790* (Philadelphia: Jewish Publication Society of America, 1953), 60; Rock, *Haven of Liberty*, 95; Leon Hühner, "Jews Interested in Privateering in America during the Eighteenth Century," *PAJHS* 23 (1915): 173–174.

18. Rock, *Haven of Liberty*, 78, 83–84; N. Taylor Phillips, "Unwritten History," *American Jewish Archives Journal* 6 (June 1954): 85.

19. Marcus, *Early American Jewry*, 1:99.

20. Jane Frances Amler, *Haym Salomon: Patriot Banker of the American Revolution* (New York: Rosen Publishing Group, 2004), 57, 80; Rock, *Haven of Liberty*, 84.

21. Rock, *Haven of Liberty*, 83–84.

22. Amler, *Haym Salomon*, 64.

23. Quotation appears in Marcus, *American Jewry: Documents*, 427.

24. Sabato Morais, "Mickve Israel Congregation of Philadelphia," *PAJHS* 1 (1893): 14–17. On the meaning of "Mikveh Israel," see Laura Arnold Leibman, *Messianism, Secrecy, and Mysticism: A New Interpretation of Early American Jewish Life* (London: Valentine Mitchell, 2012), 33–34.

25. "Items relating to Congregation Shearith Israel, New York," *PAJHS* 27 (1920): 33–34; Constitution of New York, April 20, 1777. For Moses's service as the Shearith Israel president in 1784, see 26 Elul 5544, "Congregation Shearith Israel 18th–20th Century," RG 370, reel 1, YIVO.

26. William Pencak, *Jews and Gentiles in Early America, 1654–1800* (Ann Arbor: University of Michigan Press, 2005), 66.

27. Jonathan D. Sarna, *American Judaism: A History* (New Haven, CT: Yale University Press, 2004), 29.

28. Joseph R. Rosenbloom, *A Biographical Dictionary of Early American Jews: Colonial Times through 1800* (1960; repr., Lexington: University of Kentucky Press, 2015), 120; Chernow, *Alexander Hamilton*, 199–201; Richard Sylla and David J. Cowen, eds., *Alexander Hamilton on Finance, Credit, and Debt* (New York: Columbia University Press, 2018), 59.

29. Rosenbloom, *Biographical Dictionary*, 128–129; Marcus, *Early American Jewry*, 2:193.

30. Samuel Rezneck, *Unrecognized Patriots: The Jews in the American Revolution* (Westport, CT: Greenwood Press, 1975), 50–52.

31. Following the British exit from Philadelphia in 1778, that city became a nexus for exiled Jews from Newport, New York, Charleston, and Savannah—see Pencak, *Jews and Gentiles*, 211.

32. Marcus, *Early American Jewry*, 2:193, 196, 201.

33. Marcus, *Early American Jewry*, 2:193–195.

34. Marcus, *Early American Jewry*, 2:194–195.

35. Marcus, *Early American Jewry*, 2:196–198; *LPAH*, 5:319n3; Alexander Hamilton to Jeremiah Wadsworth, April 7, 1785, *PAH*, 3:601.

36. Jeremiah Wadsworth to Alexander Hamilton, April 3, 1785, *PAH*, 3:600.

37. Alexander Hamilton to Jeremiah Wadsworth, April 7, 1785, *PAH*, 3:602.

38. Chernow, *Alexander Hamilton*, 133–134.

39. Quotation appears in Allan McLane Hamilton, *The Intimate Life of Alexander Hamilton* (New York: Charles Scribner's Sons, 1910), 259–260.

40. *LPAH*, 5:319n3; Marcus, *Early American Jewry*, 2:198, 201; Rock, *Haven of Liberty*, 45. Hamilton had a formal relationship with Moses's firm before becoming a trustee, having already represented the firm in a lawsuit—see *LPAH*, 5:319n3.

41. Marcus, *Early American Jewry*, 2:198–203.

42. Rosenbloom, *Biographical Dictionary*, 128–129; Rezneck, *Unrecognized Patriots*, 72.

43. John B. Church to Alexander Hamilton, April 5, 1786, *PAH*, 3:657.

44. Vere Langford Oliver, ed., *Caribbeana: Being Miscellaneous Papers Relating to the History, Genealogy, Topography, and Antiquities of the British West Indies* (London: Mitchell Hughes and Clarke, 1910–1919), 1:324–328.

45. James Thomas Flexner, *The Young Hamilton: A Biography* (Boston: Little, Brown, 1978), 29.

46. The back of a letter from Alexander to his brother James Jr. dated June 23, 1785—housed in the Alexander Hamilton Papers, Manuscript and Archives Division, New York Public Library—indicates that James was living on St. Thomas.

47. Alexander Hamilton to James Hamilton, June 22, 1785, *PAH*, 3:617–618.

48. H. U. Ramsing suggests that James Jr. "probably died in 1786"—see *Alexander Hamilton's Birth and Parentage*, trans. into English by Mrs. S. Vahl (1951), 29.

49. Robert McCaughey, *Stand, Columbia: A History of Columbia University in the City of New York, 1754–2004* (New York: Columbia University Press, 2003), 50–52. Quotation appears in the 1787 charter, reprinted in John B. Pine, *Charters, Acts of the Legislature, Official Documents and Records*, rev. ed. (New York, 1920), 45.

50. *A History of Columbia University, 1754–1904* (New York: Columbia University Press, 1904), 67–68, 42; Flexner, *Young Hamilton*, 62.

51. Pine, *Charters, Acts of the Legislature*, 12, 22, 46. The 1784 charter was religiously pluralistic with respect to faculty but—unlike the 1787 charter that superseded it—made no provision regarding the presidency: "no professor shall in any wise whatsoever be accounted ineligible, for, or by reason of any religious tenet or tenets, that he may or shall profess, or be compelled by any by-law or otherwise to take any religious test-oath whatsoever," p. 40.

52. Martha Mitchell, *Encyclopedia Brunoniana* (Providence, RI: Brown University Library, 1993), 137; Richard P. McCormick, *Rutgers: A Bicentennial History* (New Brunswick, NJ: Rutgers University Press, 1966), 155. Brown required that its president be Baptist until 1926; Rutgers, that its president be of the Reformed Church until 1920.

53. Pine, *Charters, Acts of the Legislature*, 46.

54. Pine, *Charters, Acts of the Legislature*, 45n1; McCaughey, *Stand, Columbia*, 55.

55. Pine, *Charters, Acts of the Legislature*, 44; Frederic Cople Jaher, *A Scapegoat in the New Wilderness: The Origins and Rise of Anti-Semitism in America* (Cambridge, MA: Harvard University Press, 1996), 125.

56. Jacob Rader Marcus, *The Handsome Young Priest in the Black Gown: The Personal World of Gershom Seixas* (Cincinnati: American Jewish Archives, 1970), 23. The second Jewish board member at Columbia was Benjamin Cardozo, a descendant of Seixas and later a member of the U.S. Supreme Court.

57. Pine, *Charters, Acts of the Legislature*, 46. James Duane was the mayor; (Henry) Brockholst Livingston was the future U.S. Supreme Court justice.

58. Gershom Seixas served as a trustee from 1787 to 1815 (see Leon Hühner, "Jews in Connection with the Colleges of the Thirteen Original States Prior to 1800," *PAJHS* 19 [1910]: 119), while Hamilton served from 1787 to 1804 (see *PAH*, 25:581–582n6).

59. Marcus, *Handsome Young Priest*, 1, 8, 11; Rosenbloom, *Biographical Dictionary*, 95 (see entry for Rachel Levy) and 154–155; Max I. Dimont, *The Jews in America: The Roots, History, and Destiny of American Jews* (New York: Simon and Schuster, 1978), 92.

60. "Items Relating to the Seixas Family," *PAJHS* 27 (1920): 171.

61. Sarna, *American Judaism*, 33.

62. "Items Relating to Gershom M. Seixas," *PAJHS* 27 (1920): 126.

63. Pencak, *Jews and Gentiles*, 65; N. Taylor Phillips, "The Levy and Seixas Families of New-port and New York," *PAJHS* 4 (1896): 205.

64. Marcus, *American Jewry: Documents*, 130–132. On Moses's wealth, see Rock, *Haven of Liberty*, 84.

65. Gershom Seixas to Hayman Levy, December 21, 1783, Papers of Seixas Family, *P-60, box 1, folder 10, AJHS.

66. Marcus, *Handsome Young Priest*, 1.

67. "Items Relating to Gershom M. Seixas," 135. Seixas was still having issues with his salary in 1785, complaining to the trustees, "I require some certain assurances of my salary being punc-tually paid when due" and noting that he was still owed backpay from 1776—see Gershom Seixas to the Trustees of K. K. Shearith Israel, September 22, 1785, Papers of Seixas Family, *P-60, box 1, folder 10, AJHS.

68. "Items Relating to Gershom M. Seixas," 129. Idle chatter during prayer was not unique to New York Jewry. Benjamin Rush attended a Jewish wedding in Philadelphia and was struck by "the freedom with which some of them conversed with each other during the whole time of this part of their worship"—see Benjamin Rush to Julia Rush, June 27, 1787, in *The Jew in the American World*, ed. Jacob Rader Marcus (Detroit: Wayne State University Press, 1996), 140.

69. Marcus, *Handsome Young Priest*, 4–5, 27.

70. Marcus, *Handsome Young Priest*, 21–22, 25.

71. Quotation appears in Shalom Goldman, "Two American Hebrew Orations, 1799 and 1800," *Hebrew Annual Review* 13 (1991): 39.

72. Hühner, "Jews in Connection with the Colleges," 102, 106, 118–120.

73. For Hamilton's call for the convention, see Address of the Annapolis Convention, [Sep-tember 14, 1786], *PAH*, 3:686–690.

74. Melvin I. Urofsky and Paul Finkelman, *March of Liberty: A Constitutional History of the United States* (New York: Oxford University Press, 2011), 1:94–97.

75. Urofsky and Finkelman, *March of Liberty*, 1:100–102.

Chapter 5

1. *Pennsylvania Gazette* (Philadelphia), August 29, 1751, 2.

2. William Pencak, "Jews and Anti-Semitism in Early Pennsylvania," *Pennsylvania Magazine of History and Biography* 126 (July 2002): 380.

3. Quotation appears in Susan E. Klepp and Karin Wulf, eds., *The Diary of Hannah Callender Sansom* (Ithaca, NY: Cornell University Press, 2009), 114. See also Pencak, "Jews and Anti-Semitism," 381.

4. Quotations appear in Edwin Wolf (2nd) and Maxwell Whiteman, *The History of the Jews of Philadelphia from Colonial Times to the Age of Jackson* (Philadelphia: Jewish Publication So-ciety of America, 1956), 45.

5. Quoted in Jacob Rader Marcus, *The Colonial American Jew, 1492–1776* (Detroit: Wayne State University Press, 1970), 3:1132.

6. Pencak, "Jews and Anti-Semitism," 371.

7. Frame of Government of Pennsylvania, May 5, 1682.

8. *Pennsylvania Evening Post* (Philadelphia), September 10, 1776, 448.

9. *Pennsylvania Evening Post* (Philadelphia), September 24, 1776, 476.

10. *Pennsylvania Evening Post* (Philadelphia), September 26, 1776, 479.

11. Quotation appears in Morton Borden, *Jews, Turks, and Infidels* (Chapel Hill: University of North Carolina Press, 1984), 11.

12. Spinoza denied that he was an atheist—see Steven Nadler, *Spinoza: A Life* (New York: Cambridge University Press, 1999), 246.

13. Constitution of Pennsylvania, September 28, 1776.

14. Borden, *Jews, Turks, and Infidels*, 11; William Pencak, *Jews and Gentiles in Early America, 1654–1800* (Ann Arbor: University of Michigan Press, 2005), 217.

15. Quotation appears in Wolf and Whiteman, *Jews of Philadelphia*, 106.

16. Pencak, "Jews and Anti-Semitism," 386–387.

17. Benjamin Franklin to Joseph Priestley, August 21, 1784, in *The Writings of Benjamin Franklin*, ed. Albert Henry Smyth (1906; repr., New York: Macmillan, 1907), 9:267. When Massachusetts chose to include a religious test in its state constitution, Franklin wrote to a different English theologian criticizing the measure while failing to admit that he had supported a similar provision in his own state constitution four years earlier—see Benjamin Franklin to Richard Price, October 9, 1780, *PBF*, 33:389–390. Pennsylvania eventually repealed its exclusionary oath. Historian Thomas S. Kidd claims that Franklin "successfully worked to have that religious test repealed anyhow," but none of the four sources cited in Kidd's accompanying endnote credit Franklin for having repealed the Pennsylvania oath—see *Benjamin Franklin: The Religious Life of a Founding Father* (New Haven, CT: Yale University Press, 2017), 225, 265n45. Whether Franklin actively labored for its repeal or simply acquiesced to majority sentiment that had turned against the oath, he probably did oppose it—and for the same reason he had articulated in the foregoing letter to Joseph Priestley. It is unknown whether Franklin was present at the federal Constitutional Convention on the particular day that the delegates voted to ban religious tests. Pennsylvania's delegation favored the measure, but there are reasons to think Franklin may have been absent: (1) Madison's notes make no mention of him on that date, (2) only half of Pennsylvania's eight delegates had to be in attendance to qualify as a quorum, and (3) Franklin's health was poor. If he was present, then Franklin stood with the majority of delegates in approving the ban, since Pennsylvania's delegation was uniformly in favor.

18. Benjamin Franklin to William Franklin, December 19, 1767, *PBF*, 14:341–342.

19. Benjamin Franklin to Jean-Baptiste LeRoy, March 14, 1768, *PBF*, 15:82–83.

20. Benjamin Franklin to John Adams, November 26, 1781, *PJA*, 12:86.

21. Benjamin Franklin to John Adams, December 14, 1781, *PJA*, 12:137, 139.

22. Benjamin Franklin to John Adams, December 14, 1781, *PJA*, 12:139.

23. Walter Isaacson, *Benjamin Franklin: An American Life* (New York: Simon & Schuster, 2003), 468.

24. Proposal for the Great Seal of the United States, [before August 14, 1776], *PBF*, 22:562–563.

25. *Pennsylvania Gazette*, August 21, 1782, 363. The piece is signed "Silvester" but was the work of Francis Hopkinson—see *The Miscellaneous Essays and Occasional Writings of Francis Hopkinson, Esq.* (Philadelphia: T. Dobson, 1792), 1:263. See also Pencak, *Jews and Gentiles*, 3.

26. *Independent Gazetteer* (Philadelphia), March 20, 1784, 3.

27. Pencak, "Jews and Anti-Semitism," 396.

28. Jacob Rader Marcus, ed., *The Jew in the American World* (Detroit: Wayne State University Press, 1996), 97–98.

29. Marcus, *Jew in the American World*, 97–98.

30. Pennsylvania eventually did repeal the restrictions on office holding in 1790—see Jane Frances Amler, *Haym Salomon: Patriot Banker of the American Revolution* (New York: Rosen Publishing Group, 2004), 92.

31. *Independent Gazetteer* (Philadelphia), March 13, 1784, 3. The Fisher quotation appears in this piece.

32. *Independent Gazetteer* (Philadelphia), March 13, 1784, 3.

33. *Independent Gazetteer* (Philadelphia), March 13, 1784, 3.

34. *Independent Gazetteer* (Philadelphia), March 13, 1784, 3.

35. "Cursory Remarks on Men & Manners in Georgia," in Max J. Kohler, "Phases in the History of Religious Liberty in America with Particular Reference to the Jews.—II," *PAJHS* 13 (1905): 25.

36. Borden, *Jews, Turks, and Infidels*, 11.

37. Pencak, *Jews and Gentiles*, 166.

38. "Cursory Remarks on Men & Manners," 28.

39. Ira Rosenwaike tallies "about a dozen families" in Savannah, home to Georgia's Jewish community, as of 1790 in "An Estimate and Analysis of the Jewish Population of the United States in 1790," *PAJHS* 50 (September 1960): 33. If these families were comparable in size to Jewish families in New York, then Savannah had approximately sixty Jews. Even if there were some isolated Jews living elsewhere in Georgia, Jews still constituted less than one-tenth of 1 percent of Georgia's population, which the 1790 federal census fixed at 82,548.

40. *Georgia Gazette*, January 13, 1785, in Kohler, "Phases in the History of Religious Liberty," 30. For Georgian Jews' support of the Revolution (including Mordecai's) and Levi Sheftall's identity as "A Real Citizen," see Pencak, *Jews and Gentiles*, 163, 167.

41. David A. Gerber, "Anti-Semitism and Jewish-Gentile Relations in American Historiography and the American Past," in *Anti-Semitism in American History*, ed. David A. Gerber (Urbana: University of Illinois Press, 1986), 14–16; Jonathan D. Sarna, *American Judaism: A History* (New Haven, CT: Yale University Press, 2004), 28.

42. Sarna, *American Judaism*, 37.

43. Dana Rabin, "The Jew Bill of 1753: Masculinity, Virility, and the Nation," *Eighteenth-Century Studies* 39 (Winter 2006): 157, 159.

44. Quotation appears in Todd M. Endelman, *The Jews of Georgian England, 1714–1830: Tradition and Change in a Liberal Society* (Ann Arbor: University of Michigan Press, 1999), 274.

45. Borden, *Jews, Turks, and Infidels*, 11–13; Hasia R. Diner, *A Time for Gathering: The Second Migration, 1820–1880* (Baltimore: Johns Hopkins University Press, 1992), 150; Leonard Dinnerstein, *Antisemitism in America* (New York: Oxford University Press, 1994), 14–15; David G. Dalin, "Jews, Judaism, and the American Founding," in *Faith and the Founders of the American Republic*, ed. Daniel L. Dreisbach and Mark David Hall (New York: Oxford University Press, 2014), 64. Quotations appear in Borden, *Jews, Turks, and Infidels*, 12. Note that the Rhode Island Constitution of 1842 did not take legal effect until 1843.

46. Quotation appears in Pencak, *Jews and Gentiles*, 66.

47. New York Constitution of 1777.

48. Jacob R. Marcus, *American Jewry: Documents, Eighteenth Century* (Cincinnati: Hebrew Union College Press, 1959), 294–297.

49. John Webb Pratt, *Religion, Politics, and Diversity: The Church-State Theme in New York History* (Ithaca, NY: Cornell University Press, 1967), 107.

50. Pencak, *Jews and Gentiles*, 66.

51. Jonathan Den Hartog, "John Jay and Religious Liberty," *Faulkner Law Review* 7 (Fall 2015): 66–67.

52. John Jay to John Murray, October 12, 1816, in *The Correspondence and Public Papers of John Jay*, ed. Henry P. Johnston (New York: G. P. Putnam's Sons, [1890–1893]), 4:393.

53. Address to the American Bible Society, May 8, 1823, in *The Life of John Jay: With Selections from His Correspondence and Miscellanous Papers*, ed. William Jay (New York: J. & J. Harper, 1833), 1:504–505. Jay's profile as a proponent of religious freedom is further mitigated by his hostility toward Catholicism. He fought to have the New York state constitution bar all Catholics from citizenship unless they forswore allegiance to the pope. And although he failed to win acceptance of that measure in 1777, Jay did manage to include a constitutional requirement that Catholic immigrants to New York had to disavow the pope—not just politically but ecclesiastically—to become naturalized citizens of the state. See Hartog, "John Jay," 67–68.

54. *Israel Vindicated; Being a Refutation of the Calumnies Propagated Respecting the Jewish Nation; in which the Objects and Views of The American Society for Ameliorating the Condition of the Jews are Investigated. By an Israelite.* (New York: Abraham Collins, 1820), vi, 16. Although the anonymous author described himself as an "Israelite," Jonathan Sarna speculates that Jews actually hired a Gentile ghostwriter to produce the pamphlet—see "The Freethinker, the Jews, and the Missionaries: George Houston and the Mystery of *Israel Vindicated*," *AJS Review* 5 (1980): 113–114.

55. Constitution of Massachusetts, 1780. See also John Witte Jr., "One Public Religion, Many Private Religions: John Adams and the 1780 Massachusetts Constitution," in *The Founders on God and Government*, ed. Daniel L. Dreisbach, Mark D. Hall, and Jeffry H. Morrison (Oxford: Rowman & Littlefield, 2004), 38.

56. John Adams to Thomas Jefferson, November 14, 1813, *PTJR*, 6:618.

57. John Adams to the President of Congress, No. 99, July 23, 1780, *PJA*, 10:27.

58. Thursday. [*sic*] Jany. 16th. 1766, *PJAD*, 1:295.

59. John Adams to John Bondfield, May 14, 1780, *PJA*, 9:311.

60. John Adams to John Jay, February 13, 1784, *PJA*, 16:33.

61. John Adams to Thomas Jefferson, June 6, 1786, *PJA*, 18:333.

62. John Adams to Benjamin Rush, October 22, 1812, quoted in Joseph J. Ellis, *Passionate Sage: The Character and Legacy of John Adams* (New York: W. W. Norton, 1993), 107.

63. John Adams to the *Boston Patriot*, June 1812, Adams Family Papers, Massachusetts Historical Society. Note: this document is filed under 12 May 1809, on reel 407.

64. John Adams to Mordecai M. Noah, March 15, 1819, in Hilton Obenzinger, *American Palestine: Melville, Twain, and the Holy Land Mania* (Princeton, NJ: Princeton University Press, 1999), 33.

65. Dalin, "Jews, Judaism," 65.

66. John Adams to Mordecai M. Noah, July 31, 1818, quoted in Simon Wolf, *Mordecai Manuel Noah: A Biographical Sketch* (Philadelphia: The Levytype Company, 1897), 34.

67. John Adams to Francis Adrian Vanderkemp, December 31, 1808, quoted in Isidore S. Meyer, "John Adams Writes a Letter," *PAJHS* 37 (1947): 200.

68. Otto to Vergennes, New York, January 2, 1786, quoted in George Bancroft, *History of the Formation of the Constitution of the United States* (New York: D. Appleton, 1882), 1:476–477.

69. Adam Gordon, "Journal of an Officer who Travelled in America and the West Indies in 1764 and 1765," in *Travels in the American Colonies*, ed. Newton D. Mereness (New York: Macmillan, 1916), 410.

70. Johann David Schoepf, *Travels in the Confederation*, trans. Alfred J. Morrison (1788; repr., Philadelphia: William J. Campbell, 1911), 1:57, 86–87, 73; quotation appears on 57.

71. David O. Stewart, *The Summer of 1787: The Men Who Invented the Constitution* (New York: Simon & Schuster, 2008), 42.

72. Schoepf, *Travels in the Confederation*, 1:58–60.

73. Quotation appears in Charles S. Olton, "Philadelphia's First Environmental Crisis," *Pennsylvania Magazine of History and Biography* 98 (January 1974): 99.

74. Schoepf, *Travels in the Confederation*, 60, 68–69.

75. Schoepf, *Travels in the Confederation*, 59–60; Ron Chernow, *Alexander Hamilton* (New York: Penguin Press, 2004), 229–230. Quotation appears in the former source.

76. George Mason to George Mason Jr., May 27, 1787, in *The Records of the Federal Convention of 1787*, ed. Max Farrand (New Haven, CT: Yale University Press, 1911), 3:28.

77. Schoepf, *Travels in the Confederation*, 99.

78. Stewart, *Summer of 1787*, 41–42.

79. Elaine G. Breslaw, *Lotions, Potions, Pills, and Magic: Health Care in Early America* (New York: New York University Press, 2012), 95.

80. Quotations appear in Olton, "Philadelphia's First Environmental Crisis," 99.

81. Stewart, *Summer of 1787*, 42–43.

82. Chernow, *Alexander Hamilton*, 227.

83. Manasseh Cutler, "New York and Philadelphia in 1787," *Pennsylvania Magazine of History and Biography* 12 (April 1888): 103.

84. Henry Wansey, *The Journal of an Excursion to the United States of North America in the Summer of 1794* (Salisbury, UK: J. Easton, 1796), 111.

85. Chernow, *Alexander Hamilton*, 241.

86. Schoepf, *Travels in the Confederation*, 112–113.

87. Schoepf, *Travels in the Confederation*, 69.

88. Chernow, *Alexander Hamilton*, 228.

89. Isaac Markens, *The Hebrews in America: A Series of Historical and Biographical Sketches* (New York: Isaac Markens, 1888), 63.

90. Dalin, "Jews, Judaism," 67; Lance J. Sussman, *Isaac Leeser and the Making of American Judaism* (Detroit: Wayne State University Press, 1995), 54; Joseph R. Rosenbloom, *A Biographical Dictionary of Early American Jews: Colonial Times through 1800* (1960; repr., Lexington: University of Kentucky Press, 2015), 141.

91. Marcus, *Jew in the American World*, 99–100.

92. The delegates approved the ban on religious tests on August 30, 1787—see Gerald V. Bradley, "The No Religious Test Clause and the Constitution of Religious Liberty: A Machine That Has Gone of Itself," *Case Western Reserve Law Review* 37 (1986–1987): 692.

93. Borden, *Jews, Turks, and Infidels*, 5.

94. Borden, *Jews, Turks, and Infidels*, 15.

95. Farrand, *Records of the Federal Convention*, 3:227.

96. Bradley, "No Religious Test Clause," 691–692.

97. Alexander Hamilton to Rufus King, August 28, 1787, *PAH*, 4:238.

98. Chernow, *Alexander Hamilton*, 236, 241; quotation appears on 241.

99. *New-Haven Gazette, and the Connecticut Magazine*, November 22, 1787, 317. The synagogue was vandalized on September 15, 1787. The delegates completed their draft that day, then recessed the following day for the Christian Sabbath, and convened again on September 17 to sign the Constitution.

100. James Madison to Thomas Jefferson, October 17, 1788, *PJMC*, 11:297.

101. "A Watchman," *Worcester Magazine*, February 7, 1788, *DHRC*, 5:880–881.

102. Quotation appears in Susan Jacoby, *Freethinkers: A History of American Secularism* (New York: Owl Books, 2005), 29.

103. Jonathan Elliot, ed., *The Debates in the Several State Conventions on the Adoption of the Federal Constitution* (Philadelphia: J. B. Lippincott, 1861), 2:119.

104. "A Rhode-Island Man," *Newport Mercury*, February 25, 1788, *DHRC*, 24:105.

105. Elliot, *Debates in the Several State Conventions*, 4:199.

106. Excerpt from the *New York Daily Advertiser* reprinted in the *Connecticut Courant and Weekly Advertiser* (Hartford), January 28, 1788, 3.

107. *DHRC*, 15:402n1.

108. Pencak, *Jews and Gentiles*, vi.

Chapter 6

1. This conversation was recounted in Abraham Yates Jr. to Abraham G. Lansing, May 28, 1788, *DHRC*, 20:1115. A rumor circulated generations later that Hamilton had been asked why the delegates made no mention of God in the Constitution and Hamilton remarked, "We forgot it"—see George Duffield Jr., *The God of Our Fathers: An Historical Sermon Preached in the Coates' Street Presbyterian Church, Philadelphia, on Fast Day, January 4, 1861* (Philadelphia: T. B. Pugh, 1861), 15. There is no contemporaneous evidence that corroborates this rumor.

2. That the Jews generally allied with the Federalists and many of Hamilton's opponents relied on antisemitism complicates conventional depictions of the former political camp as elitist and the latter as democratic. For a discussion of the Jewish-Federalist alliance and the prejudice toward Jews among Hamilton's opponents at that point in history, see William Pencak, *Jews and Gentiles in Early America, 1654–1800* (Ann Arbor: University of Michigan Press, 2005), vi, 10–11.

3. "A Note on Certain of Hamilton's Pseudonyms," *William and Mary Quarterly* 12 (April 1955): 282; Ron Chernow, *Alexander Hamilton* (New York: Penguin Press, 2004),

246–250; Lorri Glover, *Fate of the Revolution: Virginians Debate the Constitution* (Baltimore: Johns Hopkins University Press, 2016), 35–36.

4. Chernow, *Alexander Hamilton*, 261–268.

5. Robert A. McGuire and Robert L. Ohsfeldt, "Self-Interest, Agency Theory, and Political Voting Behavior: The Ratification of the United States Constitution," *American Economic Review* 79 (March 1989): 224n10.

6. Pauline Maier, *Ratification: The People Debate the Constitution, 1787–1788* (New York: Simon & Schuster, 2010), 394–395.

7. Laura Rigal, "'Raising the Roof': Authors, Spectators, and Artisans in the Grand Federal Procession of 1788," *Theatre Journal* 48 (October 1996): 253.

8. Quotation appears in Sarah Alcock, *A Brief History of the Revolution* (Philadelphia: Sara Alcock, 1843), 108. The *hazzan*, or "Rabbi," as Rush inaccurately described him, was Jacob Raphael Cohen—see *DHRC*, 18:269n3.

9. Quotation appears in George Morgan Hills, *History of the Church in Burlington, New Jersey*, 2nd ed. (Trenton, NJ: W. S. Sharp, 1885), 715.

10. Quotation appears in Michael I. Meyerson, *Endowed by Our Creator: The Birth of Religious Freedom in America* (New Haven, CT: Yale University Press, 2012), 150.

11. Sarah H. J. Simpson, "The Federal Procession in the City of New York," *New York Historical Society Quarterly* 9 (July 1925): 40.

12. Meyerson, *Endowed by Our Creator*, 148–149; Howard B. Rock, *Haven of Liberty: New York Jews in the New World, 1654–1865* (New York: New York University Press, 2012), 87.

13. Peter Collin to Nicholas Low, July 16, 1788, *DHRC*, 21:1595.

14. Adrian Bancker to Evert Bancker, July 20, 1788, *DHRC*, 21:1327.

15. The closest date to 1788 for which we have estimates of the Jewish population of New York is 1794, when Jews were 1.1 percent of the city's population—see Hyman B. Grinstein, *The Rise of the Jewish Community of New York, 1654–1860* (Philadelphia: Jewish Publication Society of America, 1945), 469. Jews who had been exiled from New York during the war almost invariably returned to the city after Evacuation Day of 1783, so the Jewish percentage of New York in 1788 was likely not far afield from its 1794 number.

16. *New York Daily Advertiser*, August 2, 1788, *DHRC*, 21:1645–1646.

17. Frank Moss, *The American Metropolis: From Knickerbocker Days to the Present Time* (New York: Collier, 1897), 1:275, 260, 285. The poem appears on 1:280.

18. Comte de Moustier to Comte de Montmorin, August 2, 1788, *DHRC*, 18:309.

19. Chernow, *Alexander Hamilton*, 268.

20. Thanksgiving Proclamation, [October 3, 1789], *PGWP*, 4:131–132.

21. Jacob Rader Marcus, *The Handsome Young Priest in the Black Gown: The Personal World of Gershom Seixas* (Cincinnati: American Jewish Archives, 1970), 18–20.

22. Gershom Seixas, *A Religious Discourse Delivered in the Synagogue in this City, on Thursday the 26th November, 1789* (New York: Archibald McLean, 1789), 12–14.

23. Seixas, *A Religious Discourse*, 13, 15, 4.

24. 20 Sh'vat 5521, "Congregation Shearith Israel 18th–20th Century," RG 370, reel 1, YIVO; Rock, *Haven of Liberty*, 46.

25. Jacob R. Marcus, *American Jewry: Documents, Eighteenth Century* (Cincinnati: Hebrew Union College Press, 1959), 149–151, 155. It is unclear whether the 1790 constitution was an extension of democratic reforms initiated in 1784 or largely novel. According to one Shearith Israel record from 1784, it was "resolved unanimously that every person who congregates with us, as Jews, of the Age of 21 years & upwards shall be entitled to vote for a Parnass [president]"—see 23 Elul 5544, "Congregation Shearith Israel 18th–20th Century," RG 370, reel 1, YIVO. However, another record from 1787 stipulated, "Trustees shall annually choose from their own Board two of their number to serve in [the] synagogue as פרנסים [presidents]"—see 13 Nisan 5547, "Congregation Shearith Israel 18th–20th Century," RG 370, reel 1, YIVO. In either case, the 1790 constitution was unquestionably democratic relative to the synagogue's pre-Revolution *haskamot*.

26. Marcus, *American Jewry: Documents*, 154–156.

27. Marcus, *American Jewry: Documents*, 148.

28. Jonathan D. Sarna, "The Impact of the American Revolution on American Jews," *Modern Judaism* 1 (September 1981): 156; Marcus, *American Jewry: Documents*, 176; Pencak, *Jews and Gentiles*, 72. Quotation appears in the first source.

29. Jonathan D. Sarna, *American Judaism: A History* (New Haven, CT: Yale University Press, 2004), 42.

30. Saul Cornell identifies the claim that the Constitution promoted aristocracy as one of the nine most frequently recurring Anti-Federalist arguments in *The Other Founders: Anti-Federalism and the Dissenting Tradition in America, 1788–1828* (Chapel Hill: University of North Carolina Press, 1999), 30. Scholars have long debated to what extent the Constitution was democratic or elitist. Charles Beard famously contends that the Constitution was a victory of the moneyed elite in a class struggle against the poor in *An Economic Interpretation of the Constitution of the United States* (New York: Macmillan, 1913). In a similar vein, Jackson Turner Main argues that the Anti-Federalists championed democratic values in *The Anti-Federalists: Critics of the Constitution, 1781–1788* (Chapel Hill: University of North Carolina Press, 1961). Gordon Wood meanwhile holds that "the Constitution was intrinsically an aristocratic document designed to check the democratic tendencies of the period" in *The Creation of the American Republic, 1776–1787* (1969; repr., Chapel Hill: University of North Carolina Press, 1998), 513. Robert A. McGuire and Robert L. Ohsfeldt advance a neo-Beardian interpretation in "Economic Interests and the American Constitution: A Quantitative Rehabilitation of Charles A. Beard," *Journal of Economic History* 44 (June 1984): 509–519. These claims have long provoked counterarguments, such as Forrest McDonald's *We the People: The Economic Origins of the Constitution* (Chicago: University of Chicago Press, 1958). A more recent example is Akhil Reed Amar's *America's Constitution: A Biography* (New York: Random House, 2005), where he locates the democratic character of the Constitution in its ratification, noting that ratification required the consent of the governed to a degree unprecedented in its time: "This was the most democratic deed the world had ever seen" (p. 5).

31. 276–A. George Mason's Objections, *Massachusetts Centinel*, November 21, [1787], DHRC, 14:151–152.

32. *Charleston City Gazette*, May 29, 1788, DHRC, 27:379.

33. As Kate Elizabeth Brown demonstrates, despite accusations from contemporaries and historians alike that Hamilton was "contemptuously elitist," in fact "Hamilton was openly and consistently concerned with the problem of securing individuals' rights under republican government"—see *Alexander Hamilton and the Development of American Law* (Lawrence: University Press of Kansas, 2017), 174, 205.

34. Alexander Hamilton to William Hamilton, May 2, 1797, *PAH*, 21:78.

35. For a discussion of the founders' fear of anarchy, see Andrew Shankman, *Original Intents: Hamilton, Jefferson, Madison, and the American Founding* (New York: Oxford University Press, 2018), 9–22.

36. Conjectures about the New Constitution, [September 17–30, 1787], *PAH*, 4:276–277.

37. Herbet E. Sloan, "Hamilton's Second Thoughts: Federalist Finance Revisited," in *Federalists Reconsidered*, ed. Doron Ben-Atar and Barbara B. Oberg (Charlottesville: University Press of Virginia, 1998), 63, 68. Washington was acutely aware that as his was the first presidential administration, it would necessarily create precedents that would shape future generations, thereby magnifying the gravity of his administration's actions.

38. Roger James Sharp, *American Politics in the Early Republic: The New Nation in Crisis* (New Haven, CT: Yale University Press, 1993), 9–10; Chernow, *Alexander Hamilton*, 391–392.

39. Cornell, *Other Founders*, 170–171.

40. Abraham H. Venit, "An Unwritten Federalist History," *New England Quarterly* 21 (June 1948): 243n5. See also Karl-Friedrich Walling, *Republican Empire: Alexander Hamilton on War and Free Government* (Lawrence: University Press of Kansas, 1999), 168.

41. Shankman, *Original Intents*, 2; Stanley Elkins and Eric McKitrick, *The Age of Federalism: The Early American Republic, 1788–1800* (New York: Oxford University Press, 1993), 77; Sharp, *American Politics*, 48.

42. Gordon S. Wood, *Empire of Liberty: A History of the Early Republic, 1789–1815* (2009; repr., New York: Oxford University Press, 2011), 95. For the completion and submission dates, see *PAH*, 6:65. For the number of pages, see Alexander Hamilton, "Report Relative to a Provision for the Support of Public Credit," January 9, 1790, box 23, reel 21, frames 1205–1229, AHP.

43. "Report Relative to a Provision for the Support of Public Credit," January 9, 1790, *PAH*, 6:69–71, 99, 106; quotation appears on 106.

44. "Report Relative to a Provision for the Support of Public Credit," *PAH*, 6:70.

45. Wood, *Empire of Liberty*, 97.

46. *Pennsylvania Gazette*, February 17, 1790, 2.

47. Chernow, *Alexander Hamilton*, 297–298, 301.

48. "Report Relative to a Provision for the Support of Public Credit," *PAH*, 6:73–78.

49. *Poughkeepsie (NY) Journal*, January 9, 1793, 1.

50. *Pennsylvania Gazette*, March 17, 1790, 3.

51. Laura Arnold Leibman, *Messianism, Secrecy, and Mysticism: A New Interpretation of Early American Jewish Life* (London: Valentine Mitchell, 2012), 243–245.

52. *New York Journal*, April 26, 1790, 2.

53. Benjamin Rush to James Madison, April 10, 1790, *PJMC*, 13:146.

54. Chernow, *Alexander Hamilton*, 323–326.

55. Chernow, *Alexander Hamilton*, 327–330. For the menu, see Laura Kumin, *The Hamilton Cookbook: Cooking, Eating, and Entertaining in Hamilton's World* (New York: Post Hill Press, 2017), 49–50. The Funding Act became law on August 4, 1790.

56. Chernow, *Alexander Hamilton*, 330–331.

57. "Final Version of the Second Report on the Further Provision Necessary for Establishing Public Credit (Report on a National Bank)," December 13, 1790, *PAH*, 7:310–311, 309, 333, 323–324.

58. Wood, *Empire of Liberty*, 144–145.

59. United States Constitution, Article I, Section 8.

60. "Opinion on the Constitutionality of the Bill for Establishing a National Bank," February 15, 1791, *PTJ*, 19:278.

61. For the number of pages, see Alexander Hamilton, "Report on the Constitutionality of a Bank," draft and two copies, February 23, 1791, box 24, reel 21, frames 1674–1702, AHP.

62. "Final Version of an Opinion on the Constitutionality of an Act to Establish a Bank," *PAH*, 8:102–103.

63. Wood, *Empire of Liberty*, 144–145.

64. Richard Sylla and David J. Cowen, eds., *Alexander Hamilton on Finance, Credit, and Debt* (New York: Columbia University Press, 2018), 185; Chernow, *Alexander Hamilton*, 357.

65. *General Advertiser* (Philadelphia), July 14, 1791, 2.

66. Pencak, *Jews and Gentiles*, 232.

67. See, for instance, *New Hampshire Gazetteer* (Exeter), August 5, 1791, 2; *Norwich (CT) Packet*, August 18, 1791, 1–2.

68. Chernow, *Alexander Hamilton*, 355.

69. Robert Morris to Benjamin Franklin, July 13, 1781, *PBF*, 35:263; Notes on Debates, *PJMC*, 6:434n10.

70. Marcus, *American Jewry: Documents*, 289.

71. W. A. Shaw, *The History of Currency, 1252 to 1894: Being an Account of the Gold and Silver Moneys and Monetary Standards of Europe and America, Together with an Examination of the Effects of Currency and Exchange Phenomena on Commercial and National Progress and Well-Being*, 2nd ed. (London: Wilsons and Milne, 1896), 250–251.

72. "Final Version of the Report on the Establishment of a Mint," [January 28, 1791], *PAH*, 7:571, 570.

73. "Final Version of the Report," 7:588–589; Chernow, *Alexander Hamilton*, 349.

74. Arthur Nussbaum, "The Law of the Dollar," *Columbia Law Review* 37 (November 1937): 1059–1060.

75. Chernow, *Alexander Hamilton*, 356.

76. Alexander Hamilton to George Washington, January 31, 1795, *PAH*, 18:238.

77. Joseph L. Blau and Salo W. Baron, *The Jews of the United States, 1790–1840: A Documentary History* (New York: Columbia University Press, 1963), 1:103.

78. Jacob Mark and Company to Alexander Hamilton, [December 11, 1794], *PAH*, 17:438.

79. Alexander Hamilton to Edmund Randolph, *PAH*, 17:438n3.

80. Edmund Randolph to Alexander Hamilton, December 23, 1794, *PAH*, 17:462.

81. Jacob Mark and Company to Alexander Hamilton, [January 21, 1795], *PAH*, 18:161–162.

82. Alexander Hamilton to Edmund Randolph, January 25, 1795, *PAH*, 18:184–185. Congressional legislation also led Hamilton, in his capacity as treasury secretary, to leave unsettled an outstanding wartime debt with a Jew named Mordecai Sheftall, whose claim was one of ten that Hamilton informed Congress could not be paid under existing statutory law—see "Report on Several Petitions Barred by the Acts of Limitation," [February 27, 1794], *PAH*, 16:99–100.

83. Robert E. Wright, *Hamilton Unbound: Finance and the Creation of the American Republic* (Westport, CT: Greenwood Press, 2002), 97, 196–197.

84. *National Gazette* (Philadelphia), February 23, 1793, 135.

85. Sylla and Cowen, *Finance, Credit, and Debt*, 70; Chernow, *Alexander Hamilton*, 480–481.

86. Hamilton's rival, Jefferson, outlived him by more than two decades, allowing Jefferson to deride Hamilton without rebuttal from Hamilton himself. Jefferson's juxtaposition of Hamilton as a lackey for the elite and himself as a true democrat continues to inform perceptions of both founders. Even Hamilton sympathizers throughout history have conceded, too readily, that he sided with the ruling class at the expense of the masses—see Stephen F. Knott, *Alexander Hamilton and the Persistence of Myth* (Lawrence: University Press of Kansas, 2002), 4–5, 25–26, 74–77, 88. See also Brown, *Alexander Hamilton*, 174–175.

87. James Madison's Version, [June 18, 1787], *PAH*, 4:192.

88. *The Federalist* No. 36, [January 8, 1788], *PAH*, 4:483.

Chapter 7

1. Richard Labunski, *James Madison and the Struggle for the Bill of Rights* (New York: Oxford University Press, 2006), 252.

2. Labunski, *James Madison*, 9.

3. *The Federalist* No. 84, [May 28, 1788], *PAH*, 4:706–707.

4. Labunski, *James Madison*, 240, 243, 246, 251–252.

5. By 1790, Pennsylvania, South Carolina, and Georgia had replaced earlier, prejudicial state constitutions with more religiously inclusive ones. But other states such as Delaware and New Jersey had not yet revised their constitutions, which contained discriminatory clauses. Rhode Island, New Hampshire, Maryland, and North Carolina would restrict Jewish suffrage well into the nineteenth century. A majority of states barred Jews from practicing law. For discussion of civil restrictions on Jews' rights, see Leonard Dinnerstein, *Antisemitism in America* (New York: Oxford University Press, 1994), 14–15.

6. Jews were not the only religious minorities who had encountered prejudice and sought reassurance from the president. Baptists, Catholics, and Quakers wrote to Washington, and invariably received warm replies that touted religious liberty. See, for instance, George Washington to the United Baptist Churches of Virginia, [May 1789], *PGWP*, 2:423–425; George Washington to the Society of Quakers, [October 13, 1789], *PGWP*, 4:185; George Washington to Roman Catholics in America, [March 15, 1790], *PGWP*, 5:235. Note that the page numbers in the latter two sources reflect the current renumbering from the editors of the *PGWP*.

7. Melvin I. Urofsky, *A Genesis of Religious Freedom: The Story of the Jews of Newport, RI and Touro Synagogue, Including Washington's Letter of 1790* (New York: George Washington Institute for Religious Freedom, 2013), 79.

8. "Items Relating to Correspondence of Jews with George Washington," *PAJHS* 27 (1920): 217–218. For the Savannah letter and Washington's reply, see George Washington to the Savannah, Ga., Hebrew Congregation, [June 14, 1790], *PGWP*, 5:520. Note that the page number in the latter source reflects the current renumbering from the editors of the *PGWP*.

9. "Items Relating to Correspondence," 217–218.

10. "Items Relating to Correspondence," 219.

11. "Items Relating to Correspondence," 219.

12. "Items Relating to Correspondence," 220.

13. Gershom Seixas to the Trustees of K. K. Shearith Israel, September 22, 1785, Papers of Seixas Family, *P-60, box 1, folder 10, AJHS. See also "Items Relating to Gershom M. Seixas," *PAJHS* 27 (1920): 130–131.

14. "Items Relating to Correspondence," 219–220.

15. "Items Relating to Correspondence," 221.

16. Jonathan D. Sarna, *American Judaism: A History* (New Haven, CT: Yale University Press, 2004), 20, 29, 39.

17. Urofsky, *Genesis of Religious Freedom*, 69, 74; T. H. Breen, *George Washington's Journey: The President Forges a New Nation* (New York: Simon & Schuster, 2016), 202–204.

18. Melvin I. Urofsky and Paul Finkelman, *A March of Liberty: A Constitutional History of the United States* (New York: Oxford University Press, 2011), 1:95–96, 106.

19. See, for instance, *New-Hampshire Recorder, and the Weekly Advertiser*, April 3, 1789, 2.

20. For the best discussion of the complex reasons for Rhode Island's resistance to the Union, see generally Irwin H. Polishook, *Rhode Island and the Union, 1774–1795* (Evanston, IL: Northwestern University Press, 1969).

21. *Bulletin of the Newport Historical Society*, no. 84 (July 1932): 11.

22. William Loughton Smith, "Journal of William Loughton Smith," in *Proceedings of the Massachusetts Historical Society*, October 1917–June 1918, vol. 51 (Boston: Massachusetts Historical Society, 1918), 36.

23. *Bulletin of the Newport Historical Society*, no. 84 (July 1932): 12.

24. *Newport Mercury*, August 23, 1790, 1.

25. *Bulletin of the Newport Historical Society*, no. 84 (July 1932): 12.

26. Morris A. Gutstein, *The Story of the Jews of Newport: Two and a Half Centuries of Judaism, 1658–1908* (New York: Bloch Publishing Co., 1936), 208.

27. "A Tour to the Eastern States," *Columbian Magazine: or, Monthly Miscellany*, September 1789, 535.

28. *Newport Herald*, August 19, 1790, 3.

29. Jacob Isaacks to George Washington, August 17, 1790, *PGWP*, 6:278–279.

30. *Newport Mercury*, August 23, 1790, 1; Smith, "Journal," 36.

31. *Bulletin of the Newport Historical Society*, no. 84 (July 1932): 13.

32. *Newport Mercury*, August 23, 1790, 1; Smith, "Journal," 36.

33. *Bulletin of the Newport Historical Society*, no. 84 (July 1932): 13.

34. Urofsky, *Genesis of Religious Freedom*, 80; *Bulletin of the Newport Historical Society*, no. 84 (July 1932): 15.

35. For a discussion of Jewish Masonry, see Laura Arnold Leibman, *Messianism, Secrecy, and Mysticism: A New Interpretation of Early American Jewish Life* (London: Vallentine Mitchell,

2012), 248–274. Although the Caribbean had a larger Jewish population than North America in the eighteenth century, Masonry was more common among North American Jews. Nevis is not known to have had Jewish Masons.

36. *Newport Mercury*, August 23, 1790, 1–2.

37. Moses Seixas to George Washington, August 17, 1790, *PGWP*, 6:286n1. Note that the letter was dated August 17 but read aloud in a ceremony on August 18.

38. Smith, "Journal," 37.

39. *Newport Mercury*, August 23, 1793, 2.

40. Douglas Southall Freeman, *George Washington: A Biography* (New York: Charles Scribner's Sons, 1954), 6:276.

41. Jeffry H. Morrison, *The Political Philosophy of George Washington* (Baltimore: Johns Hopkins University Press, 2009), 158.

42. George Washington to the Hebrew Congregation in Newport, Rhode Island, [August 18, 1790], *PGWP*, 6:285. A point of clarification is in order concerning the timing of the letter, which itself is undated (the *PGWP* estimates August 18). In a 1960 article, Paul Boller suggests that Washington read the Newport letter in person on August 18 during his stay in Rhode Island in "George Washington and Religious Liberty," *William and Mary Quarterly* 17 (October 1960): 503. Yet Boller provides no evidence for this claim, and indeed the historical record indicates otherwise. Four addresses were delivered to Washington for the occasion: (1) Judge Marchant's (although it was read by someone else), (2) the Christian clergy's joint address, (3) Moses Seixas's speech on behalf of the Masonic lodge, and (4) Seixas's other declaration on behalf of the Hebrew Congregation. On August 23, a local weekly newspaper published a report on Washington's visit and included the text of Washington's replies to Marchant, the Christian clergy, and the lodge—see *Newport Mercury*, August 23, 1790, 1–2. The text of Washington's letter to the Touro Synagogue did not appear in the *Newport Mercury* until the September 13 issue (p. 1). This three-week discrepancy suggests that Washington did have speeches prepared for the day of his visit but the Newport letter was not among them. Moreover, Washington's use of the past tense "experienced" in referencing his visit accords with the notion that he produced the letter to the Touro Synagogue after the trip. Lastly, the letter appears in the hand of the president's secretary, Tobias Lear, who did not accompany Washington to Rhode Island, indicating that the president dictated the letter once he returned to New York—see Fritz Hirschfeld, *George Washington and the Jews* (Newark: University of Delaware Press, 2005), 33.

43. Eli Faber, *A Time for Planting: The First Migration, 1654–1820* (Baltimore: Johns Hopkins University Press, 1992), 129.

44. George Washington to the Hebrew Congregation in Newport, Rhode Island, [August 18, 1790], *PGWP*, 6:285.

45. On the letter's significance, see Morrison, *Political Philosophy*, 161–162; David G. Dalin, "Jews, Judaism, and the American Founding," in *Faith and the Founders of the American Republic*, ed. Daniel L. Dreisbach and Mark David Hall (New York: Oxford University Press, 2014), 68–69; Urofsky, *Genesis of Religious Freedom*, 82.

46. As Jacob Katz explains, "Jews were on probation. Improvement in their situation was the bait dangled before their eyes—should they live up to expectations"—see *Out of the Ghetto: The Social Background of Jewish Emancipation, 1770–1870* (Cambridge, MA: Harvard University Press, 1973), 192.

47. It is worth noting that neither the Newport letter nor the ratification of the Bill of Rights in 1791 emancipated Jews at the state level. Several states maintained restrictions on Jews well into the nineteenth century. The Newport letter helped lay the foundation for the expansion of rights to Jews at the state level, and more than in just an abstract sense. In 1826, Maryland legislators waged an acrimonious battle over the "Jew Bill" that would afford the state's Jewish inhabitants full equality under the law. A lawmaker read aloud from the Newport letter on the floor of the Maryland State House, and the bill ultimately passed—see E. Milton Altfeld, *The Jew's Struggle for Religious and Civil Liberty in Maryland* (Baltimore: M. Curlander, 1924), 178–179. The U.S. Supreme Court did not begin applying the First Amendment to state governments until 1925, by which point the last state constraints on Jews had already been lifted. In the mid-twentieth century, the American Jewish Committee published a survey of antisemitism in the United States entitled *To Bigotry No Sanction: A Documented Analysis of Anti-Semitic Propaganda* (1940; repr., New York: American Jewish Committee, 1944) and prefaced with excerpts from the Newport letter. Numerous judges have drawn from the letter's prose in recent decades to uphold the free exercise of faith, not just for Jews but other religious minorities as well—see, for instance, Michaelson ex rel. Lewis v. Booth, 437 F. Supp. 439 (D.R.I. 1977); Barbosa-Orona v. Flores-Dasta, 843 F. Supp. 2d 230 (D.P.R. 2012); Sands v. Morongo, 53 Cal. 3d 863, 809 P.2d 809, 281 Cal. Rptr. 34 (1991), cert. denied, 112 S. Ct. 3026 (1992).

48. George Washington to the Hebrew Congregation in Newport, Rhode Island, [August 18, 1790], *PGWP*, 6:285.

49. Morrison, *Political Philosophy*, 144.

50. *Herald of Freedom* (Boston), September 7, 1790, 202–203; *Daily Advertiser* (New York), September 14, 1790, 2–3; *Gazette of the United States* (New York), September 15, 1790, 596; *Maryland Journal* (Baltimore), September 21, 1790, 3; *Virginia Gazette and Alexandria Advertiser*, September 23, 1790, 3; *Columbian Herald or the Independent Courier of North America* (Charleston, SC), September 25, 1790, 2–3; *Poughkeepsie (NY) Journal*, September 25, 1790, 1; *Middlesex Gazette, or, Fœderal Adviser* (Middletown, CT), October 2, 1790, 1; *Connecticut Gazette* (New London), October 8, 1790, 1; *Hampshire Gazette* (Northampton, MA), October 13, 1790, 4; *Newport Mercury*, September 13, 1790, 1.

51. Paul F. Boller Jr., "George Washington and the Jews," *Southwest Review* 47 (Spring 1962): 122; Hirschfeld, *George Washington and the Jews*, 143.

52. Quotation appears in Boller, "George Washington and the Jews," 120.

53. George Washington to Tench Tilghman, March 24, 1784, *PGWC*, 1:232.

54. Scholars have speculated with no hard proof that Jefferson, Madison, or the presidential aide David Humphreys informed or even ghostwrote the letter—see *PTJ*, 19:610n8; Stuart Leibiger, *Founding Friendship: George Washington, James Madison, and the Creation of the American Republic* (Charlottesville: University Press of Virginia, 1999), 121–122; Freeman, *George Washington*, 6:275n136; Hirschfeld, *George Washington and the Jews*, 32.

55. Jacob Rader Marcus, *United States Jewry, 1776–1985* (Detroit: Wayne State University Press, 1989), 1:120.

56. Alexander Hamilton's Final Version of the Report on the Subject of Manufactures, [December 5, 1791], *PAH*, 10:254.

57. Comments on Jews, [n.d.], *PAH*, 26:774.

58. George Washington to the Hebrew Congregations of Philadelphia, New York, Charleston, and Richmond, [December 13, 1790], *PGWP*, 7:63–64.

59. "Items Relating to Correspondence," 222.

60. George Washington to the Hebrew Congregations, 7:61–62.

61. *Pennsylvania Packet, and Daily Advertiser* (Philadelphia), December 15, 1790, 3; *Federal Gazette and Philadelphia Daily Advertiser*, December 16, 1790, 2; *Gazette of the United States* (Philadelphia), December 18, 1790, 673; *New-York Packet*, December 18, 1790, 2; *Maryland Journal and Baltimore Advertiser*, December 24, 1790, 3; *Salem (MA) Gazette*, January 4, 1791, 1; *Times, and Patowmack Packet* (Georgetown, MD), December 22, 1790, 3.

62. For the nationalistic bent of American Jews and Hamilton, see respectively William Pencak, *Jews and Gentiles in Early America, 1654–1800* (Ann Arbor: University of Michigan Press, 2005), 11; Ron Chernow, *Alexander Hamilton* (New York: Penguin Press, 2004), 157.

63. Morton Borden typifies this line of argumentation in *Jews, Turks, and Infidels* (Chapel Hill: University of North Carolina Press, 1984), 10.

64. For the importance of the Farewell Address, see Vincent Phillip Muñoz, *God and the Founders: Madison, Washington, and Jefferson* (New York: Cambridge University Press, 1999), 54; Morrison, *Political Philosophy*, 164–165.

65. John Avlon, *Washington's Farewell: The Founding Father's Warning to Future Generations* (New York: Simon & Schuster, 2017), 46–50.

66. Avlon, *Washington's Farewell*, 79.

67. Leibiger, *Founding Friendship*, 209–211.

68. Victor Hugo Paltsits, *Washington's Farewell Address* (New York: New York Public Library, 1935), 25–26.

69. Avlon, *Washington's Farewell*, 79, 83.

70. Introductory Note: To George Washington, [May 10, 1796], *PAH*, 20:172–173. That Hamilton had drafted the Farewell Address remained a closely guarded secret for many years after his death. Washington's admirers were disinclined to extend credit to an advisor whose memory did not elicit the same degree of admiration as that of the first president. Eliza Hamilton filed a lawsuit to retrieve papers that could prove her husband's authorship, and eventually they came into her possession. The Hamilton family did not initially make known the evidence of Alexander's involvement in the Farewell Address, owing to resistance from George C. Washington, grandnephew of the president and proprietor of George Washington's papers. Eventually, James Hamilton authorized a former congressman to produce a full account of the Hamilton-Washington collaboration. See Paltsits, *Washington's Farewell Address*, 75–94; Horace Binney, *An Inquiry into the Formation of Washington's Farewell Address* (Philadelphia: Parry & McMillan, 1859).

71. Avlon, *Washington's Farewell*, 78, 83–84, 86; Paltsits, *Washington's Farewell Address*, 47–49. Quotation appears in George Washington to Alexander Hamilton, August 25, 1796, *PAH*, 20:307.

72. Quotation appears in Paltsits, *Washington's Farewell Address*, 192.

73. Paltsits, *Washington's Farewell Address*, 124.

74. *The Stand* no. II, [April 4, 1798], *PAH*, 21:391.

75. The French Revolution, [1794], *PAH*, 17:587.

76. The sole study focusing on Hamilton's religious views suggests that "this period in his life hardly deserves to be praised as an era of Christian thought and practice"—see Douglass Adair and Marvin Harvey, "Was Alexander Hamilton a Christian Statesman?," *William and Mary Quarterly* 12 (April 1955): 316.

77. In the secondary literature about religious freedom in this era, James Madison and Thomas Jefferson eclipse all other founders. Only recently have scholars afforded sustained attention to George Washington's place in the religious landscape—see Mary V. Thompson, *"In the Hands of a Good Providence": Religion in the Life of George Washington* (Charlottesville: University of Virginia Press, 2008); Muñoz, *God and the Founders*, 49–69; Morrison, *Political Philosophy*, 135–172. A predecessor to these studies is Paul Boller, *George Washington and Religion* (Dallas: Southern Methodist University Press, 1963). The literature on Hamilton, when it mentions religion at all, does so in passing and usually only to note his apparent ambivalence to organized Christianity. But his indifference toward Christianity did not mean he was apathetic about religion.

78. See Muñoz, *God and the Founders*, 50.

79. George Washington to George Mason, October 3, 1785, *PGWC*, 3:292–293.

80. For an overview of the bill and of James Madison's role in defeating it, see Milton R. Konvitz, "Separation of Church and State: The First Freedom," *Law and Contemporary Problems* 14 (Winter 1949): 53–54.

81. It is telling that the ideal of separation of church and state gained traction in the mid-nineteenth century not because of broad concern about protecting religious minorities but rather due to Protestant anxiety about Catholic immigrants who, it was feared, would subjugate America to papal authority—see Philip Hamburger, *Separation of Church and State* (Cambridge, MA: Harvard University Press, 2002), 191–192, 234.

82. Bishop presented his ideas in a book, excerpts of which were printed in the press—see Abraham Bishop, *Proofs of Conspiracy, Against Christianity, and the Government of the United States, Exhibited in Several Views of the Union of Church and State in New-England* (Hartford, CT: John Babcock, 1802), 53, 54, 94; *National Aegis* (Worcester, MA) August 11, 1802, 1.

83. Nehemiah Dodge, *A Discourse, Delivered at Lebanon, in Connecticut, on the Fourth of March, 1805, at the New Meeting House; Before a Large Concourse of Respectable Citizens, Met in Honor of the Late Presidential Election of Thomas Jefferson* (Norwich, CT: Sterry & Porter, 1805), 7, 28.

84. Jonathan J. Den Hartog, *Patriotism and Piety: Federalist Politics and Religious Struggle in the New American Nation* (Charlottesville: University of Virginia Press, 2015), 6.

85. It is worth noting that not everyone considered ancient Israel an archetype to avoid. Prominent thinkers on both sides of the Atlantic actively advertised their ideas about statecraft as derived from the Israelites. They exalted the Hebrew Bible as a constitutional text that ought to serve as a model for modern countries just as it had for ancient Israel, and they described it as harmonious with civic values such as religious tolerance and the rule of law. Unsurprisingly, they concurred with the Hamiltonian view that religious and civic morality were intertwined. See, for instance, Eric Nelson, *The Hebrew Republic: Jewish Sources and the Transformation of European Political Thought* (Cambridge, MA: Harvard University Press, 2010); Eran Shalev, *American Zion: The Old Testament as a Political Text from the Revolution to the Civil War* (New

Haven, CT: Yale University Press, 2013); Nathan R. Perl-Rosenthal, "The 'Divine Right of Re-publics': Hebraic Republicanism and the Debate over Kingless Government in Revolutionary America," *William and Mary Quarterly* 66 (July 2009): 535–564; James P. Byrd, *Sacred Scripture, Sacred War: The Bible and the American Revolution* (New York: Oxford University Press, 2013), 70–72; Samuel Langdon, *The Republic of the Israelites an Example to the American States* (Exeter, NH: Lamson and Ranlet, 1788); Joseph Huntington, *God Ruling for the Most Glorious End: A Sermon, in Presence of his Excellency, and both Houses of Assembly* (Hartford, CT: Hudson & Goodwin, 1784), 24–25.

86. *The Examination*, no. 15, [March 3, 1802], *PAH*, 25: 554, 554n4.

87. Shalev, *American Zion*, 17–18.

88. Hamburger, *Separation of Church and State*, 10–11.

89. See, for instance, A Bill for Establishing Religious Freedom, *PTJ*, 2:545–547.

90. Thomas Jefferson to the Danbury Baptist Association, January 1, 1802, *PTJ*, 36:258.

91. Donald L. Drakeman, *Church, State, and Original Intent* (New York: Cambridge University Press, 2009), 259–260; Irving Brant, "Madison: On the Separation of Church and State," *William and Mary Quarterly* 8 (January 1951): 3. Quotation appears in Thomas Jefferson to the Danbury Baptist Association, January 1, 1802, *PTJ*, 36:258.

92. Thomas Jefferson to William Short, August 4, 1820, in *Letters and Addresses of Thomas Jefferson*, ed. William B. Parker and Jonas Viles (Buffalo, NY: National Jefferson Society, 1903), 268–269.

93. Thomas Jefferson to Charles Thomson, January 9, 1816, *PTJR*, 9:341.

94. Thomas Jefferson to Benjamin Rush [enclosure], April 21, 1803, *PTJ*, 40:253.

95. Jefferson once wrote, "In every country and in every age, the priest has been hostile to liberty. He is always in alliance with the despot abetting his abuses in return for protection to his own"—see Thomas Jefferson to Horatio G. Spafford, March 17, 1814, *PTJR*, 7:248.

96. Thomas Jefferson to John Taylor, June 4, 1798, *PTJ*, 30:389.

97. Thomas Jefferson to Lafayette, May 14, 1817, *PTJR*, 11:354.

98. Samuel Rabinove, "The Right of Religious Liberty for One Is a Right for Others and a Responsibility for All," *Journal of Law and Religion* 8 (1990): 243.

99. Thomas Jefferson to Mordecai Noah, May 28, 1818, in *American Jewish History: A Primary Source Reader*, ed. Gary Phillip Zola and Marc Dollinger (Waltham, MA: Brandeis University Press, 2014), 48.

100. Thomas Jefferson to Jacob de la Motta, September 1, 1820, in Zola and Dollinger, *American Jewish History*, 48–49.

101. For two other examples of Jefferson acknowledging the plight of antisemitism to Jewish correspondents, see Thomas Jefferson to Isaac Harby, January 6, 1826, in *A Selection from the Miscellaneous Writings of the Late Isaac Harby, Esq.*, ed. Henry L. Pinckney and Abraham Moise (Charleston, SC: James S. Burges, 1829), 35–36; and Jefferson's line concerning "persecution and oppression" as quoted in Hirschfeld, *George Washington and the Jews*, 56. Not all of Jefferson's correspondence with or about Jews was as positive. After the inventor Jacob Isaacks demonstrated in person to Jefferson his process for desalinating water, Jefferson, then secretary of state, issued a report to Congress about Isaacks's demonstration, a disclosure that Isaacks felt had robbed him of an opportunity to profit from his innovation. Isaacks wrote to Jefferson on

March 19, 1792, "You must be thoroughly sensible of the injury that report has done me by making it of public use without any advantage to the discoverer, and I am now deprived of selling
my secret to private persons"—see *PTJ*, 19:623–624. See also Hirschfeld, *George Washington and
the Jews*, 132–133. Notably, Jefferson demonstrated kindness to David Salisbury Franks but pri-
vately raised doubts about his capacity for self-restraint. Franks wrote to Jefferson that "my heart
feels every sentiment of gratitude and attachment to you for the many marks of friendship which
you have shown me since my stay in France" on February 10, 1787, *PTJ*, 11:135. Jefferson, however,
had earlier raised concerns to Madison about Franks's temperament for diplomacy, writing on
February 14, 1783, "He appears to have a good enough heart, an understanding somewhat better
than common but too little guard over his lips. I have marked him particularly in the company
of women where he loses all power over himself and becomes almost frenzied. His temperature
would not be proof against their allurements were such to be employed as engines against
him"—see *PTJ*, 6:241.

102. Robert M. Healey, "Jefferson on Judaism and the Jews: 'Divided We Stand, United, We
Fall!,'" *American Jewish History* 73 (June 1984): 360.

103. A Bill for the Naturalization of Foreigners, [October 14, 1776], *PTJ*, 1:559.

104. A Bill for Establishing Religious Freedom, June 18, 1779, *PTJ*, 2:546, 552n3. Note that
Jefferson drafted the bill in 1777 and submitted it to the legislature in 1779, which did not pass
it into law until 1786.

105. James Madison to Frederick C. Schaeffer, December 3, 1821, *PJMR*, 2:433.

106. Jonathan D. Sarna, *Jacksonian Jew: The Two Worlds of Mordecai Noah* (New York:
Holmes & Meier, 1981), 15, 8; "Mordecai Noah's Mission to Algiers: Spanish-American Relations
and the Fate of a Jewish Consul in Madison's Administration, February 20, 1815," *PJMP*, 9:11.
Quotations appear in the former source.

107. Sarna, *Jacksonian Jew*, 16.

108. Sarna, *Jacksonian Jew*, 17; "Mordecai Noah's Mission to Algiers," 9:11.

109. Sarna, *Jacksonian Jew*, 18–19.

110. Sarna, *Jacksonian Jew*, 19–20.

111. James Monroe to James Madison, April 22, 1815, *PJMP*, 9:199.

112. James Madison to James Monroe, April 24, 1815, *PJMP*, 9:206.

113. James Monroe to Mordecai M. Noah, April 25, 1815, reprinted in Mordecai M. Noah,
Travels in England, France, Spain, and the Barbary States in the Years 1813–14 and 15 (New York:
Kirk and Mercein, 1819), 376.

114. Sarna, *Jacksonian Jew*, 27–29.

115. Mordecai M. Noah to James Madison, May 6, 1818, *PJMR*, 1:252.

116. James Madison to Mordecai M. Noah, May 15, 1818, *PJMR*, 1:286.

117. "Mordecai Noah's Mission to Algiers," 9:14.

118. Noah, *Travels in England*, 379–381.

119. Sarna, *Jacksonian Jew*, 32.

120. Expense Account as Delegate in Congress, *PJMC*, 4:109.

121. James Madison to Edmund Randolph, August 27, 1782, *PJMC*, 5:87.

122. James Madison to Edmund Randolph, September 30, 1782, *PJMC*, 5:170.

123. Expense Account as Delegate in Congress, *PJMC*, 4:108n2.

124. James Madison to Jacob De La Motta, August [post-7], 1820, *PJMR*, 2:81.

125. James Madison to Thomas Jefferson [enclosure], September 10, 1824, *PJMR*, 3:374. After graduating from Princeton, the twenty-year-old Madison opted to stay on campus for another seven months pursuing additional study under the college president. He recalled having spent at least part of that time "acquiring a slight knowledge of the Hebrew, which was not among the College Studies"—see "James Madison's Autobiography," *William and Mary Quarterly* 2 (April 1945): 197; Ralph Ketcham, *James Madison: A Biography* (1971; repr., Charlottesville: University Press of Virginia, 1990), 51.

Chapter 8

1. Ron Chernow, *Alexander Hamilton* (New York: Penguin Press, 2004), 479–483, 501.

2. *Daily Advertiser* (New York), February 28, 1795, 2.

3. *LPAH*, 2:36, 41–43; Ira Rosenwaike, *Population History of New York City* (Syracuse, NY: Syracuse University Press, 1972), 16.

4. John Lambert, *Travels through Canada, and the United States of North America, in the Years 1806, 1807, & 1808*, 2nd ed. (London: C. Cradock and W. Joy, 1814), 2:63–64.

5. Quotation appears in Allan McLane Hamilton, *The Intimate Life of Alexander Hamilton* (New York: Charles Scribner's Sons, 1910), 75.

6. Gotthard Deutsch, "Oath More Judaico," in *The Jewish Encyclopedia: A Descriptive Record of the History, Religion, Literature, and Customs of the Jewish People from the Earliest Times to the Present Day* (New York: Funk and Wagnalls, 1901–1906), 9:367–368.

7. Max Schloessinger, "Kol Nidre," in *Jewish Encyclopedia*, 7:539, 541.

8. Quotation appears in Max J. Kohler, "Civil Status of the Jews in Colonial America," *PAJHS* 6 (1897): 99.

9. Naomi W. Cohen, *Jews in Christian America: The Pursuit of Religious Equality* (New York: Oxford University Press, 1992), 57–58. Quotation appears in the Third Constitution of New York, 1846, Article I, Section 3.

10. As early as 1796, Hamilton wrote to George Washington that Le Guen was fearful of "a rupture between the two countries" that would "prejudice him in a suit which I am directed to bring for him"—see Alexander Hamilton to George Washington, [June 16, 1796], *PAH*, 20:225.

11. Also serving on Le Guen's legal team was Richard Harison. Hamilton and Harison had both attended King's College and served as members of New York's ratifying convention in 1788—see *LPAH*, 1:311n76.

12. *LPAH*, 2:50–51. For the advertisements, see "Just Imported," September 15, 1794, *Daily Advertiser* (New York), 1; and subsequent editions of the same paper from September 17; October 14–18, 20, 27, 30, 31; November 6, 7, 10, 11, 15, 24, 26, 29; December 2–6, 8, 10–13, 15, 17, 20, 22; January 1, 3, 6, 24, 29; and February 2.

13. *LPAH*, 2:54–59; quotations appear on 58.

14. *LPAH*, 2:58–59, 72, 80n140, 81. For the two Jewish witnesses—Abraham Gomez and Moses Lopez—see Joseph R. Rosenbloom, *A Biographical Dictionary of Early American Jews: Colonial Times through 1800* (1960; repr., Lexington: University of Kentucky Press, 2015), 43, 99; William Johnson, *Reports of Cases Adjudged in the Supreme Court of Judicature of the State of New*

York; from January Term 1799, to January Term 1803, Both Inclusive; Together with Cases Determined in the Court for the Correction of Errors, during That Period (New York: Isaac Riley, 1808–1812), 1:475.

15. *LPAH*, 2:63–67.

16. Isaac Gouverneur to William Mararty, August 26, 1796, Ms. Letterbook (1796–1798), GKP, 78.

17. Isaac Gouverneur to L. Dupuy, August 29, 1796, Ms. Letterbook (1796–1797), GKP, 79–80.

18. Louis Le Guen to Alexander Hamilton, [April 24, 1797], *PAH*, 21:56.

19. "To the Public," *Commercial Advertiser* (New York), October 19, 1797, 3.

20. "To the Public," 3.

21. *LPAH*, 2:67, 73; quotation appears on 73.

22. *LPAH*, 2:67–68.

23. Isaac Gouverneur to Alexander Hamilton, *Commercial Advertiser* (New York) January 11, 1798, 3.

24. "For This Gazette," *New-York Gazette and General Advertiser*, January 11, 1798, 2.

25. Gouverneur & Kemble to Jacob Lewis, December 12, 1797, Ms. Letterbook (1796–1797), GKP, 529.

26. *LPAH*, 2:67–68.

27. *LPAH*, 1:18. The lieutenant governor served as the president of the senate.

28. *LPAH*, 2:86.

29. James Thomas Flexner, *The Young Hamilton: A Biography* (Boston: Little, Brown, 1978), 62.

30. Alexander Hamilton to Eliza Hamilton, February 5, 1800, box 19, reel 17, AHP. See also John C. Hamilton, *History of the Republic of the United States of America, as Traced in the Writings of Alexander Hamilton and of His Contemporaries*, 2nd ed. (Philadelphia: J. B. Lippincott, 1864), 7:706–707.

31. John C. Hamilton, *History of the Republic*, 7:706–707. Hamilton had long exhibited anxiety about Le Guen's prospects for continued success in the courts. When Gouverneur and Kemble pressed on with further litigation after losing to Le Guen in January 1798, Le Guen was more optimistic than Hamilton. As Hamilton wrote to his wife, "Le Guen is much buoyed up. It is to be hoped he may not have cause to be proportionally depressed"—Alexander Hamilton to Elizabeth Hamilton, [March 1, 1798], *PAH*, 21:360.

32. *LPAH*, 2:86–87.

33. *LPAH*, 2:83.

34. For the Morris-Hamilton friendship, see Chernow, *Alexander Hamilton*, 240. Morris delivered the eulogy at Hamilton's funeral in 1804.

35. William Kent, *Memoirs and Letters of James Kent, LL.D.: Late Chancellor of the State of New York, author of "Commentaries on American law," etc.* (Boston: Little, Brown, 1898), 322.

36. John C. Hamilton, *History of the Republic*, 7:707–708; quotation appears on 708.

37. There is substantial misunderstanding about the meaning of the following statement that Hamilton made in court: "Why distrust the evidence of the Jews? Discredit them, and you destroy the Christian religion." Chernow suggests this language was evidence of Hamilton's sympathy for Jews in *Alexander Hamilton*, 18, as does David G. Dalin in "Jews, Judaism, and the American Founding," in *Faith and the Founders of the American Republic*, ed. Daniel L. Dreisbach

and Mark David Hall (New York: Oxford University Press, 2014), 70. This claim by Chernow and Dalin is misleading on two counts. Hamilton was, in fact, quoting from Morris's closing argument. Morris's actual words had been slightly different from how Hamilton quoted them: "Why were these Jew witnesses considered as unworthy of credit? Are they persecuted or degraded? These Jews are in a capacity to be everything! Destroy the credit of the Jews, and you destroy the Christian religion!" Moreover, Morris's remarks were part of a closing argument that was delivered "sarcastically," in the words of Hamilton's grandson. For Morris's original line, Hamilton's quotation of him, and the grandson's description of Morris as sarcastic, see John C. Hamilton, *History of the Republic*, 7:708, 710. That Morris's comments—which appear on their face to praise Jews—were sarcastic rather than literal explains why Hamilton accused him of antisemitism. As the editor of Hamilton's law papers correctly concludes, "It is obvious that counsel for Gouverneur and Kemble, having regard for the predominantly lay membership of the Senate, saw fit to interlard discussion of the law with appeals to racial and national prejudice. The purpose was of course to discredit the testimony of Le Guen's witnesses and Le Guen himself"—see *LPAH*, 2:116.

38. John C. Hamilton, *History of the Republic*, 7:708. While the full transcript of the proceeding is not extant, the following appears in Alexander Hamilton's notes taken during Morris's discussion of the witnesses' Judaism: "*Objections emphatically* to the *credibility of their witnesses*"—see *LPAH*, 2:128.

39. *LPAH*, 2:137. Note that these words appear in Hamilton's recording of opposing counsel's argument during the trial.

40. John C. Hamilton, *History of the Republic*, 7:709.

41. John C. Hamilton, *History of the Republic*, 7:710–711.

42. *LPAH*, 2:84.

43. [From G. Morris Diary], 3, box 31, folder G-157, The Law Practice of Alexander Hamilton Papers, RBML.

44. Kent, *Memoirs and Letters*, 321.

45. Louis Le Guen to Alexander Hamilton, May 1, 1800, *PAH*, 24:438–439. Le Guen's letter indicates that Hamilton received $1,500 for the case while Burr took in $4,196.66 in some combination of legal fees and personal loans. Robert Troup understood that Hamilton, unlike Burr, had refused a higher sum, but Troup mistakenly claimed that Hamilton accepted $2,500 and Burr closer to $6,000—see Robert Troup to Rufus King, May 27, 1801, in *The Life and Correspondence of Rufus King: Comprising His Letters, Private and Official, His Public Documents and His Speeches*, ed. Charles R. King (New York: G. P. Putnam's Sons, 1896), 3:460. Meanwhile, P. S. Duponceau, a Frenchman who had fought for American independence, also had the gist of Le Guen's financial arrangement with Hamilton and Burr, but Duponceau erroneously suggested that Hamilton took only $1,000 compared to Burr's $8,000—see John C. Hamilton, *History of the Republic*, 7:712–713. See also Allan McLane Hamilton, *Intimate Life*, 171.

46. Kent, *Memoirs and Letters*, 321.

47. *LPAH*, 2:88.

48. For an example of a case in which Hamilton relied on Jewish witnesses, see James Ormond v. David Smith (1795), series JN519-17, New York State Supreme Court of Judicature judgment rolls and other documents on parchment, 1684–1848 (bulk 1765–1810), bundle 27, #C-10, NYSA; *LPAH*, 5:30. The witnesses Benjamin Seixas and Bernard Hart were both Jews.

49. *LPAH*, 5:36–37.

50. George Caines, *Cases Argued and Determined in the Court for the Trial of Impeachments and Correction of Errors in the State of New York in February, 1805* (New York: Isaac Riley, 1807), 2:196–197.

51. *LPAH*, 5:36n1.

52. Jonathan Burrall to Alexander Hamilton, [January 25, 1796], *PAH*, 20:50. See also Charles Wilkes to Alexander Hamilton, [January 25, 1796], *PAH*, 20:51.

53. Francis Lewis v. Aaron Burr, box 31, folder G-57, The Law Practice of Alexander Hamilton Papers, RBML. Note that this quotation comes from a legal document known as a "special verdict" that Hamilton principally wrote and to which the opposing counsel added some commentary—see *LPAH*, 2:17.

54. Caines, *Cases Argued and Determined*, 2:197.

55. Caines, *Cases Argued and Determined*, 2:199–200.

56. *LPAH*, 2:54n22.

57. *LPAH*, 2:54n22. As a case involving a Jew on each side, *Gomez v. Lopez* neatly illustrates that even a legal counselor with philosemitic sympathies sometimes found himself on the opposing side of a Jewish litigant. Hamilton was more likely to represent than oppose Jews in court, but instances of the latter were inevitable. See, for instance, United States v. the Ship Huron, Francis Hill, and Ephraim Hart, Claimants (1801), discussed in *LPAH*, 2:823–825. Similarly, lawyers who often worked together on one case were on opposing sides in the next. For lawyers and litigants alike, the New York legal world was small.

58. Rosenbloom, *Biographical Dictionary*, 150.

59. George Caines, *New York Term Report of Cases Argued and Determined in the Supreme Court of That State* (New York: Isaac Riley, 1805), 2:117–118. The flour was worth $2,200, and so under the terms of the agreement, the suppliers were to compensate Roget for the $50 difference between the value of the note and that of the flour.

60. Caines, *New York Term Report*, 2:118–119.

61. Caines, *New York Term Report*, 2:120.

62. Howard B. Rock, *Haven of Liberty: New York Jews in the New World, 1654–1865* (New York: New York University Press, 2012), 80; Jonathan D. Sarna, "The Impact of the American Revolution on American Jews," in *The American Jewish Experience*, ed. Jonathan D. Sarna (New York: Holmes & Meier, 1986), 20–21.

63. N. Taylor Phillips, "The Levy and Seixas Families of Newport and New York," *PAJHS* 4 (1896): 205.

64. David de la Sola Pool, *Portraits Etched in Stone: Early Jewish Settlers, 1682–1831* (1952; repr., New York: Columbia University Press, 1953), 399.

65. *LPAH*, 5:471, 485.

66. Eric Sloane and Edward Anthony, *Mr. Daniels and the Grange* (New York: Funk & Wagnalls, 1968), 56.

67. Jonathan Gill, *Harlem: The Four Hundred Year History from Dutch Village to Capital of Black America* (New York: Grove Press, 2011), 64; Chernow, *Alexander Hamilton*, 641–642.

68. Chernow, *Alexander Hamilton*, 642. "The Grange" was also the name of the Scottish castle that Hamilton's paternal ancestors owned.

69. Gordon S. Wood, *Empire of Liberty: A History of the Early Republic, 1789–1815* (2009; repr., New York: Oxford University Press, 2011), 174–177; William Pencak, *Jews and Gentiles in Early America: 1654–1800* (Ann Arbor: University of Michigan Press, 2005), vi, 7, 74, 231, 233.

70. James Rivington, "Preface," in Henry James Pye, *The Democrat; or Intrigues and Adventures of Jean Le Noir, From his Inlistment as a Drummer in General Rochembeau's Army, and arrival at Boston, to his being driven from England in 1795, after having borne a conspicuous Part in the French Revolution, and after a great variety of Enterprizes, Hazards and Escapes during his stay in England, where he was sent in quality of Democratic Missionary* (New York: James Rivington, 1795), 1:vii.

71. *Porcupine's Gazette* (Philadelphia), October 16, 1797, 771. For a discussion of the antisemitism directed at the politician in question, see Pencak, *Jews and Gentiles*, 234, 236–237.

72. Leonard B. Glick, *Marked in Your Flesh: Circumcision from Ancient Judea to Modern America* (New York: Oxford University Press, 2005), 98–102.

73. *American Mercury* (Hartford, CT), May 26, 1803, 2.

74. "The Appeal No. V," *Mercury and New-England Palladium* (Boston), June 4, 1802, 1.

75. Pencak, *Jews and Gentiles*, 244–246.

76. *Pittsburgh Gazette*, September 17, 1802, 3. For a discussion of this episode, see Carl E. Prince, "John Israel: Printer and Politician on the Pennsylvania Frontier, 1798–1805," *Pennsylvania Magazine of History and Biography* 91 (January 1967): 53.

77. Enclosure: [Notes on Conduct with Great Britain], [April 10, 1797], *PAH*, 21:41.

78. *The Stand*, no. 3, [April 7, 1798], *PAH*, 21:402–403.

79. Jonathan J. Den Hartog, *Patriotism and Piety: Federalist Politics and Religious Struggle in the New American Nation* (Charlottesville: University of Virginia Press, 2015), 2.

80. Alexander Hamilton to James A. Bayard, April [16–21], 1802, *PAH*, 25:605–606. See also Gerald Stourzh, *Alexander Hamilton and the Idea of Republican Government* (Stanford, CA: Stanford University Press, 1970), 125.

81. Alexander Hamilton to Eliza Hamilton, [April 19, 1797], *PAH*, 21:51; Alexander Hamilton to Eliza Hamilton, [March 16, 1801], *PAH*, 25:349; Alexander Hamilton to Eliza Hamilton, March [16–17], 1803, *PAH*, 26:95.

82. Chernow, *Alexander Hamilton*, 205.

83. Rules for Philip Hamilton, [1800], *PAH*, 25:289.

84. William Berrian, *An Historical Sketch of Trinity Church, New York* (New York: Stanford and Swords, 1847), 188–189, 359.

85. As Douglass Adair and Marvin Harvey explain, "After he became famous as a lawyer, Hamilton gratuitously handled Trinity's legal business . . . although not a member of the congregation"—see "Was Alexander Hamilton a Christian Statesman?," *William and Mary Quarterly* 12 (April 1955): 314n5.

86. Chernow writes, "Nominally Episcopalian, he was not clearly affiliated with the denomination and did not seem to attend church regularly or take communion"—see *Alexander Hamilton*, 205. Trinity Church has a logbook of communicants from 1801 that lists "Elizabeth Hamilton" but has no entry for Alexander.

87. Adair and Harvey, "Was Alexander Hamilton a Christian Statesman?," 311.

88. Continental Congress Unsubmitted Resolution Calling for a Convention to Amend the Articles of Confederation, [July 1783], *PAH*, 3:425.

244 NOTES TO PAGES 184–187

89. Alexander Hamilton to George Washington, October 21, 1799, *PAH*, 23:545.

90. Purchase of Louisiana, [July 5, 1803], *PAH*, 26:131.

91. Chernow, for instance, argues that by the 1790s, "Hamilton had probably fallen under the sway of deism, which sought to substitute reason for revelation and dropped the notion of an active God who intervened in human affairs"—see *Alexander Hamilton*, 205.

92. Alexander Hamilton to Oliver Wolcott Jr., December 16, 1800, *PAH*, 25:257.

93. Noemie Emery, *Alexander Hamilton: An Intimate Portrait* (New York: G. P. Putnam's Sons, 1982), 201–203; Karl-Friedrich Walling, *Republican Empire: Alexander Hamilton on War and Free Government* (Lawrence: University Press of Kansas, 1999), 276.

94. *Albany (NY) Register*, April 24, 1804, 2.

95. Aaron Burr to Alexander Hamilton, June 18, 1804, *PAH*, 26:242–243.

96. William Coleman, ed., *A Collection of the Facts and Documents Relative to the Death of Major-General Alexander Hamilton; With Comments: Together with the various Orations, Sermons, and Eulogies, That Have Been Published or Written on His Life and Character* (New York: Hopkins and Seymour, 1804), 2–7.

97. Statement on Impending Duel with Aaron Burr, [June 28–July 10, 1804], *PAH*, 26:278–279.

98. Craig Bruce Smith, *American Honor: The Creation of the Nation's Ideals during the Revolutionary Era* (Chapel Hill: University of North Carolina Press, 2018), 214.

99. Richard Bell, "The Double Guilt of Dueling: The Stain of Suicide in Anti-Dueling Rhetoric in the Early Republic," *Journal of the Early Republic* 29 (Fall 2009): 384.

100. Smith, *American Honor*, 217.

101. Joanne B. Freeman, *Affairs of Honor: National Politics in the New Republic* (New Haven, CT: Yale University Press, 2001), xvi.

102. Statement on Impending Duel with Aaron Burr, *PAH*, 26:280.

103. Statement on Impending Duel with Aaron Burr, *PAH*, 26:280.

104. Freeman, *Affairs of Honor*, 163.

105. Coleman, *Collection of the Facts*, 230.

106. Nathaniel Pendleton's Amendments to the Joint Statement Made by William P. Van Ness and Him on the Duel between Alexander Hamilton and Aaron Burr, [July 19, 1804], *PAH*, 26:338.

107. Alexander Hamilton to Eliza Hamilton, [July 10, 1804], *PAH*, 26:308. Hamilton had written another letter to be given to Eliza if he died in which he urged her, "Fly to the bosom of your God and be comforted"—see Alexander Hamilton to Eliza Hamilton, [July 4, 1804], *PAH*, 26:293.

Epilogue

1. William Coleman, ed., *A Collection of the Facts and Documents Relative to the Death of Major-General Alexander Hamilton; With Comments: Together with the Various Orations, Sermons, and Eulogies, That Have Been Published or Written on His Life and Character* (New York: Hopkins and Seymour, 1804), 18.

2. Quotation appears in Aaron Burr to Charles Biddle, July 18, 1804, in *Political Correspondence and Public Papers of Aaron Burr*, ed. Mary-Jo Kline (Princeton, NJ: Princeton University Press, 1983), 2:887.

3. David Hosack to William Coleman, August 17, 1804, *PAH*, 26:344.

4. Ron Chernow, *Alexander Hamilton* (New York: Penguin Press, 2004), 703–704.

5. John Sedgwick, *War of Two: Alexander Hamilton, Aaron Burr, and the Duel That Stunned the Nation* (New York: Berkley Books, 2015), 341–342.

6. Chernow, *Alexander Hamilton*, 706.

7. David Hosack to William Coleman, August 17, 1804, *PAH*, 26:345; Coleman, *Collection of the Facts*, 48.

8. Coleman, *Collection of the Facts*, 49–50. Douglass Adair and Marvin Harvey argue that the bishop's reluctance was rooted partly in his concern "to take especial care that such [deathbed] conversions do indeed represent a new spiritual birth" rather than a convenient, last-ditch bid for grace—see "Was Alexander Hamilton a Christian Statesman?," *William and Mary Quarterly* 12 (April 1995): 309.

9. Quotation was recounted in David Hosack to William Coleman, August 17, 1804, *PAH*, 26:347.

10. Chernow, *Alexander Hamilton*, 708.

11. Quotations appear in Coleman, *Collection of the Facts*, 56–57, 128.

12. Aaron Burr to Charles Biddle, July 18, 1804, in Kline, *Political Correspondence*, 2:887. For Burr's exile, see Chernow, *Alexander Hamilton*, 716–720.

13. On the eve of Adams's bid for reelection to the presidency in 1800, Hamilton publicly alleged that Adams suffered from "great and intrinsic defects in his character," which included "a vanity without bounds, and a jealousy capable of discoloring every object"—see Letter from Alexander Hamilton, Concerning the Public Conduct and Character of John Adams, Esq. President of the United States, [October 24, 1800], *PAH*, 25:186, 190.

14. Friday, September 20, 1776, *PJAD*, 3:435.

15. In a multivolume biography of his father, John Hamilton wrote in 1864 that Alexander was led "often to declare in the social circle his estimate of Christian truth. 'I have examined carefully,' he said to a friend from his boyhood, 'the evidence of the Christian religion; and if I was sitting as a juror upon its authenticity, I should unhesitatingly give my verdict in its favor.' To another person, he observed, 'I have studied it, and I can prove its truth as clearly as any proposition ever submitted to the mind of man'"—see *History of the Republic of the United States of America, as Traced in the Writings of Alexander Hamilton and of His Contemporaries*, 2nd ed. (Philadelphia: J. B. Lippincott, 1864), 7:790. Alexander may have made these comments, but neither quote that John offered is possible to verify. There is no record during Alexander's lifetime of his articulating these sentiments or any similar in nature. That John wrote the biography at the request of his pious mother (see Chernow, *Alexander Hamilton*, 727) may have led him to embellish his father's engagement with Christianity. John also painted a poignant scene of his father wherein Alexander passed the final evening before his death sharing a bed with an orphan boy with whom he recited the Lord's Prayer, a claim that Chernow acknowledges "may have embroidered the truth"—see *Alexander Hamilton*, 699.

16. Coleman, *Collection of the Facts*, 59.

17. Diane Ashton, *Rebecca Gratz: Women and Judaism in Antebellum America* (Detroit: Wayne State University Press, 1997), 24.

18. Rebecca Gratz to Rachel Gratz, July 18, 1804, item 31 in "Index to American Judaica Collection of Mark Boartman," AJA.

246 NOTES TO PAGES 189–192

19. Ashton, *Rebecca Gratz*, 14, 56.

20. Coleman, *Collection of the Facts*, 57–59, 66–67.

21. Rebecca Gratz to Rachel Gratz, July 18, 1804.

22. For a general discussion of Jews as modernizers globally, see Yuri Slezkine, *The Jewish Century* (Princeton, NJ: Princeton University Press, 2004).

INDEX

Note: Page numbers in *italics* indicate figures.

Varick, Richard, 64, 65

Virginia: Jefferson and citizenship for foreigners, 155; no religious test for holding office, 95–96; public dollars and religious education in, 150; ratification of the Bill of Rights and, 136; Statute for Religious Freedom of, 155; synagogue in Richmond, 120, 136, 146, 147

Voltaire, 105

Wadsworth, Jeremiah, 81

Washington, George: Burr and, 75; Constitutional Convention and, 109, 111; Farewell Address of, 148–151; Franks and, 64–66;

Hamilton in Revolutionary War and, 59–60, 70; image on flags, 117; public reading of Declaration of Independence, 58; reaction to death of, 190; synagogues' collective letter to, 136–139, 146–148; Thanksgiving Proclamation of 1789, 118; trip to Rhode Island and Newport letter to synagogue, 139, 140–146, 233n42, 234n47

Woodward, William E., 203n57

Worcester Magazine, 112

Yates, Abraham, Jr., 114

Zuntz, Alexander, 178–179